PROPERTY AND COMMUNITY

PROPERTY AND COMMUNITY

EDITED BY GREGORY S. ALEXANDER
EDUARDO M. PEÑALVER

OXFORD
UNIVERSITY PRESS

OXFORD
UNIVERSITY PRESS

Oxford University Press, Inc., publishes works that further Oxford University's objective of excellence in research, scholarship, and education.

Oxford New York
Auckland Cape Town Dar es Salaam Hong Kong Karachi Kuala Lumpur Madrid Melbourne
Mexico City Nairobi New Delhi Shanghai Taipei Toronto

With offices in
Argentina Austria Brazil Chile Czech Republic France Greece Guatemala Hungary Italy
Japan Poland Portugal Singapore South Korea Switzerland Thailand Turkey Ukraine
Vietnam

Published by Oxford University Press, Inc.
198 Madison Avenue, New York, New York 10016

Library of Congress Cataloging-in-Publication Data

Property and community / edited by Gregory S. Alexander and Eduardo M. Peñalver
p. cm.
Includes bibliographical references and index.
ISBN 978-0-19-539157-2 (hardback: alk. paper)
1. Right of property—Philosophy. I. Alexander, Gregory S., 1948–
II. Penalver, Eduardo Moisés, 1973–
K721.5.P759 2010
346.04'32—dc22 2009032660

Note to Readers
This publication is designed to provide accurate and authoritative information in regard to the subject matter covered. It is based upon sources believed to be accurate and reliable and is intended to be current as of the time it was written. It is sold with the understanding that the publisher is not engaged in rendering legal, accounting, or other professional services. If legal advice or other expert assistance is required, the services of a competent professional person should be sought. Also, to confirm that the information has not been affected or changed by recent developments, traditional legal research techniques should be used, including checking primary sources where appropriate.

(Based on the Declaration of Principles jointly adopted by a Committee of the American Bar Association and a Committee of Publishers and Associations.)

To our wives, Kim and Sital,
who have supported us so much

CONTENTS

ACKNOWLEDGMENTS

The genesis of this book was a conference on "Property and Instrumentality," held at the London School of Economics Faculty of Law, July 20–21, 2007, and jointly sponsored by Cornell Law School and the LSE Faculty of Law. The co-organizers of the conference were Gregory S. Alexander (Cornell) and Alain Pottage (LSE).

The papers delivered at the conference, while uniformly stimulating and excellent, turned out to pursue two disparate topics. One was the relationship between property and governance; the other was property's relationships with community in its various meanings. After the conference, when the space between these two core topics had become clear, the conference co-organizers, who had originally planned to publish a single volume based on the all of the papers, realized that the better strategy was to publish two separate volumes focused on each of the two topics, recognizing that this artificial separation would mean sacrificing to a certain extent the conversation that all of the papers had with each other. This book, then, represents the community dimension, as it were, of that memorable conference.

We wish to thank both Cornell Law School and the LSE Faculty of Law for their support, including generous financial support and, in the case of LSE, for very congenial space and helpful logistical support for the conference. In particular, we wish to single out Deans Stewart Schwab and Hugh Collins for their personal support and encouragement for the enterprise. Finally, we wish to offer special thanks to Alain Pottage, without whose intelligence, imagination, and enthusiasm neither the conference nor this book would have come to fruition. Working with him was an honor and a pure pleasure.

CONTRIBUTORS

Gregory S. Alexander, a nationally renowned expert in property law, is the A. Robert Noll Professor of Law at Cornell University and has taught at Cornell since 1985. Alexander has been a Fellow at the Center for Advanced Study in the Behavioral Science, in Palo Alto, California and at the Max-Planck-Institute for Comparative and International Law, in Hamburg and Heidelberg, Germany. Professor Alexander is a prolific and recognized writer, the winner of the American Publishers Association's 1997 Best Book of the Year in Law award for his work, *Commodity and Propriety*. His most recent book is *The Global Debate Over Constitutional Property: Lessons for American Takings Jurisprudence.*

Hanoch Dagan is the Dean of the Tel Aviv University Faculty of Law and the founding director of the Zvi Meitar Center for Advanced Legal Studies at TAU. He is also a member of the American Law Institute and of the International Academy of Comparative Law. Professor Dagan wrote *Unjust Enrichment: A Study of Private Law and Public Values* and *The Law and Ethics of Restitution* (both with Cambridge University Press) as well as numerous articles on property, restitution, and private law theory. His articles were published in leading legal journals such as *Yale Law Journal, Columbia Law Review, New York University Law Review, California Law Review, Virginia Law Review, Michigan Law Review, Cornell Law Review,* and *University of Toronto Law Journal.* His forthcoming book—*Property, State, and Community*—will be published with Oxford University Press in 2011.

Kevin Gray was elected a Fellow of the British Academy in 1999. He has been a Professor of Law in the University of Cambridge since 1993 and is Dean of Trinity College Cambridge. He is also an Adjunct Professor in the National University of Singapore. He was formerly Drapers Professor of Law in the University of London and a Senior Research Fellow in the University of Oxford. He has held visiting fellowships and professorships at the Australian National University (on numerous occasions) and at the Universities of Leiden, New South Wales, Osaka, Stellenbosch, Tasmania and Tilburg. He has written extensively on property law and theory, family law, human rights and the environment, and is a co-author of Gray and Gray, *Elements of Land Law.* In 2008 he was awarded a Major Research Fellowship by the Leverhulme Trust.

David Lametti is the Associate Dean (Academic) and Associate Professor of Law, Faculty of Law, McGill University. He is a past Director of the Institute of Comparative Law and a founding Member of the Centre for Intellectual Property Policy (CIPP). He teaches and writes in the areas of Civil and Common law property, intellectual property and property theory. His work to date has attempted to understand the parameters or traditional and intellectual resources in analytic terms, linking them to their underlying justifications and ethical goals. He obtained a B.A. in Economics and Political Science from the University of Toronto in 1985, and received his Common and Civil law degrees from McGill in 1989. He received an LL.M. from the Yale Law School in 1991, and a Doctorate in Law from Oxford University in 1999. He was a clerk to Justice Peter Cory of the Supreme Court of Canada in 1989–90.

Avital Margalit is a graduate of Tel Aviv University in Law (LL.B) and in Sociology and Psychology (B.A), and a graduate of Boalt Hall School of Law, University of California at Berkeley (LL.M, J.S.D). She teaches courses on property law and the sociology of law at the Law Faculty of Bar Ilan University. Her research focuses on the social and cultural aspects of property relationships, co-operative societies and the legal history of the Kibbutz.

Eduardo M. Peñalver joined the Cornell faculty in 2006 after teaching from 2003–05 at Fordham Law School and spending 2005–06 as a visiting professor at Yale Law School. Professor Peñalver received his B.A. from Cornell University and his law degree from Yale Law School. He was a Rhodes Scholar at Oxford and a law clerk for Supreme Court Justice John Paul Stevens. His research interests focus on property and land use, as well as law and religion. He is particularly interested in the ways property both fosters and reflects communal bonds. His forthcoming book *Property Outlaws* (co-authored with Sonia Katyal) will be published by Yale University Press in early 2010.

Joseph William Singer began teaching at Boston University School of Law in 1984 and has been teaching at Harvard Law School since 1992. He was appointed Bussey Professor of Law in 2006. Singer received a B.A. from Williams College in 1976, an A.M. in political science from Harvard in 1978, and a J.D. from Harvard Law School in 1981. He clerked for Justice Morris Pashman on the Supreme Court of New Jersey from 1981 to 1982 and was an associate at the law firm of Palmer & Dodge in Boston, focusing on municipal law, from 1982 to 1984. He teaches and writes about property law, conflict of laws, and federal Indian law, and has published more than 40 law review articles. He was one of the executive editors of the 2005 edition of *Cohen's Handbook of Federal Indian Law*. He has written a casebook and a treatise on property law, as well as two theoretical books on property called *Entitlement: The Paradoxes of Property* and *The Edges of the Field: Lessons on the Obligations of Ownership*.

Nomi M. Stolzenberg holds the Nathan and Lilly Shapell Chair in Law at the University of Southern California Law School, where she has taught courses on property law, family law, law and religion, and law, language and ethics. A strong proponent of multidisciplinary research and teaching, she helped establish the USC Center for Law, History and Culture. She is a member of the Association for the Study of Law, Culture and the Humanities, and serves on the editorial boards of Theory and Research in Education and the Journal of Law, Culture, and the Humanities. Her research spans a range of interdisciplinary interests, including law and religion, cultural pluralism, law and liberalism, and law and literature. She has published a number of works on property and community, including "The Property of Culture" (Daedalus 2000), "A Tale of Two Villages" (*Nomos xxxix: Ethnicity and Group Rights*, Shapiro & Kymlicka, eds., N.Y.U. Press); "The Puzzling Persistence of Community" (in *from ghetto to emancipation*, University of Scranton Press, Myers & Rowe, eds.); and "The Return of the Repressed: Illiberal Groups in a Liberal State" (*Journal of Contemporary Legal Issues*), and on law and religion ("The Profanity of Law" in *Law and the Sacred*, Sarat, Douglas and Umphrey, eds., Stanford U. Press, and "He Drew A Circle That Shut Me Out," *Harvard Law Review*). She is currently working on a book on the interaction between the American liberal legal regime and traditional Jewish law and culture in the ultra-Orthdox Satmar community of Kiryas Joel.

A. J. van der Walt graduated from Potchefstroom University in 1985 with a thesis on ownership, possession and holdership. He completed an LLM degree in Property Law at the University of the Witwatersrand in 1986 with a dissertation on the conservation of the built-up environment. He has taught Property Law, Legal Philosophy and Legal History at Potchefstroom University, the University of South Africa and Stellenbosch University. Since 2008 he holds the South African Research Chair in Property Law at Stellenbosch University. He has been the recipient of the Alexander von Humboldt fellowship on several occasions and has been a visiting fellow commoner in Trinity College, Cambridge. Professor Van der Walt is author, co-author or editor of and contributor to more than 20 books on legal history, research methodology and property law, and has published more than 100 articles in legal journals. He has presented more than 50 papers at international conferences or as guest lecturer. He was co-organiser of the international colloquium on property law presented by the University of Maastricht in the Netherlands in September 1995 and co-editor of the collected papers of the colloquium. His most recent work is mainly concerned with constitutional property, land reform and property theory. His most recent books include *Constitutional Property Clauses: A Comparative Analysis* (1999); *Constitutional Property Law* (2005) and *Property in the Margins* (2009).

INTRODUCTION

GREGORY S. ALEXANDER AND EDUARDO M. PEÑALVER

The relationship between individuals and communities—all manner of communities, but especially the state[1]—is a central preoccupation of property theory. Across a broad range of property thought—from utilitarian to Lockean to Hegelian—scholars have expended enormous efforts explaining what owners can do with their property and the extent to which the community or the state can participate in those decisions. The mountainous literature on the subject of regulatory takings is a testament to scholars' interest in questions concerning the relationship between individuals and community as mediated through property.

The nexus between theories of property and community is perhaps tightest in Hegelian property theory, where property practically stands in the place of the individual herself. Within such a conception, working out the contours of an owner's rights becomes the delineation of the proper relationship between the individual and the community around her. Although the connection is admittedly less direct within other theoretical frameworks, discussions of property rights, from whatever perspective, necessarily reflect ideas about the proper domain and limits of individual and community power.

Property stands so squarely at the intersection between the individual and community because systems of property are always the creation of some community. As property theorists of all stripes have long recognized, "[i]n the world of Robinson Crusoe property rights play no role."[2] Moreover, systems of property have as their subject matter the allocation among community members of rights and duties with respect to resources that human beings need in order to survive and to flourish.[3] These allocative decisions are crucially important both to individuals, owners and nonowners alike, and to the community as a whole. Jeremy Waldron is therefore surely correct when he says that "our interest

1. Our conception of communities is intentionally capacious, embracing the state as well as smaller groups, including families, voluntary associations, and the like. As our discussion below of human flourishing and the social matrices that are necessary for the development of the capabilities that are necessary for human flourishing should make clear, we emphasize the role of small groups, such as families and friends. That said, we also emphasize that the state, which we consider to be a community, plays an important role here as well. *See* Part 3 *infra*.

2. Harold Demsetz, *Toward a Theory of Property Rights*, 57 Am. Econ. Rev. 347, 347 (1967).

3. *See* Jeremy Waldron, The Right to Private Property 32 (1988) (describing the problem of "allocation" as the central concern of property law).

in property is effectively an interest in the political and economic structure of society."[4] In other words, whenever we discuss property, we are unavoidably discussing the architecture of community and of the individual's place within it.

Even though the relationship between individuals and community stands at the conceptual center of property theory, the normative theories of community underlying discussions of property are frequently left implicit. This is particularly common in discussions of private ownership, which is to say in most contemporary property scholarship. In such discussions, the focus is often fixed firmly on the person of the "owner," and all others reduced to the amorphous category of "nonowner." This way of talking about ownership obscures the possibility that the "community" may have a moral status that is distinct from those of neighboring owners or nonowning individuals.

I. TWO APPROACHES TO PROPERTY AND COMMUNITY

Two approaches dominate discussions about community and property within contemporary property scholarship: law and economics' utilitarian theory and liberal contractarianism. In this introduction, we will briefly describe the contours of these theories, and then, drawing on the papers in this volume, discuss some of their shortcomings. Finally, we will propose some alternative approaches. We do not intend the discussion in this introduction to be comprehensive on any of these scores. Instead, the task we set for ourselves is merely to situate the papers in this volume within a broader conversation about property and community and, hopefully, in the process, to encourage the reader to seek out the richer, fuller discussions contained within the individual papers.

A. Utilitarian Theory

Utilitarian theory, of which normative law and economics is perhaps the most prominent contemporary exemplar, has as its ultimate aim the maximization of aggregate welfare, understood most commonly as the satisfaction of individual preferences. Utilitarian analysis of community is refracted through this maximizing lens. Although theorists have approached the deceptively simple goal of welfare maximization through a variety of strategies, three broadly shared features of the utilitarian analysis of community are particularly significant for our purposes: the centrality of the individual within utilitarian calculus; the contractarian tendencies that this methodological individualism engenders; and, finally, utilitarian discussions of the appropriate boundaries of community.

---

4. *Id.* at 328.

Within normative economic theory, individual preferences are the sole source and measure of value. Economic theories, of course, differ widely in terms of how they go about measuring those preferences, but they all share this fundamental focus.[5] Utilitarian theories typically have little to say, however, about how individuals come to have the preferences they do, generally treating their preferences as exogenous, or given, when in reality they often respond to the very distributive questions with which economists concern themselves.[6]

The result of this constellation of commitments is to instrumentalize the utilitarian account of community. Within utilitarian theory, community is only valuable insofar as it contributes to the satisfaction of some individual's preferences. Conversely, community or sociality is never, for the economic theorist, an end in itself.

The central utilitarian question, then, is whether a particular community or a particular model of community will enhance or diminish individual preference satisfaction. Because the individual is in the best position to know what his preferences are and what sorts of communal attachments will satisfy them, utilitarian theorists of community stress the importance of permitting individuals to choose for themselves the communities into which they will enter.[7]

Perhaps the most interesting and complex discussions of community within utilitarian theory concern the question of what might be termed community ecology. The landscape of options available to individuals as they go about satisfying their preferences may have a significant impact on aggregate welfare. Utilitarians, then, must be concerned about maintaining the sorts of communal landscapes that will be most conducive to maximizing individual preference satisfaction.

The most prominent example of this concern in action is in the body of literature elaborating on and refining the Tiebout hypothesis. According to Charles M. Tiebout, when conditions permit individuals to vote among local communities by selective entrance into or exit from those communities, the relationship between local communities and their potential residents comes to resemble a competitive market in which individual preferences are more likely to be satisfied than in an alternative in which individuals lack the ability

---

5. *See* Amartya Sen, DEVELOPMENT AS FREEDOM 67–68 (1999).

6. *See* Martha C. Nussbaum, WOMEN AND HUMAN DEVELOPMENT 136–48 (2000). Some economic theorists do favor correcting actual preferences and replacing them in utilitarian calculus with preferences that are idealized in some way. *See, e.g.*, J. C. Harsanyi, RATIONAL BEHAVIOR AND BARGAINING EQUILIBRIUM IN GAMES AND SOCIAL SCIENCES (1977).

7. *See, e.g.*, James M. Buchanan, PROPERTY AS A GUARANTOR OF LIBERTY 16 (1993); Robert C. Ellickson, *Cities and Homeowners Associations*, 130 U. PA. L. REV. 1519 (1982).

to "vote with their feet."[8] Although Tiebout was concerned with markets for local government, the same basic argument holds for private communities as well. A landscape in which communities must compete with each other for membership, the argument goes, will be one in which individual preferences are more likely to be satisfied than they would be in a communal landscape in which they had few options from which to choose.[9]

The consequence of this approach for utilitarian discussions of the state is a tendency toward suspicion of state power, insofar as the state is a community that the individual has not chosen.[10] Utilitarian suspicion of state power is likely to be extremely sensitive to the state's scale and context. Based on the Tiebout hypothesis, a utilitarian is likely to subject to a greater degree of scrutiny demands made by large, unchosen communities that are, as a consequence of their unchosen nature, less susceptible to the discipline of competition.

In sum, the utilitarian conception of community is instrumental and procedural. Community is valuable, but not intrinsically so. Rather, it has value only insofar as it contributes to the satisfaction of individual preferences, whatever they might be. The best way to ensure that a community will act so as to satisfy those preferences is to maintain a robust "market" for communities, both public and private, within which individuals are free to enter and exit communities in accordance with their own preferences. Where such a market is absent, or where individual choice is impaired, utilitarian theorists believe, there is a lesser likelihood that communities will act in ways that are welfare-maximizing.

B. Classical Liberal Contractarian Theory

Like the utilitarian, the classical liberal contractarian conception of community begins with the individual. The results of the classical contractarian's analysis end up resembling in many ways the utilitarian discussion of community. The liberal, contractarian discussion of the relationship between individuals and the communities to which they belong begins with the mature individual in an idealized state of maximal negative liberty and with the total absence of involuntary communal commitments or obligations. From this starting point, liberal contractarian theorists typically seek to derive rules for society that preserve as much of this hypothetical state of nature as possible, at least as to the individual's experience of liberty, while permitting everyone to gain from the benefits of community life. They demand that the move from this hypothetical (and idealized)

8. *See* Charles M. Tiebout, *A Pure Theory of Local Expenditures*, 64 J. Pol. Econ. 416 (1956); *see also* William A. Fischel, The Homevoter Hypothesis ch. 3 (2001).

9. *See* Fischel, *supra* note 8, at 58–59, 63; Robert C. Ellickson, *Alternatives to Zoning: Covenants, Nuisance Rules, and Fines as Land Use Controls*, 40 U. Chi. L. Rev. 681, 710–19 (1973); Clayton P. Gillette, *Courts, Covenants, and Communities*, 61 U. Chi. L. Rev. 1375, 1388–92 (1994).

10. *See* Gerald E. Frug, *The City as a Legal Concept*, 93 Harv. L. Rev. 1057, 1076 (1980).

situation of isolation and freedom to one of social obligation should be either the result of actual choice or, when an external constraint is imposed, should require that the constraint itself be justified by the need to preserve (or enhance) every individual's enjoyment of liberty.[11]

Randy Barnett's libertarian political theory provides a contemporary illustration of these moves. On the one hand, Barnett praises voluntary associations and welcomes the substantial restrictions they often impose on individual liberty, but he does so only to the extent that joining such associations is in fact voluntarily. "Under conditions of unanimous consent," he argues, "liberty is not inconsistent with both heavy regulation and even the prohibition of otherwise rightful conduct."[12]

Accordingly, like many property libertarians, he celebrates the restraints on individual freedom assumed by those who join private residential communities. At the same time, however, he is extremely suspicious of the state, precisely because he views it as an unchosen community from which exit is extremely costly. "The larger the land area," Barnett observes, "the higher the cost of exit and thus the less meaningful is 'tacit' consent to the jurisdiction of the lawmaking process. Most modern cities are probably too large, but even if they are small enough, states are certainly too large to command meaningful unanimous consent."[13] Consequently, he favors dramatically limiting the power of virtually all territorially defined governments to intrude upon individual liberty. Drawing heavily on Lockean political theory, Barnett argues that the principal purpose of government must be limited to the protection of a constellation of negative individual liberties, such as private property and freedom of contract, the operation of which helps us to preserve the individual liberty present in the prepolitical state of nature.[14]

From where does Barnett derive the content of these negative liberties? From an implicit account of the human person as an uncoerced individual, living free from the constraints of involuntary community life. It is for this reason that Barnett, like other classical liberals, talks about the appropriate terms on which individuals hypothetically "enter" society.[15] One can only "enter" society, even hypothetically, if one was not already there to begin with. Liberal contractarians understand the being who enters into society and trades away her preexisting liberty to be a fully formed, rational, and autonomous individual.[16]

---

11. *See* John Locke, Two Treatises of Government Bk. II, §§ 123–31 (Peter Laslett ed., 1988) (1690).

12. *See* Randy E. Barnett, Restoring the Lost Constitution 43 (2004).

13. *Id.*

14. *Id.* at 75.

15. *See id.* at 69–76.

16. *See* 2 Charles Taylor, *Atomism, in* 2 Philosophy and the Human Sciences: Philo-sophical Papers 187, 187–89 (1985).

C. Conclusion

Although these two influential approaches to community differ from each other in important respects, they also share a number of common features. Most importantly, within both theories, the individual stands ontologically prior to the community. Communities are voluntary associations of individuals pursuing "convergent" ends that are themselves independent of the community and rooted in the individual's own preexisting goals and desires. (The exception in this regard is the state, and precisely because the state is not a voluntary community, it is subject to a degree of suspicion and limitation not accorded other communities.) As a result of this basic orientation, both approaches treat the good of the community as derivative of the good of individuals, and therefore as fundamentally instrumental.

Finally, when they turn to exploring the relationship between individuals and their communities, both approaches adopt what amounts to a procedural stance. Utilitarian theories of community do not associate any substantive ends with the maximization of utility. Instead, they focus on the freedom with which individuals may locate, enter, and exit communities and the existence of robust competition among communities for members. Similarly, contractarians do not posit substantive accounts of the proper relationship between individuals and their community. Rather, relying on actual agreements or hypothetical bargains struck in the state of nature or some other such evaluative device, they elaborate procedural norms to adjudicate the demands that communities may make on their members and their members' property.

II. PROBLEMS WITH THE LAW AND ECONOMICS AND CLASSICAL LIBERAL ACCOUNTS OF COMMUNITY

Each of these dominant approaches to understanding the relationship between property and community struggles in its own way to give an adequate account of community life. For starters, the tendency of many law and economics scholars to rely on a rational-actor model of human behavior leads them to predict that individuals will, as far as possible, avoid contributing to cooperative community endeavors when they can instead free-ride on the efforts and sacrifices of others. In practice, this model has proved unable to explain the observed incidence of cooperative participation in community life. More importantly, however, both classical liberal and economic theories of community fail to provide an adequate standpoint from which to criticize oppression or dysfunction within seemingly consensual communal arrangements.

A. Community and the Rational Actor

Although, as we discussed above, the existence of a robust community ecology is important to utilitarian accounts of community, and in particular to the operation of the Tiebout model, the conception of human behavior that is most frequently employed within the economic analysis of law is ill-suited to sustain such an ecology. The problem arises from the mismatch between the so-called rational actor model of individual decision-making and the demands that all successful communities must be able to place on their members if they are to function effectively. In short, the sort of person that traditional law and economics imagines us to be is not the sort of person who is likely to contribute to the creation of a diverse and vibrant communal landscape.

According to traditional economic accounts, human beings are rational maximizers of self-interest. That is, in making their decisions about what to do and how to act, they ask themselves which course of action is likely to yield the best outcome for *them*. The best outcome for a given individual will be the one that maximizes his net wealth, happiness, or preference satisfaction.

The problem posed to the notion of community by this theory of individual behavior is that (1) successful communities require substantial cooperative effort in order to generate benefits for their members, and (2) the rational actor is not someone who is likely to want to contribute to those efforts. The cooperation that sustains communities demands individual sacrifice, but the rational actor will be the sort of person who sits back and lets others engage in the hard work of cooperating, in the hopes of being able to enjoy the benefits that result for all members of the community. In a society made up of rational actors, we would expect a great deal of free-riding and, as a consequence, a fairly bleak communal landscape as communities struggle to convince (or, if possible, coerce) rational actors not to default on their communal commitments in the hopes that others will pick up the slack.

Some economic theorists have been able to formulate scenarios in which rational actors can predictably generate cooperative outcomes. Perhaps most famously, Robert Axelrod has demonstrated that voluntary cooperation is a possible outcome when self-interested, rational actors employ a tit-for-tat strategy in an iterated prisoner's dilemma game of indefinite duration.[17] Of course, as he concedes, universal defection is also a stable equilibrium in such situations. The emergence of cooperation on his theory is possible, but it is both fragile and uncertain.

As Elinor Ostrom and others have noted, however, actual observations of human behavior in situations where self-dealing might be expected routinely find far more cooperation than the traditional rational actor models, like Axelrod's, predict.[18] For example, experimental economists observing human

---

17. *See generally* Robert Axelrod, The Evolution of Cooperation (1984).

18. *See* Elinor Ostrom, *A Behavioral Approach to the Rational Choice Theory of Collective Action*, 92 Am. Pol. Sci. Rev. 1 (1998); Samuel Bowles & Herbert Gintis, *The Evolution of Strong Reciprocity: Cooperation in Heterogenous Populations*, 65 Theoretical Population Biology 17 (2004).

behavior in the laboratory routinely find that people cooperate in one-shot prisoners' dilemma games, notwithstanding the rational actor model's robust theoretical predictions of universal defection. Similarly, in so-called ultimatum games, players routinely make substantial sacrifices in order to punish what they interpret to be unfair behavior by their opponents.[19] Finally, while the rational actor model predicts that mere communication between subjects in a prisoners' dilemma game would have absolutely no impact on subjects' tendencies to cooperate, providing participants with the opportunity to communicate typically yields significantly higher levels of cooperation.[20] The upshot of this research is that human beings, either by nature or nurture, are much more cooperative and more likely to participate in community endeavors than the rational actor model predicts.

The descriptive failures of the rational actor model are not fatal to efforts to formulate a broadly utilitarian analysis of the relationship between property and community. Such descriptive shortcomings can be remedied by turning to more sophisticated behavioral models or a broader conception of the values that self-interested human beings will pursue. And, in recent years, legal economists have taken both tacks. Some, drawing on the work of the new institutional economists, have responded to experimental observations of human altruism to formulate conceptions of human behavior characterized by "bounded self interest" and "bounded rationality." Others have turned to broader definitions of the sort of value that "rational actors" will pursue. One influential account, for example, defines the value rational actors will pursue (almost tautologically) to include anything that a person might desire, in the process recasting seemingly altruistic behavior as (by definition) self-interested efforts to satisfy other-regarding desires.

Even with more sophisticated modeling of what human beings are likely to want, however, the touchstone for normative economic discussions of human beings' communal involvement remains satisfaction of individual desires. In this sense, and as we noted above, utilitarian approaches share much with the classical liberal conception of community, which places voluntary choice at its normative center. A crucial problem with these approaches is that by taking individuals as they find them, they make it extremely difficult to develop a basis from which to criticize the choices people make, particularly when the choices appear to be informed and when the only people harmed by the choices are the choosers themselves.

---

19. *See* Ernst Fehr et al., *Strong Reciprocity, Human Cooperation, and the Enforcement of Social Norms*, 13 HUMAN NATURE 1, 10–11 (2002) (summarizing studies of ultimatum game behavior).

20. *See* Ostrom, *A Behavioral Approach, supra* note 18, at 6–7.

B. Preserving a Critical Standpoint

The utilitarian focus on community as a means to satisfy individual preferences and the classical liberal focus on the voluntary assumption of community life reflect impoverished understandings of the nature and importance of community. The communities in which we find ourselves, often without any meaningful choice on our part, play crucial roles in the formation of our preferences, the extent of our expectations, and the scope of our aspirations. While membership in certain communities can obviously be based upon contract or voluntary agreement, the very possibility of these voluntary associative relationships depends upon our prior and continuing (and frequently involuntary) participation in or exposure to communal institutions that impart to us the information, resources, and capacities necessary to understand and engage in voluntary choice to begin with.

Not only do unchosen communities play a vital role in the formation of our ability to engage in subsequent choosing, there can be little doubt that people's desires, and therefore their choices, are often distorted by experiences of abuse or material deprivation within those communities. As Amartya Sen has put it, "[a] person who is ill-fed, undernourished, unsheltered and ill can still be high up in the scale of happiness or desire-fulfillment if he or she has learned to have 'realistic' desires and to take pleasure in small mercies."[21]

In light of the unreliable guidance desires provide to our normative assessments, it is often the case that seemingly voluntary choices to contribute to or remain in particular communities can be a very poor basis for determining the scope of an individual's social obligations. In order to be able to judge individual preferences and choices as healthy or unhealthy, what we require is an objective account of human well-being.[22] As we will discuss in the next section, although they differ in many of their details, several of the papers in this volume converge in relying on just such an account in formulating their conception of the proper relationship between individuals, their property, and the communities to which they belong (or aspire to belong).

III. ALTERNATIVES TO CLASSICAL LIBERAL AND UTILITARIAN APPROACHES TO PROPERTY AND COMMUNITY

In recent years legal scholars have developed theories of the relationship between property and community that are alternatives to both the utilitarian and classical liberal approaches. Although these theories depart from utilitarianism and classical liberalism in important respects, they share with those traditions certain

---

21. Amartya Sen, COMMODITIES AND CAPABILITIES 21 (1985).

22. Objectivity here can mean as little as an account of well-being that is not rooted solely in an individual's subjective states.

fundamental commitments. First, like classical liberalism and utilitarianism, they start with the individual, taking seriously the individual's moral agency. Second, like those approaches, these alternative theories stress the importance of individual freedom and individual well-being.

Beyond these shared commitments, important differences quickly emerge. Unlike the other approaches, particularly classical liberalism, these alternative theories of property and community view the individual in a social context, not in isolation. That is, these theories take seriously the understanding of human beings as social animals whose very sociality enables their autonomy. They reject the tendency of classical liberal theorists to view the person who enters into society as already a fully formed, rational, and autonomous moral agent. Rather, they regard membership in society as both inherent in the human condition and necessary for the development of moral agency. In his essay in this volume, for example, David Lametti analyzes the social functions that Aristotle and Thomas Aquinas understood as central to the institution of private property.[23] Lametti argues that each of them conceived of private property as promoting virtue and, through the cultivation of virtue, of the common good. For example, he discusses Aristotle's view that ownership of private property fosters virtues, such as liberality and moderation,[24] that the virtue of individuals would enable the city to flourish, and that the city's flourishing would in turn contribute to the flourishing of its citizens.[25]

The relationship between human sociality and property is more implicit in Joseph Singer's "good neighbor" conception of property, according to which property rights are socially situated and defined.[26] Singer understands property rights as inherently relational. Like Lametti's Aristotelian approach, however, Singer's conception rests on a vision of the self as necessarily social rather than isolated or atomistic.

Hanoch Dagan's paper, even more so than Singer's, explicitly situates the self within communities while simultaneously celebrating the affirmative value of liberal autonomy. He rejects the alienated or isolated conception of the self and stresses the fact of membership in communities. Yet he is quick to add that the freedom to join and to exit from multiple communities as one sees fit is necessary for individual autonomy.

23. *See* David Lametti, *The Objects of Virtue infra.*

24. *Id.*, at 7–8.

25. *Id.*, at 17. ("The virtue in the city is founded on the virtue of individuals and virtue of individuals is based on the virtue of the city. Each forms the other through laws and education, and the actions of virtuous individuals leading to a virtuous state of character aimed at the good.").

26. Singer at 59.

These theories reject the view adopted by classical liberals (and at least some utilitarians[27]) that communities not created by contractual agreement stand in need of special justification. They recognize that the value of communities cannot be reduced to contractual satisfaction of individual desires because they are always, at least in part, constitutive of personal identity. Dean Dagan, for example, states that "communities are important human goods exactly because they are so significant to the *identities* of individual people."[28] Individual selves are constituted in part by their membership and participation in multiple and sometimes overlapping communities over the course of their lives.

The nonstrategic and noncontractual character of many communities means that social relations within them will transcend demands for immediate or short-term reciprocity. It further means that members of such communities, which include but are not limited to political communities, have obligations to fellow members of their communities. These obligations result from membership itself. What members give to fellow community members are not in the nature of market exchanges, where a calculated return of greater value is expected. There may well be an expectation of reciprocity, but, as Dagan notes, the expectation may well operate over an extended period of time, perhaps even extending over multiple lifetimes. Moreover, the form that such long-term reciprocity takes means that compensation may be very different in kind from what was given. Indeed, it may come from a member of the community other than the one to whom it was given, and, in some ways, its "value" relative to the original contribution is less important than that it is received at all.[29]

Our earlier discussion of utilitarian accounts of community pointed out that utilitarianism, including its latter-day variant, law-and-economics theory, seeks to maximize a single scalar end, or value, namely, social or aggregate welfare. We also noted that in modern welfare economics literature, social welfare is commonly defined in terms of the satisfaction of individual preferences. In contrast, the alternative accounts of community described in this volume are pluralist in their conception of value. That is, they recognize that there are multiple ends that communities legitimately seek to serve. In addition, unlike utilitarians, the theories of community at work in this book further recognize that the values underlying communities may be instrumental or noninstrumental, or both. Indeed, on one view communities are always at least noninstrumentally valuable insofar as they involve cooperative activity and such activity is considered valuable for its own sake.[30]

27. BARNETT, RESTORING THE LOST CONSTITUTION, *supra* note 7; Ellickson, *Cities and Homeowners Associations, supra* note 7.

28. Dagan at 45 (emphasis in original).

29. *Id.* at 46.

30. *Id.* at 50.

The plurality of values served by communal attachments stems in part from the rich variety of types of communities that exist in most societies, a point that we will discuss below. In our society, families, for example, at least in their healthier moments, are based on love, the kind of love that may lead to self-sacrifice. Other, less tightly knit communities are based on shared values ranging from friendship to professional values such as craft. As the alternative accounts of community recognize, this plethora of values served by and realized in different sorts of communities means that no single metric, even one as seemingly capacious as preference satisfaction, can do justice to explaining what makes community valuable.

IV. IMPLICATIONS OF THESE ALTERNATIVES FOR PROPERTY: PROPERTY AND OBLIGATION

These methodological differences with both classical liberalism and utilitarianism yield much richer theories of the obligations that property owners owe to their communities, and of the rights they ought to enjoy. Joseph Singer's paper on property norms, for example, discusses how those norms shape the contours of social relationships. Singer points out that whereas classical liberal and utilitarian theorists take individual interests as given and beyond evaluation, both lawmakers and ordinary people in fact do not treat all interests equally. In ordinary life, he argues, people constantly make moral evaluations about interests and draw distinctions among them. Property norms both inform and rely on those distinctions to shape the character of our relationships with members of our communities.

V. MEANINGS AND DILEMMAS OF PROPERTY-BASED COMMUNITY

The term "community" can be used to refer to a concept,[31] a regulative ideal,[32] or a social institution or practice, but all too frequently scholars do not make clear

---

31. Referring to community as a concept, Andrew Mason has usefully distinguished between "ordinary" community and "moralized" community. *See* Andrew Mason, COMMUNITY, SOLIDARITY, AND BELONGING: LEVELS OF BELONGING AND THEIR NORMATIVE SIGNIFICANCE 21–27 (2000). By "ordinary" community, Mason means a group who act or cooperate together in pursuit of shared goals or at least who possess common interests. *Id.*, 21. A "moralized" community has two additional conditions: (1) solidarity, or mutual concern, i.e., its members must give each other's interests some degree of noninstrument weight, and (2) no systematic exploitation among members. *Id.*, at 27.

32. As a regulative or normative ideal, theorists like Michael Sandel have used the term as an alternative to the political and moral vision of "atomist" individualists, whose central doctrine is, as Charles Taylor explains, "a principle ascribing rights to men as binding

in which sense they are using the term. The essays in this volume discuss community primarily as a social institution, although some authors at times use it in the other two senses as well. As a social institution, community exhibits a remarkable diversity of forms, covering a wide spectrum of practices.[33] The social practices and institutions that are the subject of the essays in this volume are confined to territorial or geographic communities. Even so confined, the term "community" remains maddeningly ambiguous. Its use ranges from small face-to-face groups in which personal relationships are close and characterized by a high degree of mutuality and identification to the so-called "global community." Part of the difficulty stems from the famous distinction drawn by Ferdinand Tönnies between *Gemeinschaft* and *Gesellschaft*,[34] the former referring to small-scale, preindustrial groups whose social relations are intimate, while the latter refers to the contractual and impersonal relationships typical of industrial societies. Although most social scientists today regard that distinction as unhelpful, it continues to influence some discussions of community by a tendency to dichotomize conceptions of community as either hopelessly weak or "tightly knit," with the latter often romanticized as the ideal toward which communities ought to aspire.

Several contributors to this volume avoid this error by addressing three core dilemmas that community, both as a social institution and as a regulative ideal, faces. These dilemmas are (1) the insider/outsider problem, or the problem of exclusion; (2) the problem of effacement; and (3) the problem of internal governance. Not all of the papers discuss or provide solutions to these core dilemmas, but many of them do shed light on the problems. In so doing, they clarify the multiple meanings of community itself.

A. The Insider/Outsider Dilemma

Communities often exclude.[35] Jeremy Waldron expresses a common concern when he states that "Communitarianism has an inherent 'us'/'them' logic, a tendency to define itself by contrast with the 'other.'" Precisely because communities at all levels (other than the global) are based on shared commitments to

---

unconditionally . . . [b]ut . . . do[es] not accept as similarly unconditional a principle of belonging or obligation." Taylor, PHILOSOPHICAL PAPERS: *supra* note 16, at 188. Arguing against the primacy of rights, communitarians like Taylor have propounded what he calls a "social thesis," which holds that the very affirmative of our right creates for us an obligation to belong to and sustain the right kind of society, i.e., the kind of society that nurtures people's capabilities to develop as free and autonomous moral agents.

33. *See* Amnon Lehavi, *How Property Can Create, Maintain, or Destroy Community*, 10 THEORETICAL INQUIRIES IN LAW 43, 46–61 (2009).

34. Ferdinand Tönnies, COMMUNITY AND CIVIL SOCIETY (Jose Harris ed., 2001).

35. *See* Jeremy Waldron, *Community and Property for Those Who Have Neither*, 10 THEORETICAL INQUIRIES IN LAW 161, 191 (2009); Gregory S. Alexander, *Dilemmas of Group Autonomy: Residential Associations and Community*, 75 CORNELL L. REV. 1, 52–53 (1989).

some goods that are constitutive of their identity, communities must, in effect if not consciously, exclude members of the larger society to which they belong, precluding those "others" from participating in the group's internal life. By excluding others, communities limit, sometimes drastically so, their capacity to develop sympathy for others. In this sense they contradict community as a regulative ideal. We may call this the paradox of community.[36] It is evident at the level of small-scale groups (consider urban neighborhoods, particularly those with strong ethnic, racial, or religious identities) and at the level of national communities (think of the intense resistance to immigration of certain groups in the United States, France, and elsewhere).

Several of the papers in this volume deal with this insider/outsider dilemma in various ways as it bears on property. Andre van der Walt discusses it in terms of the marginalized position of those members of society who are property-less. Van der Walt defines "marginality" as "legal positions not characterized or dominated by the presence of rights, possessions, privilege and power."[37] He argues that the law of property, indeed the legal system generally, provides a central position to those who possess property while at the same time rendering those who do not have property socially, economically, and legally weak, vulnerable, and dependent. Conventional legal theory, with its singular focus on owning or not owning property, creates insiders and outsiders. Property theories based on need or social responsibility, he argues, are flawed insofar as they fail to address the central role that law and society give to owning property. In doing so, they reinforce the socially marginal position of those who do not own property. Van der Walt argues in favor of a different perspective, one that "de-centers" ownership of property by focusing on marginality. The purpose of such an approach, he stresses, is not to ignore or to devalue property rights but "to imagine a perspective on property that includes . . . the interests of those who are not 'normally' considered part of the property elite, without automatically reducing them to the status of weakness and dependency."[38] So, for example, a marginality approach to nuisance law in South Africa would focus not on the social relations between those who are equally privileged and powerful but instead on the social relations between inhabitants of so-called informal townships (usually poor Black residents) located near established wealthier (and usually white) residential areas.[39] Marginality analyses of this sort, van der Walt forcefully argues, are essential to the project of contextually embedding social justice issues in traditional property discourse.

In her fascinating paper on the Israeli "facts-on-the-ground" policy, Nomi Maya Stolzenberg considers the problem of exclusion at the level of

---

36. *See* Alexander, *Dilemmas of Group Autonomy, supra* note 35, at 52.

37. A. J. van der Walt, *Property and Marginality, infra* at 98.

38. *Id.* at 99.

39. *Id.* at 99–100.

national communities. The facts-on-the-ground policy was designed to influence the terms of any ultimate political resolution between Israel and the Palestinians in Israel's favor. The effect of strengthening the Israeli political community in this way would be to exclude Palestinians from parts of what had previously been Palestinian land. Stolzenberg argues that the insider/outsider dilemma that the facts-on-the-ground policy creates cannot be understood, let alone resolved, on the basis of a property framework. Property, like community, is frequently exclusionary.[40] Looking at the dilemma in terms of property only exacerbates the problem by fostering zero-sum thinking that emphasizes exclusionary ethnic and religious identification. What is needed, Stolzenberg argues, is a richer understanding of the logic of property that underlies the facts-on-the ground policy, a logic whose moral and practical ambiguities exclude the possibility of binary categories.

B. The Effacement Dilemma

A second dilemma that communities, including property-based communities, pose is what we call the effacement dilemma. This dilemma is in a sense the mirror image of the insider/outsider dilemma, for it involves the problem of internal relations within communities. Restrictions are important for maintaining, symbolically and instrumentally, the community's identity, not only in its public face but also within itself. Restrictions on specific forms of behavior—for example, what religious practices are permitted, what types of books may be read, whether alcohol and tobacco may be consumed—often create the community's boundary on its own internal consciousness. What Roberto Unger calls the "paradox of group cohesion"[41] exists because of the commitment of community as a normative ideal to enable the self to flourish rather than to oppress the self. As Unger points out, "By its very nature, community is always on the verge of becoming oppression."[42]

Hanoch Dagan focuses directly on this problem in his contribution to this volume. Discussing community as a normative ideal rather than as an existing social practice, Dagan criticizes conceptions of community that require community members to make personal sacrifices for the well-being of their community. "The greater good, on behalf of which calls for sacrifice are made," Dagan writes, "tends to efface individuals."[43] "[S]elflessness," he argues, "is not a virtue we should celebrate."[44] Self-sacrifice may be morally blameworthy, Dagan believes, insofar as it "harm[s] the very people for whom [self-sacrificers] care by teaching 'the permissibility of their own exploitation by submitting to, and even supporting,

---

40. *See* Waldron, *Community and Property*, *supra* note 35, at 20.

41. Roberto Mangabeira Unger, KNOWLEDGE AND POLITICS 266 (1975).

42. *Id.*

43. Dagan, *Re-Imagining Takings*, at 44.

44. *Id.*

their subservient role.'"[45] Dagan emphasizes the importance of maintaining the right of each community member to exit the community to avoid self-sacrifice and oppression.

C. The Internal Governance Dilemma

The third dilemma concerns another internal aspect of communities, but this one concerns communities as social institutions rather than as a normative ideal. How do communities govern themselves? Do they rely on formal law, or are, as recent legal and social science literature suggests,[46] do social norms do most or all of the regulatory work? Several of the papers address this question, providing different answers.

Building on recent scholarship that has focused on the role of social norms as a means of governance,[47] Kevin Gray's fascinating study of the proprietary dimensions of queuing suggests that the social norms associated with queuing perform many of the same functions as the legal rules of property do. They allocate scarce resources. One of Gray's key insights is that, as he puts it, "[q]ueueing behaviour is all about the ownership, management and conservation of the commodity of *time*."[48] The queue in its proprietary role is also about mediating social relationships, both among insiders and between insiders and outsiders. In this respect it sheds light on the social order of communities. It reflects a coordinated system of social relationships within a group of individuals. Moreover, the queue's social norms evolve in ways that "breed[] collaborative or mutually supportive sub-systems based on acts of local co-operation or 'local conspiracy' that ease the discomfort of waiting, thereby reducing the overall stress of queue discipline."[49] Gray observes that "[i]n the context of the queue the idea of 'boundary' has both a *public* and a *private* dimension." Gray explains:

> At the public level, the queue sets in place a moral geography which demarcates the waiting line as the exclusive channel of access to a desired service. . . . At the private level, the queue recognizes the spatio-temporal ownership represented by each place in the line and operates a normative convention that there may be no unconsented advancement of position within the queue.[50]

---

45. *Id.* (quoting Jean Hampton, *Selflessness and the Loss of Self, in* ALTRUISM 161 (Ellen Frankel Paul et al. eds., 1993)).

46. *See, e.g.*, Robert C. Ellickson, ORDER WITHOUT LAW: HOW NEIGHBORS SETTLE DISPUTES (1991).

47. The classic work here is, of course, Ellickson, ORDER WITHOUT LAW.

48. Kerin Gray, *Property in a Queue, infra* at 175 (emphasis in original).

49. *Id.* at 180 (citation omitted).

50. *Id.* at 189.

One of the primary conclusions that Gray draws from his study of the queue is its reliance on norms of trust and cooperation. It is, as he pithily puts it, a "self-help community."[51]

In her paper, Avital Margalit develops a new mode of analyzing commons, which she calls dynamic contextualized analysis. This new approach somewhat relaxes the categorical distinction between internal (norms) and external sources (law) of community governance. Instead, her paper argues that law is part of the internal culture of communal life. Law is culturally constitutive of commons even as the commons develops its own normative structure.

Applying this approach to the Israeli *kibbutz*, Margalit provides a richly detailed case study of the relationship between property and a form of community that is increasingly rare in the world. She emphasizes the simultaneous existence of multiple levels of legality within the *kibbutz*, and she uses the tools of legal pluralism, legal consciousness, and neo-institutionalism theory to analyze this plurality of normative orders. What she finds is that *kibbutzim* developed their own legal consciousness of indifference toward the official state rules that nominally regulated them. *Kibbutzim* created their own cultural world, and it was a world that was not entirely comfortable with the rules of the state. Rather than overtly resisting the state's rules, however, *kibbutzim* adopted a response of indifference toward the state's efforts at governance. In this way, kibbutzim were able to reach a more-or-less stable equilibrium with the state.

VI. CONCLUSION

The concepts of property and community are deeply intertwined. And yet the implications of property discussions for the conceptualization or operation of community (and vice versa) tend to be left unexplored within property scholarship. Moreover, the dominant approaches within property theory are poorly suited to the task of explaining and evaluating the interaction between property and community. The essays in this volume take a significant step toward rectifying this prior neglect. At the same time, they perform the important service of broadening the conversation to encompass theories of property and community that diverge, both methodologically and normatively, from the traditional diet of utilitarianism and classical liberalism.

---

51. *Id.* at 193.

1. THE OBJECTS OF VIRTUE

DAVID LAMETTI*

I. INTRODUCTION

Although a deep and rich property theory literature already exists, more needs to be said about the underlying ethical values of private property. In particular, the role that objects play in understanding property relations and the ways in which the uses of certain objects are affected by society's ethical choices need further elaboration.

Private property classically has been considered a part of private law, of course. Along with the law of obligations—contractual obligations and civil responsibility (and unjust enrichment for common lawyers)—private property forms the basis for the private law. Indeed, one might argue that to the extent that private property regulates the objects of social wealth[1] necessary for contractual obligations and unjust enrichment, or the means of compensation for tort, private property underlies all of private law.

Intellectual property represents a newer category of resources, arising out of the changing nature of society and how wealth is generated and valued. Hence, *droit d'auteur*—especially in its economic dimension, copyright, but also

---

* Associate Dean (Academic) and Associate Professor, Faculty of Law, McGill University, and Member, Center for Intellectual Property Policy; B.A. (Toronto); LL.B., B.C.L. (McGill); LL.M. (Yale); D.Phil. (Oxford). A previous version of this paper was presented at a workshop on private property law and intellectual property entitled, "Terminology and Property Models in the 21st Century," at the Quebec Research Centre of Private and Comparative Law, Faculty of Law, McGill University, and was subsequently presented at the Centre for Innovation, Law, and Policy, Faculty of Law, University of Toronto, the Faculty of Law Queen's University and the Università degli studi di Trento. I thank the following for their comments: Abraham Drassinower, Edward Iacobucci, Richard Corley, David Cameron, Lisa Austin, Bryan Thomas, Larissa Katz, Malcolm Thorburn, Roberto Caso, and Umberto Izzo. It was later presented at a property workshop at NYU Law School in the summer of 2008: I wish to thank (again) Larissa Katz and Lisa Austin, as well as Amnon Lehavi, Christopher Serkin, James Penner, Laura Underkuffler, and Katrina Wyman. Finally, many careful suggestions were offered by Greg Alexander, Eduardo Peñalver, Bruce Carlini and Catherine Doldirina. I wish to thank McGill's Wainwright Fund, the Social Sciences and Humanities Research Council of Canada, and Simone Bittman for her thoughtful substantive and formal suggestions, as well as for her research assistance.

1. The term is Jim Harris's: *see* JAMES W. HARRIS, PROPERTY AND JUSTICE (1996).

to a lesser degree in its noneconomic aspect, moral rights[2]—as well as patents, trademarks, trade secrets, confidential information, and domain names have some value and are commonly seen as a type of "property" right and property resource. Some might say that such ideational or intellectual resources are in the realm of "ideas" and as such are not "property." Certainly there are significant points of distinction, but it remains true that such ideational resources have significant economic value and share the attributes and even the structure of what one might call "ordinary" property: an object of value, as well as a series of rights that are attached to that object. While intellectual property governance is characterized by different normative responses—legislation (both codal and statutory), common law rules, quasi-private schemes, contracts, or contractually based schemes, or combinations thereof—basic attributes persist. Thus traditional and intellectual property constitutes resources of value, or "patrimonial" resources in civilian terms, and in both systems they are classified as "real" rights, that is, good against the whole world. And intellectual property rights are, increasingly, registered in formal registries run by both the state and private bodies. Most important is the shared rhetoric: metaphorically and often legally, the word "ownership" is used.

Of course there are real differences between property and intellectual property. There is obviously a question of intangibility, although many forms of private property are also intangible. It must also be recognized that intellectual property often concerns the privatization of public goods (such as ideas, facts, science, etc.), although historians would remind us of the enclosure movement, which had the same effect.[3] Certainly, the objective "markers" or "fences" signifying traditional property are different, and less metaphorical than the © or TM symbol, which are not as effective at excluding. And most obviously, the history and relative historical power of different forms of property is unique to each. But here, too, we must appreciate a changing world where intellectual resources do generate greater degrees of wealth.

So to some extent, the question of intellectual property governance is about defining new "property," both in terms of new objects of social wealth and the relationships—rights and duties—that are erected around these objects. On a cynical view, however, everything is property: anything with a value, any asset, is my property. This includes rights or services that might be held by me or owed to me, even if they have no attachment to an object of social wealth; the right in a sense is the object itself.[4] On the contrary, nothing is property: all property is

---

2. *Gilliam v. American Broadcasting Corp.*, 538 F.2d 14 (2d Cir. 1976); Henry Hansman and Marina Santilli, *Authors' and Artists' Moral Rights: A Comparative Legal and Economic Analysis*, 26 J. LEG. STUDIES 95 (1997).

3. JAMES BOYLE, THE PUBLIC DOMAIN: ENCLOSING THE COMMONS OF THE MIND 42 ff. (2008).

4. Indeed what in civilian scholarship is called "patrimony."

simply a relationship between and among individuals with no particular role for the object of property to play in defining the terms of the property relationship. It is fair to ascribe such a view to Thomas Grey and Wesley Hohfeld.[5] How do we escape this definitional conundrum? We need to look at the purpose of private property as an institution. What is missing is an appreciation that the institution of private property is in some sense very public, serving certain goals, individual and collective. So, while there are many structures and concepts, little will be understood if those definitions and concepts do not reflect something of the teleology of the institution of private property, and the manner in which we value resources.

My purpose in this paper is to try to illuminate more fully some of the underlying values of both forms of property. How are they similar or different? In the end, it is a question of how society views resources, and of how we value those resources. What I would like to consider, borrowing from Lon Fuller, is what one might call property law's "morality of aspiration." This in turn was inspired by Aristotle, who ought to be reinstated as a central figure in our understanding of private property. Thus framed, the question is to what do we aspire with respect to our relationship with resources? It is nothing less than a question of both individual development and societal development, and the role property plays in those processes. Private property will play this role both through use and through distribution.

Elsewhere I have argued that we need a new metaphor for private property: property is a relationship between or among individuals *through* objects of social wealth.[6] The definition of private property that embodies this metaphor places property squarely within its social context:

> Private property is a social institution that comprises a variety of contextual relationships among individuals *through objects of social wealth* and is *meant to serve a variety of individual and collective purposes.* It is characterized by allocating to individuals a measure of control over the *use* and alienation of, some degree of exclusivity in the enjoyment of, and some measure of obligation to and responsibilities for scarce and separable objects of social wealth.[7]

---

5. Thomas C. Grey, *The Disintegration of Property, in* PROPERTY: NOMOS XXII 69 (J. Roland Pennock and John W. Chapman eds., 1980); and Wesley N. Hohfeld, *Fundamental Legal Conceptions as Applied in Judicial Reasoning* (Walter Wheeler Cook ed., 1919).

6. David Lametti, *The Concept of Property: Relations Through Objects of Social Wealth,* 53 U. TORONTO L.J. 325 (2003).

7. The text continues, putting this change of metaphor in context:

> Private property is necessarily social because of its structural asymmetry *and* underlying value and purposes—human survival, human development and flourishing, and so on—coupled with its scarcity. In short, property is social because of its ethical dimensions and implications. In addition to the social aspect, virtually all writers point

The impact of this change of metaphor and definition is that it puts part of the focus on the object—its value, its uses, its context, its social aspect—without losing what one might call the private aspect of the relationship: the interrelationship of individuals. That is, the particular object of social wealth—i.e., the *thing* in property—brings unique characteristics to the private property relationship—i.e., property rights and duties. How we value, use, and understand the object is shared across society and in particular reflects shared societal values regarding resources or indeed the particular resource in question. "Property," then, is a social, contextual phenomenon concerning distributive and/or redistributive decisions, as well as decisions about proper uses. As a resource, in its allocation to a private owner (thus by definition excluding others) and in its use by that owner (thus consuming, altering the resource or the environment, changing the sum pool of objects of social wealth, etc.) necessarily has an impact on others, and thus adds a public dimension to a private relationship.

Thus understood, the source of property's social aspect is ultimately the collective values of any given society. But one must then ask what values are at play? What is the source of these values, or how are they determined? The answers to such questions can only be found in our deepest ethical beliefs. Many of these will be most evident in the discourse justifying or explaining private property. Obviously, in the practice of private property, they will play out in rules about how property is allocated and how property is used. These discourses will contain not only the rationales for favoring private property over other alternatives such as forms of common property, but will betray the larger goals and values that the institution serves.

A great deal has been written about the individual values that property rights serve: autonomy, liberty, individual actualization, development, and self-expression. There can be no doubt that such values are crucial to our understanding of the institution. Less has been written about private property's collective or communitarian values (although this is now changing).[8] Such understandings are equally important in explaining and justifying private property, and in simply understanding the institution's fullest, socially situated dimensions. It is in this direction that I wish to move.

In order to understand what may be missing in the present understanding of private property, we need to go back. I propose to look carefully at Aristotle (and, by implication, Plato) and Aquinas in order to illuminate some of the ethical

---

to the relative scarcity of objects of social wealth, its distributive impact and impact on justice, as well as its inherently controversial nature. All of these factors point clearly to a concept of property that is based on more than individual rights to exclusive use. Any attempt to describe the institution, or to frame its normative structure and assess its normative weight must take these wider interests into account. *Id.* at 326.

8. *See, e.g.*, Gregory S. Alexander and Eduardo M. Peñalver, *Properties of Community*, 10 Theoretical Inquiries in Law 127 (2009).

underpinnings of their respective theories of property. To the extent that such understandings of private property might directly or indirectly influence current property discourse—think of "virtue ethics" or neo-Aristotelian scholarship[9]—they are usefully examined. In fact it is precisely in these writers that we find clues to the misunderstood, or perhaps a less-than-well-understood, social aspect of private property.

II. ARISTOTLE ON "PRIVATE IN POSSESSION, COMMON IN USE"

As it framed the discourse for Aristotle's later treatment of private property, we need to briefly understand Plato's view. And the starting point in Plato is perhaps the most celebrated regime of property in classical political theory: the regime of common property set out by Socrates in Plato's *Republic*. While that "ideal city" was based on the common ownership or property, it is nevertheless a useful starting point for Plato's more extensive theory of property in the *Laws*, as well as for Aristotle's defense of private property against Plato's common regime.

Plato's *Republic* is celebrated for having articulated two regimes of common property. In the most rudimentary city, the so-called "city of sows,"[10] in which citizens engaged in the four primary occupations, putting all the fruits of their labor toward the common disposition, as well as in the more "luxurious city" in which other occupations were allowed, no one would possess any private property.[11] Not only would private property be held in common, but women and children would be as well. Plato felt that common property would remedy the personal evils and societal injustices brought about by vices associated with private property such as greed, immoderation, and intemperance. In addition, happiness was not to be associated with material possessions and sensual pleasures: the guardians, who would live completely in common in every aspect of life, would be the happiest citizens of all.[12]

---

9. *See* ROSALIND HURSTHOUSE, ON VIRTUE ETHICS (1999); DANIEL STATMAN ed., VIRTUE ETHICS: A CRITICAL READER (1997); and ROGER CRISP AND MICHAEL SLOTE ed., VIRTUE ETHICS (1997). *See also* ONORA O'NEILL, TOWARDS JUSTICE AND VIRTUE (1996); and CHARLES TAYLOR, THE SOURCES OF THE SELF (1989).

10. Plato's REPUBLIC 372d, 49 (Allan Bloom trans., 2d ed. 1991). Where possible, I have chosen fairly literal translations as base texts. Less literal translations are used to supplement.

11. REPUBLIC, 416d, 95–96.

12. REPUBLIC, 420b, 98; and 465d–466c, 145–46. Of course, many have argued that the structure of REPUBLIC as a whole is meant to be an allegory for the proper structuring of the human soul, and thus this property theory may not have been meant to be, in Schlatter's terms, "a serious contribution" to political thought. With Schlatter, one can

The "second-best" city described in the *Laws* does not maintain this position of complete sharing of property.[13] Here an older Plato has clearly admitted that *private* property is "by nature" and would have to be an integral part of the human city. But the scepticism regarding the negative effects of private property still lingers: after the founding of a new city upon the remains of a tyrannical regime, Plato states that the distribution of property would be the first specific to be dealt with by the new leaders. Preventing disputes over property by the settlement of ancient debts and redistributing property so that the inequality of property is minimized is aimed at avoiding disputes over property. The old Athenian interlocutor portrays avarice as a spiritual poverty far greater than material poverty: "This is the most important source of a city's preservation, and provides a sort of sturdy foundation upon which someone can later build whatever political order befits such an arrangement. But if this foundation is rotten, political activity would always encounter difficulties in the city."[14] In order to have a proper foundation, a city must therefore have enough land for every person to have a certain amount, as well as a common amount of land for the functional things that a city needs: ritual space, government space, market space, etc. Yet according to Plato, all citizens should treat their land as part of the common stock of the city.[15] Further, there would be restrictions on buying and selling, on the accumulation

---

only conclude that this is of no matter, as it has been taken seriously: RICHARD SCHLATTER, PRIVATE PROPERTY: THE HISTORY OF AN IDEA (1951), 11.

13. PLATO'S LAWS 739c–740a, 126 (Thomas L. Pangle trans., 1980):

> That city and that regime are first, and the laws are best, where the old proverb holds as much as possible throughout the whole city: it is said that the things of friends really are common. If this situation exists somewhere now, or if it should ever exist someday—if women are common, and children are common, and every sort of property is common; if every device has been employed to exclude all of what is called the "private" from all aspects of life; if, in so far as possible, a way has been devised to make common somehow the things that are *by nature* private, such as the eyes and the ears and the hands, so that they seem to see and hear and act in common; if, again, everyone praises and blames in unison, as much as possible delighting in the same things and feeling pain at the same things, if with all their might they delight in all the laws that aim at making the city come as close as possible to unity—then no one will ever set down a more correct or better definition than this of what constitutes the extreme as regards virtue. Such a city is inhabited, presumably, by gods or children of gods (more than one), and they dwell in gladness, leading such a life. Therefore one should not look elsewhere for the model, at any rate, of a political regime, but should hold on to this and seek with all one's might the regime that comes as close as possible to such a regime. If the regime we've been dealing with now [in the LAWS] came into being, it would be in a way, the nearest to immortality and second in point of unity. [My emphasis.]

14. LAWS, 736e–737a, 123.

15. LAWS, 740a, 127.

of wealth, on the quality and quantity of currency,[16] on loans, as well as absolute prohibitions on money-lending with interest and dowries.[17] Private property is thus allowed rather begrudgingly, and is strictly limited.[18]

Plato is also careful to stipulate that while there will be necessarily some difference in wealth between citizens, as well as between talents, virtues, and honors, this will be held to a strict "maximin" principle:[19] the poorest class always maintaining their minimum allotment, and the wealthiest class only being allowed to accumulate up to five times the amount of the basic allotment, after which point they would be required to turn over the surplus to the city.[20] Thus there is a clear picture of what might be called the vocation or "destination" of private property: the teleology of the institution of private property is to serve a vision of the common good, with specific norms applying this larger idea in specific circumstances.[21] So there are two visions of property found in Plato: the idealistic vision of common property described in *Republic,* and the more pragmatic scepticism toward common property in the *Laws,* couple with a restrained, limited regime of private property supporting the "common stock of the city."

Aristotle's comments on property are framed generally as a response to these theories of property set out by Plato in *Republic* and *Laws,* as well as those set out by other contemporary theorists and lawgivers[22] and those in place in contemporary regimes.[23] Using these regimes of common property as points of departure, Aristotle articulates a defense of private property in Book II of *Politics.* The extent to which common property is employed in the ideal and practical regimes set out by Plato and certain of these others is rejected for the well-constituted city. Aristotle touched upon fundamental claims pertaining to the social dimension of private property. This is manifest in his clear teleology for private property: private property ownership was meant to serve, promote, or develop virtue. Aristotle therefore has much to offer at an intuitive level about an ethical

---

16. "[T]hey should possess a kind of coin that carries value among themselves but is valueless among other human beings." LAWS, 742a, 129.

17. LAWS, 741d–742d, 128–29.

18. LAWS, 743d, 131.

19. *See* JOHN RAWLS, A THEORY OF JUSTICE 154, 150–61 (1971). For a recent application specific to property theory, *see* STEPHEN R. MUNZER, A THEORY OF PROPERTY 241–53 (1990).

20. LAWS, 744b and 744e–745b, 131–32.

21. For a modern application, *see* D. Lametti, "The *Destino* of Destination in Civil Law Property" (unpublished manuscript on file with the author).

22. Phaleas of Chalcedon and Hippodamus of Miletus are named. *See* Aristotle's THE POLITICS Book II, 1261al ff, 55 ff. (Carnes Lord trans., 1984). I will be relying on the Lord translation, also considered to quite literal. Brackets used in quotations are Lord's, except where noted.

23. Lacedaemon (Sparta), Crete, and Carthage. *See* POLITICS, *id.*

justification for private property, and more specifically about the legitimate uses of private property, and the virtues it helps to develop. The theory of private property as articulated in the text of the *Politics* can serve only as an incomplete basis for private property in the political regime. One can, however, gain specific insight into the gaps left by Aristotle, by placing his theory of property into the context of his larger ethical and political theory, namely the *Ethics*. Aristotle's social theory thus helps to explain the function of and delineate the boundaries of his property theory.

A. Property in the *Politics*

The central passage on private property in the *Politics*, which provides the setting for the often-cited formula "private in possession, common in use," is as follows:

> In general, to live together and be partners in any human matter is difficult, and particularly things of this sort. This is clear in the partnerships of fellow travelers, most of whom are always quarrelling as a result of friction with one another over everyday and small matters. Again, friction particularly arises with the servants we use most frequently for regular tasks. Having possessions in common involves, then, these and other similar difficulties, and the mode that prevails now—if provided with the adornment of character and an arrangement of correct laws—would be more than a little better. For it would have what is good in both—by both I mean what comes from having possessions in common and what from having them privately. For they should be common in some sense, yet private generally speaking. Dividing the care [of possessions] will cause them not to raise these accusations against one another, and will actually result in improvement, as each applies himself to his own; and it will be through virtue that "the things of friends are common," as the proverb has it, with a view to use. Even now this mode can be found in outline in some cities, so it is not impossible; in finely administered cities especially some of these things already exist, while others could be brought into being. [In these cities] *everyone has his own possessions, but he makes some of them useful to his friends, and some he uses as common things*. In Lacedaemon, for example, they use each other's slaves, as well as their horses and dogs, as practically their own, and anything they need by way of provisions from the fields [when they travel] in their territory. *It is evident, then, that it is better for possessions to be private, but to make them common in use*. That [the citizens] become such [as to use them in common]—this is a task peculiar to the legislator.[24]

---

24. Politics, Book II, 1263al–bl, 60–61. In the Jowett translation, the critical passages are as follows:

> For, although every man has his own property, some things he will place at the disposal of his friends, while of others he shares the use with them. . . . It is clearly better that property should be private, but the use of it common; and the special disposition of

Based on this passage, private-in-possession seems to be comprehensible at an intuitive level. Aristotle acknowledges that something in human nature makes common property difficult to have in practice, and that private property is more efficient. More importantly, private-in-possession first assumes something important about the role of property in the development of human potential and the promotion of virtue, and that these goals are fostered by an association with private possessions at an individual level. There is an underlying reason why possessions are important to those of us living in modern Western cultures, why we will defend what is our own and what is dear, and, regarding property, why we will use it in a more effective manner when it is our own. We develop certain virtues by acting with property in a certain way. This explanation is incomplete as a defense of private property because it does not fully articulate what restrictions virtue places on our use of private possessions.

In addition, private-in-possession accepts self-love, and the pleasure that emanates from it, as a natural, rational, and virtuous activity when properly moderated and aimed at just goals: "[T]he good man will be a lover of self (for he will both himself profit by doing noble acts, and will benefit his fellows), but the wicked man should not; for he will hurt both himself and his neighbors, following as he does evil passions."[25] But this is not the same as excessive self-love or self-affection, which loses sight of what is virtuous. Self-love is purposive and rational in that it leads one to take care of oneself and one's family, as well as one's property, and puts a person in a position to benefit others.

The difficulty comes in understanding the meaning of the phrase "common in use." The standard interpretation of this passage takes the words at their face value, even if "confusing": Aristotle is advocating sharing of some resources by private owners in some sense.[26] Further insight might be found in the critique of Plato. In Book II of the *Politics,* Aristotle takes issue with political regimes where common property is the norm, or where equality of property is attempted. Aristotle's critique in the *Politics* of each of the Platonic systems is centered about several similar points. Regarding the scheme of common property in *Republic,* Aristotle does recognize certain benefits under specific circumstances emanating from common property—for example, if farmers were a class unto themselves, land could be held and farmed in common and the crops divided for common consumption[27]—and acknowledges its attractive

---

the legislator is to create in men this benevolent disposition. Aristotle's THE POLITICS 26 (Benjamin Jowett trans., Stephen Everson ed., 1988).

25. Aristotle's NICHOMACHEAN ETHICS Book IX, 1169a8, 237 (David Ross trans., 1925).

26. SCHLATTER, *supra* note 12, at 15–19.

27. POLITICS, 1263al, 60.

face and its humanity.[28] Common property would probably eliminate absolute want.[29]

Aristotle then quite famously takes issue with Plato's scheme of common property, specifically the common possession of women and children. Here Aristotle presents three initial criticisms:[30] he first questions Plato's ends, he then questions Plato's means, and finally questions the effectiveness of having these important elements of society held in common, specifically in terms of its effect on the level of care and affection in society. The central critique is on the question of ends: in Aristotle's view, the goal of creating a seemingly complete unity of will in the city is neither attainable nor desirable. In positing such a scheme, Plato has misjudged the correct balance between the individual and the city:

> [With] respect to the end which he asserts the city should have, it is . . . impossible. . . . I mean that it is best for the city to be as far as possible entirely one, for this is the presupposition Socrates adopts. And yet it is evident that as it becomes increasingly one it will no longer be a city. For the city is in its nature a sort of multitude, and as it becomes more of a unity it will be a household instead of a city, and a human being instead of a household; for we would surely say that the household is more a unity than the city, and the individual than the household. So even if were able to do this, one ought not do it, as it would destroy the city.[31]

In practice, it is the fact that each person in "the multitude" brings different talents to a partnership—first to a marriage, then to a household, then to the city—that allows for greater degrees of self-sufficiency for the collectivity: "If, therefore, the self-sufficient is more choiceworthy, what is less a unity is more choiceworthy than what is more a unity."[32] Since the city is formed by human beings differing in kind, what binds them together is "reciprocal equality," a notion found in the *Ethics*, not complete unity. In this context, human fulfillment—the greatest good of each thing—and its promotion is what preserves the city. The state should therefore aim at maximum self-completeness in order to strengthen the city, and not maximum unity.[33]

---

28. POLITICS, 1263bl, 61. In general there are three possible common property schemas: (1) land be privately owned; produce put into the common stock; (2) land be common and worked in common, but produce divided and private; and (3) both land and produce be common.

29. Newman says Aristotle would have admitted as much: 1 WILLIAM L. NEWMAN, THE POLITICS OF ARISTOTLE, 163, n.3 (1887–1902).

30. I am following Newman's organization of these points. *Id.* at 160–61.

31. POLITICS, 1261al, 56.

32. POLITICS, 1261bl, 60–61.

33. In the second prong of the critique, Aristotle questions Plato's means to achieving unity. Aristotle states that a "collective mine" is difficult to define, as opposed to an

The third critique is even more explicit: Aristotle recognizes that common property will diminish the care and attention given to wives and children, and the closeness of connection to it, and will weaken affections: "What belongs in common is accorded the least care: they take thought for their own things above all, and less about things common, or only so much as falls to each individually."[34] In addition, there would also be moral problems stemming from the uncertainty of lineage: patricide, matricide, and incest. If mutual affection is necessary for the united city, collective ownership of women and children can only serve to diminish it by weakening the ties that bar people from engaging in factional conflict: "For there are two things above all which make human beings cherish and feel affection, what is one's own and what is dear; and neither of these can be available to those who govern themselves in this way."[35]

It is fair to say that these criticisms can be applied *mutatis mutandis* to the critique of common property in general.[36] While one does not, and indeed should not, love one's property in the same way one loves another human being, property is "dear" and certainly "one's own." The considerations of the unity of the state, the difficulties of assessing the collective "mine" (or, I suppose, the collective "ours"), and the loss of efficiency from according the least care to what is collective are all fairly attributed to the Aristotelian critique of common property, even though Aristotle will himself try to accommodate a role for common property in his regimes. The question, as shall be discussed later, will ultimately turn upon the balance between individual fulfillment and the ends of the community.

To these general critiques—"even apart from legislation concerning children and women"—Aristotle would add two further critiques: a common property regime fails to eliminate the bad effects generally attributed to private property and, most importantly, the loss of certain virtues associated with private possessions that common property does not foster. Regarding the first of these additional criticisms, Aristotle recognizes the attractiveness of common property when contrasted to the "ills" leveled against private property: "lawsuits against one another concerning contracts, trial involving perjury, and flattery of the rich." But on closer examination, these come about not because of property but because of "depravity." We see those with whom we hold things in common as rivals, not those who, presumably as our equals, we see as other property owners. Such an

---

"individual mine," which is comprehensible. In reality, a "collective mine"—as in "all say the same thing"—is impossible, or it does not even lead to unanimity or concord. Politics, 1261bl, 57. Aristotle means unanimity as something less than unity: as a mere means or transition point on the way to a complete end.

34. Politics, 1261bl, 57.

35. Politics, 1262bl, 59.

36. Following Newman, *supra* note 29.

argument certainly resonates in the modern liberal ear. Good fences make good neighbors.

Despite these critiques, the precise sense of "private in possession, common in use" remains difficult to determine. As we have seen, Aristotle had identified three possible common or partially common ownership scenarios,[37] but as Richard Schlatter points out, he does not really identify which of these scenarios his argument and new metaphor is meant to correct or indeed to which it might be meant to apply.[38] The idea that perhaps one should separate the land and the product is also not further applied.

Hence the metaphor "private in possession, common in use" ought to be pushed further in the direction of the last identified critique of Plato that focuses on the idea of virtue. The key to understanding this phrase is to see that it is virtue—both metaphorically and in actuality—that makes property common. Private property plays a role in the attainment of individual virtue generally both in how it should be used and also how it should be allocated and pursued.[39] Parallel to the relation between virtuous acts and virtue itself, the relation between how one should use property and the virtues that private property helps to foster is a mutually reinforcing, symbiotic one. Just as virtuous acts help one attain a virtuous disposition and a virtuous disposition helps one choose to act virtuously, acquiring and using possessions in a proper fashion will help a person to develop moderation and liberality, so liberality and moderation will help one to acquire and use private property in a virtuous fashion. This relationship indicates a purposive element in the use of property, and represents an important difference between Aristotle's conception of private property and that of modern right-based theorists. Although he has touched upon the fundamentally individual goal of personal ethical development, Aristotle's conception of private property is also grounded in the fundamentally communitarian goal of the virtuous development of the city. Aristotle's defense of private property is best understood as one attempt to address the balance between the complete unity of the city (for which he criticized Plato) and the complete particularity of the multitude.[40]

The last criticism of common property, while it shares some etymology, is anything but "liberal." It flows from an admission that one gets intrinsic pleasure

---

37. To repeat, they are: (1) land be privately owned; produce put into the common stock; (2) land be common and worked in common, but produce divided and private; and (3) both land and produce be common. Notably, a "private-private" solution is not suggested.

38. Schlatter, *supra* note 12, at 15–17.

39. Terence H. Irwin, *Aristotle's Defense of Private Property, in* A Companion to Aristotle's Politics 200, and especially 213–225 (David Keyt and Fred D. Miller Jr., eds., 1991).

40. *See infra* note 44 and accompanying text.

from considering something one's own, and that having private property allows one to cultivate the virtues of moderation and liberality:

> Further, it makes an immense difference with respect to pleasure to consider a thing one's own. It is surely not to no purpose that everyone has affection for himself; this is something natural. Selfishness is justly blamed; but this is not having affection for oneself [simply], but rather having more affection than one should—just as in the case of the greedy person; for practically everyone has affection for things of this sort. Those who make the city too much of a unity not only forfeit these things; in addition, they manifestly eliminate the tasks of two of the virtues, moderation concerning women (it being a fine deed to abstain though from a woman who belongs to another) and liberality concerning possessions. For it will not be possible to show oneself as liberal or to perform any liberal action, since the task of liberality lies in the use of possessions.[41]

In general, this certainly fits with the overall teleology expressed elsewhere in the *Politics:* private property helps to promote good behavior, and when such behavior does occur the owner demonstrates a certain virtue. There is at least a public dimension to private property, in the realm of good conduct.

The first particular point to note, then, is that there is a natural self-love that is responsible for a healthy disposition to regard something as one's own. While not explicitly stated at this juncture, presumably this proper self-love is similar to the virtue of proper self-love discussed in the *Ethics,* based on moderation and distinct from selfishness, and therefore is not responsible for the greed that emanates from too much self-love.[42] Virtue has a role in how property is disposed of, i.e., how objects of property ought to be used.

The second point is related conversely to the first; property has a role in the development of virtue. Common property eliminates some or all of the need for the virtues of moderation and liberality. We must recall that in *Republic* moderation is exercised in the example specifically with respect to women, but, as I have argued above, the virtue can be extended to "other" forms of property by preventing excessive self-love and greed, particularly to the use and extent of one's wealth. With regard to liberality, one cannot show oneself liberal if one has no possessions with which to do favors for friends or to be generous with. Generosity in turn fosters friendship, which is beneficial for the city. Private property therefore affords a means to develop virtues that would otherwise remain un- (or at least under-) developed in a common property system.

---

41. Politics, 1263bl, 61.
42. Ethics, 1168a33, 234ff.

These errors, according to Aristotle, stem from the assumption[43] that unity (as distinct from unanimity) was a possibility in the city: "Both the household and the city should be one in a sense, but not in every sense. On the one hand, as the city proceeds [in this direction], it will at some point cease to be a city, on the other hand, while remaining a city, it will be a worse city the closer it becomes to not being a city—just as if one were to reduce a consonance to unison, or a meter to a single foot."[44] Thus the root of this error is the presupposition by Socrates, already identified, of trying to make all individuals one complete unity. Such an ideal is impossible and undesirable, since a person's self-contained interest is an essential condition to the achievement of the human good.[45] Instead of making all individuals the same unity in practice, the city must be made one in virtue, through education, but left alone to dispose of what is their own.

Aristotle's correctives of the scheme set out in Plato's *Laws* offer further support. They are correctives in the sense that with regard to possessions, Aristotle does not appear to discard completely the entire system of property envisioned in the regime.[46] Given that Plato has now allowed for private possessions, albeit with restrictions, it is fair to conclude that Aristotle is less hostile to this second regime. Indeed, given that Aristotle will also set out a limited version of property aimed at promoting happiness (*eudaemonia*) and the human good, one could safely argue that with respect to private property at least the *Laws* represents a step toward the regime set out in the *Politics*.

The first corrective regards the virtue of moderation and the extent of possessions:

> As regards the extent of possessions, too, one should see whether it would not be better to determine this differently and more clearly. For [Plato] asserts that there should be as much as is needed to live with moderation, which is as if one were to say "to live well": it is too general. Moreover, it is possible to live with moderation but wretchedly. A better defining principle would be

---

43. Made especially by Plato.

44. POLITICS, 1263bl, 62.

45. Irwin, *supra* note 39, at 216.

46. Which Aristotle seems to do for the rest of the general ideas proposed in the LAWS:

> [A]lthough he wishes to make it more attainable by cities, he gradually brings it around again toward the other regime. For apart from the partnership in women and possessions, the other things he assign it are the same for both regimes: education is the same, as is the life abstention from necessary work and of common messes; only here he asserts that there should be common messes for women as well, and that the number of those possessing arms should be five thousand whereas it is a thousand there. All the discourses of Socrates are extraordinary: they are sophisticated, original, and searching. But it is perhaps difficult to do everything finely. [1265al, 64.]

> "with moderation and liberally" (for when separated the one will tend toward luxury, the other toward a life of hardship), since these alone are the choice-worthy dispositions concerning the use of property: it is not possible to use property gently or courageously, but it is possible to use it with moderation and liberally, so the dispositions connected with it must be these.[47]

Once again, and more explicitly than in his discussion of the *Politics*, Aristotle underscores the important relationship between these two virtues and the disposition and use of property. Plato's "error" was in only associating one of the relevant virtues, moderation, with private property and neglecting the other. It is important to note that this passage indicates that Aristotle meant to associate the virtue of moderation with possessions generally, and not just women and children, as argued above.[48]

The discourse on property in the *Politics* identifies the basic elements of the Aristotelian schema. However, the question of values is still underdeveloped. In addition, there are also some equally unclear notions of equality, and especially only for the ruling classes.[49] So there is still a great deal shared by Aristotle with the Plato of the *Laws:* neither is fully a "communist," nor a defender of private property for all. In particular, the larger teleology—the common in use or common in purpose—seems thin. While specific virtues are identified and fostered, and some general benefits to the community identified, more needs to be said.

B. Property in *Ethics*

In order to properly understand this, we must see how property and the city fit into Aristotle's general ethical structure and are manifested in political regimes. In other words, the *Politics* must be situated within the *Ethics*. In general, it has been said that the *Ethics* sets out the form of the good life as realized by the best persons in the ideal state, while the *Politics* tries to set out the parameters of the good state itself.[50] By situating private property in a state built upon the foundation

---

47. Politics, 1265al, 65.

48. The second corrective pertains to the (relative) equalization of property among citizens: here it is "odd" that Plato would concern himself with equality of property without restricting procreation. Since property allotments in the newly founded regime could not be split in the future, some people would necessarily be left out in the next generation, causing poverty, and in turn factional conflict and crime. The birth rate would need to be regulated, taking mortality and infertility rates into account. *See* Politics, 1265bl, 65.

49. Schlatter, *supra* note 12, at 28.

50. John L. Stocks, Aristotle's Definition of the Human Good (1919), quoted in William K. C. Guthrie, A History of Greek Philosophy (vol. VI, Aristotle: An encounter) 331, n.2 (1981).

of virtue and always striving for it, we can sketch more fully the outlines of Aristotle's theory of private property.

It should be recalled at the outset that the role of the city for Plato was to provide the basic necessities of life: self-sufficiency thus limits the goals of the city. In the city of sows, moderate desires are easily satisfied. Therefore, common property is a potentially obtainable and desirable property system in theory. T. H. Irwin also argues that there is no need for a substantive form of justice in this city; rather justice in this specialized city is merely instrumental efficiency.[51] The swollen city is still specialized, though more complex, but justice remains centered about instrumental efficiency. Later in the *Republic,* something more fundamental and enlightened—first determined by nature through the "myth of the metals" and then nature identified by those philosophers who have escaped the "cave"—determines how specialization occurs. Finally, in the City of Guardians a common good unites the individuals in the city, and justice moves beyond the ordering of the city to the ordering of the soul. But, as cities become larger and more realistic, common property encounters difficulties in practice, as Plato more or less admits in the *Laws*. More importantly, Plato's last goal of proper ordering and justice cannot succeed: common property does not allow for the development of the individual soul, and prevents the city from attaining virtue, and also justice.

In contrast, for Aristotle, the city is organized for the promotion of the fine, and the happiness (*eudaemonia*) of its citizens. The basic partnership (*koinonia*) is more than the mere provision of material needs; rather it is aimed at living well. Justice in this city must be more than the equality of possessions, or the sharing of common ones, and more than just a proper ordering of the city according to reason. It must move beyond rational ordering to one that allows virtue to flourish. In his discussion of ideal regimes, Aristotle states:

> For if it were for the sake of possessions that they participated and joined together, they would share in the city just to the extent that they shared in possessions, so that the argument of the oligarchs might be held a strong one; for [they would say] it is not just for one who has contributed one mina to share equally in a hundred minas with the one giving all the rest, whether [he derives] from those who were there originally or the later arrivals. But if [the city exists] not only for the sake of living but rather primarily for the sake of living well (for otherwise there could be a city of slaves or of animals. . . .) It is evident, therefore, that the city is not a partnership in a location and for the sake of not committing injustice against each other and of transacting business. These things must necessarily be present if there is to be a city, but not even when all of them are present is it yet a city, but [the city is] the partnership in living well both of households and families for the sake of a complete and

51. Irwin, *supra* note 38, at 205.

> self-sufficient life. . . . The political partnership must be regarded, therefore, as being for the sake of noble actions, not for the sake of living together.[52]

And those who have attained a higher degree of virtue, those who contribute more to the political arrangement, are to receive greater honors. This heightened role for the city places greater responsibility on the regime to foster what is desired for the sake of living well. The regime must foster the best of what mankind can produce, such that citizens can share in the widest sense of happiness. For its part, just having property in common or even in private, as Plato asserts, is insufficient as a criterion for living well. Rather, it is how property is used and how it affects one's character that is important.

The substantive base for living well is virtue. Aristotle defines virtue in the *Ethics* as "a state of character concerned with choice, lying in a mean, i.e., the mean relative to us, this being determined by a rational principle by which practical wisdom would determine it."[53] It is this characteristic state that helps one to choose and find the proper balance, as well as a state of being produced when one has consistently chosen well. The virtue in the city is founded on the virtue of individuals, and the virtue of individuals is based on the virtue of the city. Each forms the other through laws and education, and the actions of virtuous individuals leading to a virtuous state of character aimed at the good. "Human good turns out to be the activity of the soul exhibiting excellence, in accordance with the best and most complete,"[54] and virtue the means of attaining that good. That is, virtue is a matter of finding mean-points between extreme states of character. These states of character are options, and practical wisdom and reason, coupled with proper training form the city, allow us to choose the virtuous midpoints, and in doing so become virtuous ourselves.

Private property, at first private-in-possession, becomes common-in-use through the auspices of virtue. Since praise and blame attach only to voluntary actions, we therefore need private property to develop those aspects of character tied in some way to options concerning the use of property. This usage must be according to virtue—specifically those of moderation and liberality, as we have seen. Through these virtues, we get a clearer sense of how property should be used; virtue dictates how much property we can have, and how we must use it.

In discussing moderation, to pick but one example, Aristotle distinguishes between natural and unnatural expertise concerning the acquisition of property. Natural expertise is based on "self-generated" work such as farming, fishing, and hunting (as well as the expertise of the nomad and the pirate) and has a natural boundary of sustenance, since nature would not have made these modes

52. Politics, 1280al–1281al, 98–99.
53. Ethics, 1006b36, 39.
54. Ethics, 1098a15, 14.

of life incomplete.[55] Unnatural acquisition stems from commerce and business when such is meant to support more than natural self-sufficiency. In both theory and unvirtuous practice, wealth created by such an exchange is unlimited. Yet, those who live well would either not engage in the practice at all or would submit wealth accumulation to the limits of virtue:

> Thus in one way it appears necessary that there be a limit to all wealth; yet if we look at what actually occurs we see that the opposite happens—all who engage in business increase their money without limit. The cause of this is the nearness to one another of these [forms of expertise in business]. For they converge in the matter of use, the same thing being used in the case of either sort of expertise in business. For possessions serve the same use, though not in the same respect, but in the one case the end is increase, in the other something else. So some hold that this is the work of expertise in household management, and they proceed on the supposition that they should either preserve or increase without limit their property in money. The cause of this state is that they are serious about living, but not about living well; and since that desire of theirs is without limit, they also desire what is productive of unlimited things. Even those who also aim at living well seek what conduces to bodily gratifications, and since this too appears to be available in and through possessions, their pursuits are wholly connected with business, and this is why the other kind of business expertise has arisen. For as gratification consists in excess, they seek the sort that is productive of the excess characteristic of gratification; and if they are unable to supply it through expertise in business, they attempt this in some other fashion, using each sort of capacity in a way not according to nature.[56]

Aristotle shows a clear dislike of exchange for its own sake, implying that it is immoderate to pursue wealth for the sake mere accumulation. At the very least we can say that virtue, for Aristotle, imposes some limits on the way that property is used, by restricting accumulation beyond what is necessary. These limits follow nature: wealth created by exchange for the sake of wealth creation is unvirtuous. However the modern reader feels about restricting all secondary exchange and the disposition of those who engage in the practice, some might be at least partly sympathetic to the idea that the dictates of moderation should limit property, or that certain types of property or professions are less natural and deserve closer regulation. The general point is that Aristotle's conception of private property is not unlimited. Common-in-use means the submission to the limits placed by the virtue of moderation on the extent of private wealth, and the way in which wealth is generated.

---

55. POLITICS, 1256bl, 45–46.
56. POLITICS, 1258al, 48.

Moreover, the virtue of liberality requires us to use what property we do have for the sake of generosity to deserving friends. Liberality is "the mean with regard to wealth; for the liberal man is praised . . . with regard to the giving and taking of wealth, and in respect to the giving" and lies between the extremes of prodigality and meanness.[57] The virtue of liberality persuades us to develop our greater virtue by willingly parting with our possessions for the right reasons. This does not mean charity to those who are undeserving:

> Now virtuous actions are noble and done for the sake of the noble. The liberal man, like other virtuous men, will give for the sake of the noble, and rightly; for he will give to the right people, the right amounts, and at the right time, with all the other qualifications that accompany right giving; and that too with pleasure or without pain; for that which is virtuous is pleasant or free from pain—least of all will it be painful. But he who gives to the wrong people or not for the sake of the noble but for some other cause, will be called not liberal but by some other name. Nor is he liberal who gives with pain; for he would prefer the wealth to the noble act, and this is not characteristic of a liberal man.[58]

Giving, then, is an action that virtue regulates. But virtue also determines how one should receive:

> But no more will the liberal man take from wrong sources; for such taking is not characteristic of the man who sets no store by wealth. Nor will he be a ready asker; for it is not characteristic of a man who confers benefits to accept them lightly. But he will take from the right sources, e.g., from his own possessions, not as something noble but as a necessity, that he may have something to give. Nor will he neglect his own property, since he wishes by means of this to help others.[59]

In this statement of liberality, one again sees the limits on use placed on private possession by virtue, as well as a duty to maintain the property that one has.

In placing private property within its proper context of virtue, it is easy to see that property involves duties based on virtue, in a system without a transcendent good, but where the goal of the state is to be virtuous by being composed of and promoting virtuous individuals. In this sense, Aristotle places private property in its place as part of a larger ethical and political theory, making it common-in-use. Metaphorically, common-in-use means property aids in the development of virtue to unite the city. In actuality, it means the submission to the duty to acquire, dispose, and use possessions for the common good, in the

57. Ethics, 1119b18, 79.
58. Ethics, 1120a9–a35, 80.
59. Ethics, 1120a9–a35, 80–81.

fostering of virtue. Common-in-use is therefore only intelligible in principle within Aristotle's ethical framework.

Of course, the modern theorist or lawyer will find problems with the substance of this approach. For example, the distinction between money and property, and primary and secondary exchange might be seen as artificial or tenuous, and the rules for the accumulation of wealth might seem to be unduly harsh. Similarly, the value placed on liberality might be seen as too strong. But the important insight is that Aristotle sees private property in theory as a limited concept and one that is set within an ethical structure. This ethical structure is based on virtue and duty, as well as on individual fulfilment. Within this structure, the fact that possessions should be "private in possession, common in use" reflects a balance between individual fulfillment and the imperatives of the community.

In defense of Aristotle, one first should complete Aristotle's explicit theory of justification, as liberality is not the only virtue fostered by private property. The discussion of the virtue of moderation criticizes Plato's scheme for failing to promote moderation. As I have argued above, these arguments can be applied to private property generally, specifically to the creation of and limits upon wealth. And in the *Laws,* where Plato has some role for private possessions, moderation is also associated with private property as a limit. As set out in the passage quoted earlier, in discussing this matter in the *Laws,* Aristotle states that both moderation and liberality are necessary in determining the proper level of private possessions.[60] It seems, then, that in both cases, Aristotle's discussions revolve around the virtue of moderation, as well as liberality.

Indeed, moderation is one of the most important elements in the whole structure of Aristotelian ethics, as the pursuit of virtue itself is in every case a question of finding the mean. Moderation, Aristotle argues, is fostered by having one's own family—what is "dear." Moderation is also fostered by a private property system since one can act moderately when private, self-contained action gives a person the option to be immoderate.

Second, regarding the requirement of exclusive control in order to be generous, it is worth noting that it is rather technical to distinguish between control and ownership when the justification of private property is concerned with a person's disposition and its relation to a generous act. One does not need to focus at this stage on the definitions of ownership, exclusive control, etc., but on the quality of the generous act and the virtue upon which it is based. The point is that there is something—some virtue—in being able to use property in a certain way, whether one owns it or is "allotted" it, that is an essentially private decision, and has granted the person other options that were not so generous. At this level, Aristotle's conception of private property does much from the examples that

60. *See* the cited passage and discussion above, *supra* note 47 and accompanying text.

Irwin had cited: limitations by the state on uses, being allotted a patch of ground for a certain time or under certain conditions, etc. These would probably be private property to Aristotle, whose conception of private property was a limited one, not at all analogous to a modern conception. The possibility of fostering private generosity, therefore, might still contain some merit as an element in the justification for private property. If there are still "gaps," they flow from the failure to set out an explicit taxonomy of property rights and obligations, or more theoretically, from not setting out a full examination of the limitations imposed by virtue on the use of property.

While Irwin's conclusion that Aristotle has failed to give an impenetrable defense of private property is still generally true, by trimming down the theory to its narrowest reading, Irwin's perception of the inadequacies is stronger than it might otherwise have been. By including the argument from moderation, Aristotle's defense is more complete, and more plausible.

Further, in what follows from these text-based rejoinders, is what might be called Aristotle's "implicit" justification of private property. That is, these arguments set out in the *Politics,* while incomplete, can form part of a larger theory of justification. This larger theory, I would argue, is Aristotle's more central view of the justification for private property, and can only be understood in the larger context of Aristotle's ethical theory. Aristotle's view of property fits into his larger theory of human virtue and social ordering, reflecting the difficult but inescapable tension between the individual and the community.

C. Conclusion on Aristotle

If Irwin is correct in saying that Aristotle's theory of private property is not persuasive solely as a means of fostering private generosity, Aristotle's defense is stronger when seen as an element of an ethical theory aimed at fostering virtue generally. In this light, Aristotle has touched upon a number of insights that are crucial to our understanding of private property: that there is something difficult about making communal property regimes work in practice; that private property is important to individual development; and that private property has a limited scope, and is subject to the ethical imperatives of the city.

The important point is that on an individual level, property plays a role in how individuals develop. Private property takes its place as a means to an end in a moral and ethical structure that is directed at the central goal of overarching virtue by fostering two particular virtues, moderation and liberality. Private property is insufficient because there are other virtues that must develop as well in order for a person to be called virtuous in the universal sense. But these two smaller virtues, and therefore private property, are at least a necessary part of the larger structure. Therefore, there is a proper way individuals should develop, in consonance, with the city—in effect, directed self-development. The balance that Aristotle has achieved is better than the one posited by Plato: it recognizes the products of diversity in the city while providing a unity of purpose that strives to achieve the good life. At the level of the collective, there is a clear teleology present: the fostering of the good life or society. The fostering of individual virtues is in a sense greater than the sum of its parts, and leads to a collective state that is happy (in the sense of *eudaimonia*), just, and good.

What is perhaps underdeveloped is the focus on the object of property itself. However, it is clear that the actions taken by individuals with respect to specific objects of social wealth are to be undertaken with the common "purpose" in mind, and thus help to condition the common purpose. That is, the *use* of specific objects of property will be a manner that the community can recognize as being good, virtuous, just, etc. As such, they provide a metaphorical point of entry for virtue in property discourse.

III. AQUINAS ON PRIVATE PROPERTY

The Aristotelian notion of "private in possession, common in use" stands as a metaphor for the idea that private ownership, while private, is meant to serve a greater ethical purpose. The idea that property could have what Aristotle identifies as private and common aspects continues on through the work of the Roman and early Christian writers and comes to the fore in the work of medieval theorists writing about private property. It is this medieval synthesis, aimed at justifying or criticizing the role of the church as a property owner and drawing on the principles of Christianity as expounded by the "fathers" of the church and on the work of Aristotle, which laid the foundation for the evolution of the theory of private property down to the seventeenth century. It is the situation of property in the Christian belief and value structures that gives the Aristotelian metaphor a very clear set of principles upon which to base "common in use."

Moreover, it is during this period that the idea of private property as a natural "right" begins to gain greater currency among a number of proponents. Thus understood, the idea that private property is defensible as an institution is centered around the view that there is something about property generally and the acquisition of private property in particular that stems from human nature or from the human situation on earth and is discernable through the application of human reason. Indeed, the debate about whether private property is a natural product of the human condition and its reasonable extensions or a convention that is the product of civil society comes to fore, particular in the debates among various mendicant religious orders, university doctors, and popes over poverty within the church.[61]

---

61. William of Ockham, The Work of Ninety Days and A Dialogue: III in A Letter to the Friars Minor and Other Writings (John Kilcullen trans., Arthur S.

The development of the notion of *ius* as a type of active, subjective "right" is a story with many parallels to the changing justifications of private property; it is fundamentally linked to the theoretical history of private property. As John Finnis has pointed out, there is a watershed moment in the meaning of the word *ius* between the time of Thomas Aquinas and Francisco Suarez.[62] When Aquinas wrote in the twelfth century, *ius* was primarily an objective term meaning "what was right" or "what was just." By the time Suarez wrote three centuries later, the meaning of *ius* had shifted to being a claim right against other persons or groups. Most notably, Richard Tuck, in *Natural Rights Theories: Their Origin and Development*,[63] has located this point when the meaning of *ius* changed during and shortly after the debates over poverty among the two major mendicant orders of the Catholic church, the Franciscans and the Dominicans, and the papacy. Aquinas, a Dominican, was not an unbiased participant in the debate, which concerned not only the legal ways in which one could acquire, hold, and exchange property, but also went to the very justification for temporal and secular power and theories of the state.[64] The evolution of the concept and usage of *ius* is important to the debate on property since *ius* was invariably discussed at times as a subset of, at other times as an analogue to, and finally as a higher order of the concept of, *dominium*. Thus the history of the relationship between *ius* and *dominium* is an important one. There is no need to pronounce on the actual specific point when *ius* becomes a positive, active, and subjective right. For my purposes, it is sufficient to point out that it becomes apparent that as *ius* becomes more of a subjective right, of which one example is *dominium*, private property tends to become justified increasingly in terms of natural rights. As persons begin to make claims based on natural rights against the state, they are implicitly justifying private property in a way that places the powers of the state below the level of natural law. This is a specific playing down of the communal element that Aristotle and indeed Aquinas tried to maintain in their property narratives: it is thus important to return to what was being advanced prior to the ascendance of subjective right in property discourse.

McGrade and John Kilcullen eds., 1995); A Short Discourse on Tyrannical Government (John Kilcullen trans., Arthur S. McGrade ed., 1992).

62. Natural Law and Natural Rights 206–7 (1980).

63. Richard Tuck, Natural Rights Theories: Their Origin and Development (1979). *See also* Michel Villey, Le droit et les droits de l'homme chs. 6 and 7 (1983).

64. Two of the best examples are Marsiglio of Padua, Defensor pacis and Defensor minor: The Defender of the Peace (Annabel Brett trans. and ed., 2005) and Defensor minor and De translatione Imperii (Cary J. Nederman trans. and ed., 1993). *See also* William of Ockham, A Short Discourse on the Tyrannical Government and A Letter to the Friars Minor, *supra* note 61. These were all written as polemics against the temporal power of the papacy. And of course in popular literature, these themes and actors are woven into the narrative of Umberto Eco's *The Name of the Rose* (1983).

In terms of private property, the relation between the terms *ius* and *dominium* and their content help channel justification for the institution. If some power or *ius* over land, like *usus* or *possessio,* was tantamount to the ultimate control over an object, *dominium,* then such powers were very close to being full rights of ownership. They were more likely to be traced back to and justified in pre-civil society as a natural power. If they were conventional powers, i.e., created by human agreement or human law, and therefore different from *dominium,* then they were the products of post-civil society. These can only be tendencies at this stage, however, with important conventional justifications still to be advanced, and with the natural view never completely holding sway.

This was an important issue for the time, as one of the more important property owners was the church. Thus, the canon law tried to grapple with these issues, but was also ambiguous in its discussion regarding the source of ownership, drawing as it did from the same sources as the civil law. Following the church fathers, all property was common before the Fall, with private acquisition being allowed *after* the Fall. But were property rights given to mankind by natural law or divine law prior to human agreement, or did these come afterward? Moreover, where did the church fit into this structure of justification, and did this allow the church to be a landowner or *dominus?* Debate on these questions began increasingly to provide the forum in which private property was discussed. By this stage in time, the church had to live with the fact that the second coming was not coming soon, and that the question of *dominium* had to be dealt with.

A. Thomas Aquinas on Property and Its Purposes

These issues of classification, as well as the justification for private property of both the church fathers and Aristotle, are dealt with in the writings of Thomas Aquinas. His theory of private property, contained in the provisions of the *Summa Theologiae*[65] dealing with theft, robbery, and later usury, as well as in the parts of the *Summa Contra Gentiles*[66] dealing with poverty, represents an extremely important juncture in the history of property theory. He not only becomes the focal point for later debates on poverty (and given that he is silent or unclear on a number of issues, the cause of them), but he sets out a theory of justification for private property that became extremely influential to the later Natural Law tradition.

By melding aspects of Aristotle's property theory with an explicit form of Christian natural law, Aquinas perhaps best gave meaning to Aristotle's notion of "private in possession, common in use" by infusing the Aristotelian conception

---

65. Excerpts from the Summa Theologiae (ST) are taken from Saint Thomas Aquinas, On Law, Morality, and Politics (William P. Baumgarth and Richard J. Regan, S.J. eds., English Dominican Province trans., 1988).

66. Saint Thomas Aquinas, Summa Contra Gentiles (SCG) Book III: Providence, Parts 1 and 2 (Vernon J. Bourke trans., 1975).

of property with a very explicit teleology and a code of conduct subservient to it. His discussion contains aspects of both a natural rights justification of property in general, though for the most part, the specifics of property regimes are left to the determinations of men. As such, he stands between the two traditional poles of justification for private property: it is neither wholly natural nor wholly conventional, containing elements of both within the larger framework he sets out for law. But unlike Cicero,[67] with whom Aquinas's work has some superficial resemblance, Aquinas explicitly draws boundaries between what is natural and what is conventional.

Aquinas's discussion of private property is set out in two stages, the first of which articulates the justification for the possibility of human ownership of all property. Aquinas holds that the use of property generally by human beings is part of natural law, necessitated as it is by a human being's obligation to preserve oneself. The argument is contained in complementary discussions in the *Summa Contra Gentiles* (*SCG*) and the *Summa Theologiae* (*ST*). In Chapter 131 of the *SCG*, he outlines the natural justification in the context of a hypothetical argument against voluntary poverty:

> Natural appetite requires every animal to provide for itself in regard to the necessities of its life. . . . But men need many things for the preservation of life which cannot be found in every season. So there is a natural tendency in man to gather and keep things necessary to him. Therefore, it is contrary to natural law to throw away, under the guise of poverty, all that one has gathered together.
>
> Again, all things have a natural predilection for the things whereby their being may be preserved, because all things desire to be. But man's life is preserved by means of the substance of external goods. So, just as each man is obliged to preserve his life, so he is obliged to preserve external substance. Therefore, as it is contrary to the law of nature for a man to injure himself, so, too, is it for a man to deprive himself by voluntary poverty of the necessities of life.[68]

---

67. Cicero had said property "fell" individuals, and it remains ambiguous as to whether the distribution is a result of natural right or of human convention:

> Now no property is private by nature, but rather by long occupation (as when men moved into some empty property in the past), or by victory (when they acquired it in war), or by law, by settlement, by agreement or by lot. The result is that the land of Arpinium is said to belong to the Arpinates, and that of the Tusculum to the Tusculani. The distribution of property is of a similar kind. Consequently, since what becomes each man's own comes from what had in nature been in common, each man should hold on to whatever has *fallen* to him. If anyone else should seek any of it for himself, he will be violating the law of human fellowship. [My emphasis].

CICERO, *De Officiis* Book I: 22, 10 (E. Margaret Atkins trans., Miriam T. Griffin ed., 1991).

68. SCG, Book III: 131, paras 2 and 3, 168.

Most obviously, someone has a basic claim over resources in order to survive. However, there is scope in Aquinas for holding more than what is necessary for mere survival. While at the end of this particular discussion Aquinas did support certain types of voluntary poverty, these statements represent his opinion as they regard human nature in the natural situation and the urge to possess therein.[69] Clearly Aquinas saw the use of property as natural—*dominium naturale*—required in order for a person to provide the necessities of life. With the exception of mendicant orders dedicated to poverty, everyone would have been expected to consume and possess external goods. As such it was natural and self-evident to use property resources, though this natural inclination says nothing about whether property should be common or private.

This general ability to possess is rendered even more precise in the First Article of the *ST* dealing with theft and robbery.[70] Here Aquinas answered the question of whether it was natural and possible for man to own external things. In doing so, he applied the general Accursian distinction between ultimate *dominium directum* and *dominium utile,* ascribing the former to God and the latter to human beings:

> External things can be considered in two ways. First, as regards their nature, and this is not subject to the power of man but only to the power of God, Whose mere will all things obey. Secondly, as regards their use, and in this way man has a natural dominion over external things because, by his reason and will, he is able to use them for his own profit, as they were made on his account, for the imperfect is always for the sake of the perfect. . . . It is by this argument that the Philosopher proves that the possession of external things is natural to man.
>
> [Reply Obj.1] God has sovereign dominion over all things, and He, according to His providence, directed certain things to the sustenance of man's body. For this reason, man has a natural dominion over things as regards the power to make use of them.[71]

In this view, then, God has placed human beings below only Him in the order of creation, and has given them, as a group, the power to use all goods of the earth. Therefore, human beings can use external objects according to their will and reason for not just their mere survival, but in Aristotelian fashion, for their

69. Regarding voluntary poverty, he completes this position with correctives to represent his own views: since men come together to live in society, the division of labor does not mean that everyone has to preserve external substance in order to survive. Indeed, those who provide spiritual nourishment are giving something to the community and increasing the benefit of all. SCG, Book III: 134, paras 2, 3, and 4, 179–80.

70. ST, II-II, q. 66, art. 1, 176–77.

71. ST, 176–77.

own perfection. It is important to observe how Aquinas was using the two types of *dominium.* The *dominium naturale* given to human beings by God was dominion over use, *dominium utile,* as only God has ultimate *dominium, dominium directum,* over nature. As noted, this was the Accursian distinction applied to the relation between God and human beings, but it meant in theory that no human right over nature could be absolute because it is always subservient to the divine law and *dominium* of God. Moreover, without absolute control and given the situation of human beings on earth, the imperatives of use are normative.

Property use, in general terms, was mandated by natural law. But this first step did not go so far as to justify *private* possessions. The church fathers had held that by natural law, all property was common. Consistent with this view, the *dominium naturale* of the *SCG* and more precisely the *dominium utile* of the *ST,* in principle, seem to be consistent with this idea that the natural law points to the common ownership of all goods. It is necessary, therefore, that a second step justify private possession. In the Second Article of Question 66, in answering the question of whether it is lawful for a man to possess something individually, Aquinas raises the following objection to private ownership:

> It would seem unlawful for man to possess a thing as his own. For whatever is contrary to the natural law is unlawful. Now, according to the natural law, all things are common property, and the possession of property is contrary to this community of goods. . . . [72]

His reply not only clarified what natural law required, but laid the groundwork for justifying private property. That is, while he tended to admit that natural law generally justified common possession, natural law nevertheless did not rule out the possibility of private possessions. Here the natural law was silent or neutral. As such, private possessions could be allowed by human law, if such was reasonable: "Hence, the ownership of possessions is not contrary to the natural law but an addition thereto devised by human reason."[73]

Private ownership is an additional possibility for organizing property right, in addition to the common ownership of *dominium naturale,* where human reason determines this is in the best interest of the human community. It is human propensities and conventions that justify the bringing of private acquisition into existence. This position is consistent with religious thinkers of his time, and is reproduced in slightly different terms in later works.[74] The objections cited in the

---

72. ST, q. 66. art. 2, 177–78.

73. ST, 178.

74. *See especially* Ockham, who held that this right exists only in the post-Fall condition of humanity. In Ockham's view there are two types of lordship, divine and human; human is further divided between lordship common to the whole human race and exclusive ownership. Ockham's explanation of human lordship took place at two temporal stages, with

passage above had taken the classic account of the early fathers of the church in maintaining that *ius naturale* was common possession. After the Fall, sin or the *ius civile* and *ius gentium* mandated or necessitated human *dominium*. But Aquinas does not use the metaphor of the Fall to justify private property; rather he grounds it in the scope given by God and natural law to human reason. The substance of the two accounts is similar both beginning with a natural or divine period of common ownership and with the subsequent introduction of human law allowing private ownership.[75] The difference for Aquinas is that reason provided for private property on its own determination, while for William of Ockham reason reacted to the effects of original sin, only setting on private property when it had to do so. Aquinas's view of human nature is constant throughout his description, while Ockham effectively distinguishes between an ideal nature and a fallen one.

This second, more important, stage of the justification where private property was allowed is only comprehensible within Aquinas's larger theory of law. The natural law, derived from rules of reason, does not determine everything in human affairs. In response to the question of whether every human law is derived from the natural law, Aquinas offers the following passages that are critical to his general theory of law:

> Now, in human affairs a thing is said to be just from being right according to the rule of reason. But the first rule of reason is the law of nature. . . . Consequently, every human law has just so much of the nature of law as it derived from the law of nature. But if, at any point, it deflects from the law of nature, it is no longer a law but a perversion of the law.
>
> But it must be noted that something may be derived from the natural law in two ways: first, as a conclusion from premises; secondly, by way of

---

the mode of property holding and its explanation differing fundamentally at each. In the first stage, the pre-Fall period, private appropriation was not necessary:

> Lordship common to the whole human race is that which God gave Adam and his wife for themselves and all their posterity, power to manage and use temporal things to their own advantage. That power would have existed in the state of innocence without power to appropriate ant temporal thing to any one person or to any collectivity or to certain persons. . . .
>
> [That state] existed in the state of innocence, and would have continued if man had not sinned, but without power to appropriate anything to anyone except by use, as has been said. For since there would have been among them no avarice or desire to possess or use any temporal thing against right reason, there would have been no necessity or advantage in having ownership of any temporal thing.

[Ockham, A Short Discourse on Tyrannical Government, *supra* note 61, at 88–89.] Consequently the natural state of affairs, according to natural law, gave only common dominium, and included powers of use and management.

75. *See, e.g.*, Schlatter, *supra* note 12, at 50 (discussing Aquinas in contrast to Isidore).

> determination of certain generalities. The first way is like to that by which, in the sciences, demonstrated conclusions are drawn from the principles while the second mode is likened to that whereby, in the arts, general forms are particularized as to details; thus the craftsman needs to determine the general form of a house to some particular shape.[76]

These determinations (*determinationes*) or specifications are derived not directly through natural law, but secondarily through human reason as applied to practical problems. Thus it is according to the natural law that wrongdoers be punished, but the actual punishment is according to human determination. While it is not entirely clear, private ownership then appears to be one of the additions made to the natural law according to the dictates of human reason.

According to human reason, then, Aquinas set out the reasons why property should be private and not common, reflecting the utilitarian aspects of Aristotle's justification in *Politics*. Aquinas assigned two types of competence to man in respecting the use of exterior goods. The first is a power to acquire and dispose of private property, and hence to possess private property. Private property was to be favored for three reasons: human beings tend to take better care of their possessions when they are privately held, human affairs tend to be more ordered when persons are ultimately responsible for certain objects, and finally, because if every person is content with what is his own there will be a more peaceful state. Common property was seen as inefficient and quarrelsome. The second is a competence with regard to the use of external things. While following his Christian principles, Aquinas makes a statement similar to that made by Aristotle: "In this respect man ought to possess external things, not as his own, but as common, so that, to wit, he is ready to communicate them to others in their need."[77]

So as with Aristotle, the question of possessing or using in common is incorporated into Aquinas's discussion. Clearly, as with Aristotle, one must point out at the outset that there is a role for the state in determining common in use. A state can protect private ownership while directing its use for the common good. Thus, the dividing of property, restrictions on alienation, and succession rules might all serve the greater good.[78]

On an individual level other ethical imperatives will channel private uses. The first and most basic component of Aquinas's concept of "common" is the duty of charity. One is required to help others in need, using what is not necessary for

76. ST, II-II, q.95, art. 2, 59. *See also* Finnis, Natural Law and Natural Rights, *supra* note at 62, 284–89, for discussion and application.

77. ST, II-II, q. 66, art. 2, 179.

78. ST, I-II, q.105, art. 2, as discussed in Schlatter, *supra* note 12, at 50–51.

one's own basic needs, but rather what is extra or superfluous.[79] While what is necessary or proper to oneself is widely defined, according to Finnis, there is a still a great deal that is morally available or held in common for the poor. (As seen above, those who need property for basic survival have a moral claim to everything that is held.)[80] In the case of scarcity, where there is necessity, private possessions are no longer a bar to one taking any property necessary to one's own survival. All reverts to the common stock and the needy can take from it. Survival, an imperative of natural law for which possession generally is allowed, takes precedence over human determinations when necessity arises. This positive limitation is an important move, and will come to influence the more famous Lockean provisos in the seventeenth century. Thus, even though there is a set of imperatives that seem to justify exclusionary appropriation and the inequalities brought about by a "first come, first served" rule, these too are limited.

We must however go further, as we did with Aristotle, to a more robust understanding of "common in use" based on the role of property in Aquinas's ethics. Human communities, following the position articulated in slightly different forms by Aristotle, are natural structures given man's social nature. By fostering their development, and consistent with *dominium utile* given generally to human beings, private possessions in use are justified as part of the fostering of human virtue and the service of God's purposes. Thus, property has a function in bringing about an explicitly desired end. Unlike Aristotle, Aquinas has used Christian revelation to give explicit shape to the purposes that private property must serve. Private possessions are to be used for the betterment, the perfection of mankind. They are justifiable only in service of a good end, specifically that of virtue:

> [E]xternal riches are necessary for the good of virtue, since by them we support our body and give assistance to other people. Now, things that are means to an end must derive their goodness from the end. So, external riches must be a good for man; not, of course, the principal one, but as a secondary good. . . . Therefore, riches are good, to the extent that they advance the practice of virtue, but if the measure is departed from, so that the practice of virtue is hindered by them, then they are not to be numbered among goods, but among evils.[81]

As it had with Aristotle, virtue lay in the mean, a middle point between the excesses of vice as determined by reason. Aquinas wrote:

> that man has this natural endowment, he may use lower things for the needs of his life. Now, there is a definite measure according to which the use of the

79. This more restricted discussion of Aquinas "common-in-use" is meticulously well done in JOHN M. FINNIS, AQUINAS 188–96 (1998).

80. *Id.* at 191.

81. SCG, III: 133, 177.

aforesaid things is proper to human life, and if this measure is set aside the result is harmful to man, as is evident in the immoderate eating of food.[82]

This mean was variable, in different circumstances:

> [W]e must consider that the mean of virtue is not taken according to the amount of exterior goods that come into use, but according to the rule of reason. So, it sometimes happens that what is excessive in relation to the quantity of an external thing may be moderate in relation to the rule of reason. For no one inclines to greater things than does the magnanimous man; nor is there anyone who surpasses in greatness of expenditures the magnificent man. So, they adhere to a mean that does not consist in the amount of expense, or anything like that, but insofar as they neither exceed the rule of reason, nor fall short of it. Indeed, this rule measures not only the size of a thing that is used, but also the circumstances of the person, and his intention, the fitness of place and time, and other such things that are necessary in acts of virtue.[83]

As with Aristotle, all human beings were not created equally in spirit or talent, nor were they equal in resources. As a result, the relative means were different for different individuals. Thus, the lives of the rich magnanimous landowner and the poor mendicant friar could both be virtuous according to the respective mean of each.

The service of virtue is defined even more specifically for Aquinas than for Aristotle. Certainly virtue was aided by the promotion of generosity and liberality, as it was for Aristotle. Here private property was instrumental in serving these laudable ends. According to Aquinas, covetousness, the opposite of liberality, was not only evil and a sin but was a capital vice.[84] But, what is more, there was an explicit imperative according to the divine law that all corporeal things be used in the reverence of God.[85]

This imperative is in a way more explicit in Christian terms than in classical times because of the perceived binding nature of the divine law. In effect, the Thomistic structure Christianizes the phrase "private in possession, common in use" by making common uses those which more explicitly follow Christian imperatives as taken from revealed texts. The virtues of liberality are reinforced by the precepts of loving one's neighbor and not coveting another's possessions. There is a duty to be charitable, which is in a sense more binding to the Christian than to the Athenian or Roman, though as in these traditions the duty of charity

---

82. SCG, III: 129, 163.
83. SCG, III: 134, 181.
84. ST, II-II, q.118, arts. 1, 3, and 7, 209–14.
85. SCG, III: 121, 141.

is always according to circumstances of both the giver and the beneficiary. Giving is not required in every case.[86]

It is this requirement for just uses that allows Aquinas to skirt the issue of inequality of acquisition, or the exclusion of others once property has been acquired. Hence in reply to the words of Basil, which stated that the appropriation from the common stock by the wealthy prevents others from using what was intended for common use, Aquinas focused on the proper uses by the wealthy as the justification for allowing unequal appropriations:

> A man would not act unlawfully if by going beforehand to the play he prepared the way for others, but he acts unlawfully if by doing so he hinders others from going. In like manner, a rich man does not act unlawfully if he anticipates someone in taking possession of something which at first was common property and gives others a share, but he sins if he excluded others indiscriminately from using it. Hence Basil says, "Why are you rich while another is poor, unless it be that you may have the merit of good stewardship, and he the reward of patience?"[87]

Aquinas had perceived the problem of inequality of first acquisition, and had given his solution by linking acquisition to an active responsibility to foster the good. Indeed, the duty of stewardship is added to the type of virtuous behavior necessary to justify private allocations.

This justification based on fostering human virtue shows the obligations of and limits upon the property owners and users. If the proper use of private property lies in the mean of reason and service to higher ends, then certain completely selfish uses of private property will not be permissible. Even the quantity of acquisition is limited by reason, and the concept of superfluousness, though it would be different for different persons, and would always be checked by duties to charity and liberality. Aquinas's justification also contains elements of both the natural and conventional accounts. It is natural in the sense that human beings need some type of property in order to survive and flourish. And it is according to natural law that God gave human beings *dominium utile* over the earth, and hence some justification for a property regime. But it is human agreement that determines that the actual property regime is one of private (and not common) ownership. All of these ideas fit into the larger Thomistic theology and philosophy of politics. The goal of the Christian rule, ruling absolutely according the divine law and the precepts that could be derived from the natural law or through determinations of human reason, was to promote the common good, that is, the Good life that is God's will for human beings. The notion of duty and responsibility is imbibed in the larger notion of eternal salvation and just ordering. Thus Aquinas holds an even more explicit teleology than Aristotle,

---

86. ST, II-II, q. 71, arts. 1, 191–92. *See also* FINNIS, AQUINAS, *supra* note 79, 191–6.
87. ST, II-II, q. 66, arts. 2, 179.

toward which all things in society must be ordered. The virtues of justice and liberality, through moderation and reason, help point human beings toward the Good of salvation. Consequently, private property is an instrumental good (analogous to utility) but in the service of human development (dignity, development) within a Christian framework.

Another way to understand this discussion is to frame it in terms of the common good. What Aquinas has supplied is a more robust version of the common good as compared to Aristotle—reinjected more of the unity back into the community, if you will—and made it a positive duty to foster the common good as part of a moral rectitude or virtuous social ethic. The key concepts are responsibility and duty.[88] The language of duty is much clearer in Aquinas in the sense of what is due or *debitum,* as opposed to merely goodness for Aristotle. Hence there is a relational aspect now recognized by Aquinas to all natural right,[89] and by extension to property. Thus, the virtuous use of property is a social duty, in service of the common good, and, obviously, for Aquinas, to God.

B. Conclusion on Aquinas

Aqinas's theory is important for our purposes because he increasingly clarifies the content in the notion of duties and limits associated with private property. Insofar as property holding is generally a product of natural law, it must conform to the divine law and God's purposes for man on earth. These limit the uses to which all goods can be put; uses are now clearly restricted according to the good of the community and general Christian precepts. Insofar as private property holding is justifiable as a determination of human law, there are also limitations based on reason in accordance with the general strictures or forms of natural law. Thus all private uses must serve the ends of virtue and the common good in order to be justifiable. As such, there is a duty to charity, and surplus accumulation is limited. And the thrust of the analysis, applying familiar medieval categories of *dominium directum* and *utile,* places the effective weight of the

---

88. This point has been recently made by Mary M. Keys:

> It seems important to stress that Aquinas's connection of moral rectitude, or goodness of will, with the common good is not primarily a matter of negatives, of *not desiring* particular goods, but rather desiring especially the highest or intrinsically most common. Aquinas understands that it is socially and civicly indispensable, for instance, that individual persons specially care for particular or proper goods. . . . Aquinas argues that the particular goods of honor and glory should be valued, but moderately so: through them the good of virtue can shine forth and be made known to many, and their bestowal for public service both fosters and flows from the common good.

Mary M. Keys, Aquinas, Aristotle, and the Promise of the Common Good, 123 (2006).

89. *Id.* at 124.

common on the use or the resource, and not so much on its ownership and, hence, distribution.

The focus on the proper uses of property makes the role of objects in property relations more visible, or more central to understanding property. Hence, the proper uses of a resource such as land is more easily discernable when one considers the ethical imperatives that are attached to it through the innate understanding of Thomistic virtue. Here, for example, the concept of stewardship present in Aquinas's property theory will have a normative impact: an owner has to care for the resource entrusted to him or her. The grounding for this specific duty is nothing less that what Aquinas believes is the proper basis for any society.[90] Property's vocation is thus much more clear for Aquinas than it was for Aristotle (though it was certainly present in the latter), and pertains quite directly to a much larger political ambition for proper social ordering.

So while similar in thrust to the Aristotelian schema, there is now an explicit, and explicitly Christian, teleology to the institution of private property. Charity, generosity, sharing, and stewardship have all been added to the list of property virtues. In the end, Aquinas has Christianized virtue, but the impact is both surprisingly (or not so surprisingly) similar to Aristotle and more robust: it is a weightier notion of Christian generosity over classical liberality.

IV. BACK TO THE FUTURE

Are these elements present in the current discourse of private property and intellectual property? As I have argued at the outset and elsewhere,[91] I certainly believe this to be the case, though much current discourse has missed these underlying concepts and their import. Can we or how should we embody formally or explicitly such moral sentiments in current private property discourse, revising, of course, for the current social context (and accepted sources of values)? Put another way, what values transcend either a particular historical context or religious ethos (even if we grant that this context and this ethos have had a foundational role in the construction of our current society)?

Specifically, in my view, the gateway for entry of this ethical discourse in property discourse is precisely through the object of the property relationship,

---

90. *See also* Keys, *id.* at 236–7.

91. *Supra* note 6. *See also* David Lametti, *The Morality of James Harris's Theory of Property*, *in* THE PROPERTIES OF LAW: ESSAYS IN HONOUR OF JAMES HARRIS (Timothy A.O. Endicott, Joshua Getzler, and Edwin Peel eds., Oxford: Oxford University Press, 2006); and *The (Virtue) Ethics of Private Property: A Framework and Implications*, *in* NEW PERSPECTIVES ON PROPERTY LAW, OBLIGATIONS, AND RESTITUTION 39 (Alastair Hudson ed., London; Cavendish Press, 2003).

tangible or intangible, traditional or intellectual property. It is manifested in the ways in which society values objects, the manner in which society believes objects ought to be used (and therefore are valued), and the ways in which society—through property rules[92]—attaches strings to its uses through limits and even duties in some cases. In short, the teleology of private property is most present in the ways in which objects are valued, distributed, and governed. The value-ladened, ethical discourse is best seen with respect to the objects of property relations, be they tangible or intangible, by focusing on the actions and uses, the duties and rights, and the limits that they bear. In parallel fashion, the underlying justificatory base for private property also reflects this ethical discourse, and is similarly "balanced" among rights and duties, limits, and goals.

A possible modern label for this stance is that of "virtue ethics." It is a relatively modern term, describing the practical philosophy of many who trace their intellectual roots to Aristotle.[93] In modern philosophy, exponents include Bernard Williams and the late Iris Murdoch, and perhaps others such as Charles Taylor and Martha Nussbaum. It is practical ethics focusing on concepts such as respect, sympathy, loyalty, and fidelity, and in formal terms is neither deontological nor consequentialist. Modern property writers who might be considered to be now working in this vein include Gregory Alexander and Eduardo Peñalver.[94]

In my view, the value of objects of property relations is precisely the filtering role that they play in human relations. Our societal values are reflected in the manner in which we allocate objects, use objects, alienate objects, and share objects. What is important from the foregoing is that a society will have determined, given substance to, and in some way defined the notion of "common in use" or even "public in use."

Thus, "public in use" becomes a metaphor for the teleology given to private property and the public, ethical purposes to which private property is put. The emphasis on the object is what is unique to private property (over other aspects of social ordering reflecting often similar ethical concerns, but with a different focus). The objects of property relations, contextually understood and valued, therefore, become a specific point of entry for the community's imposition of values in property discourse. A modern notion of the virtue ethics of private property will concern itself with a wider series of ethical imperatives. These will

---

92. In Harris's terms, trespassory rules, property-duty rules, and property-limit rules: *see* HARRIS, PROPERTY AND JUSTICE, *supra* note 1, ch. 3.

93. *See* the authors cited, *supra* note 9.

94. Joseph Singer is close, but his call to traditional theology perhaps places him in the deontological camp. *See* JOSEPH W. SINGER, ENTITLEMENT: THE PARADOXES OF PROPERTY (2000).

include issues of distribution (e.g., poverty) and use (e.g., the environment, waste, uses for the good of society and, generally, property stewardship).[95]

Such concerns are already evident in property discourse. The teleology is obvious in intellectual property. The purposes of copyright protection evident in the Statute of Anne, or enshrined in the U.S. Constitution, or in the "bargain theory" of patent, or in the "use it or lose it" element of trademark theory and practice. The goals of a property institution are often explicit, defining the nature of the resource, as well as the nature of the rights that are filtered through it. Rights are thus usually clearly defined (in statutes, regulations etc.) as are often very explicit limits on those rights.

Can the same be said to be true for traditional property? While less obvious, this vocation is still present. It is certainly true that property systems will classify property according to physical attributes (realty/personalty or movable/immovable, or tangible/intangible) and that different rules will attach to these different objects, according to their classification. These classifications (and subsequent rules) will be a reflection of both general and specific societal concerns. So, for example, land and buildings get special consideration in a variety of contexts, and this is in part a reflection on the priority of regulating what has traditionally been the most important resource in society, i.e., land. This is especially true as resources become scarcer and more valuable. As we become more attuned to the environment, for example, land use will be increasingly subject to this communal concern, and the number of restrictions that reflect this dimension of "public in use" will increase or become more explicit.

In the final analysis, how we use, distribute, and govern resources will reflect the ethics of our society. Virtue should dictate how we act with respect to valuable resources. The discourse of property, how we value, distribute, and use objects, is an exercise in virtue, not only a responsibility that we have as a community given scarce resources and presumptive equality, but also a discourse in which such virtues (goals, responsibilities, and obligations) will be reflected in the norms governing property "conduct." In other words, an ethical stance is required by the nature of property itself. We therefore need to look at the object, how it is valued, how it is used, how it is distributed (or how to distribute) and

---

95. *See* the work of Eric Freyfogle, for example, *Ownership and Ecology*, 43 Case Western Reserve L. Rev. 1269 (1993) and *The Construction of Ownership* U. Ill. L. Rev. 173 [1996]. *See also* William N. R. Lucy and Catherine Mitchell, *Replacing Private Property: The Case for Stewardship*, 55 Cambridge L.J. 566 (1996); Kevin Gray, *Equitable Property* 49 Current Legal Problems 157, 161 (1996); and Edward J. McCaffery, *Must We Have the Right to Waste?, in* New Essays in the Legal and Political Theory of Property (Stephen R. Munzer ed., 2001), 76. For a civil law perspective, *see* Roderick A. Macdonald, *Relational Ownership, in* Cross-Examining Private Law 167 (Quebec Research Centre of Private and Comparative Law ed., 2008).

then "construct" our property norms around these issues. These norms are found in a wide variety of places: statutes governing property, civil codes, land use norms, environmental norms, the norms governing natural resources, and intellectual property. Hence a contextual, ethical foundation is necessary for a full understanding of private property. The concepts, definition(s), and justifications of property and intellectual property must account for this ethical stance.

Where would one look to find the substance of such a virtue ethics? The classical texts highlighted in this study present two major sources: Aristotelian ethics and Thomistic ethics. The potential sources to be tapped are wider than classical or Judeo-Christian ethics, though many substantive principles will be overlapping. Versions or reworkings of these classical or religious systems may well better resonate in the modern secular ear.[96] The substantive virtues of justice, generosity, stewardship, and development/preservation found in these systems will be manifested through the resource. The objects of property are thus the objects of virtue.

96. As evidenced in this volume and in their other works.

2. REIMAGINING TAKINGS LAW

HANOCH DAGAN*

I. INTRODUCTION

Takings law, composed of the law of eminent domain and the regulatory takings doctrine, attracts the attention not only of lawyers and judges but also of property theorists and political philosophers since it is widely understood as one of property's most defining features. Takings law indeed deserves this characterization because it both epitomizes the relationship of ownership and government and heavily participates in generating the governance structure that ownership constructs.

The thick literature on takings law tends to fall into rather predictable and, I argue, quite disappointing camps. Libertarian authors maintain that compensation should be required each time the taking's impact on the owner is disproportionate to the burden, if any, carried by other beneficiaries of the intended public use of the public action at hand. Their liberal opponents, who hold that property should serve not only liberty but also such values as social responsibility and distributive justice, seek to restrict the range of takings law as much as possible. They imply that the connection between takings and these competing values is simple: social responsibility and distributive justice are better served when the doctrines of eminent domain and regulatory takings become increasingly limited. This debate is now deadlocked.

This chapter seeks to reimagine a truly liberal takings doctrine, which deviates dramatically from the positions of both camps. Unlike the former, it disputes the desirability and even the intelligibility of both the notion that ownership should only promote individual liberty and the strict takings doctrine said to follow this libertarian utopia. Unlike the latter, it insists that takings law should not fall back to a doctrine of no, or almost no, compensation that, I will argue, is counterproductive to the very commitment to social responsibility and distributive justice. Rather, in order to successfully integrate social responsibility and distributive justice into takings doctrine, and also other important property values such as autonomy, personhood, and utility, we need to opt for a regime of partial

* Dean and Professor of Law, Tel-Aviv University Buchmann Faculty of Law. Thanks to Greg Alexander, Mark Fenster, Tali Margalit, Eduardo Peñalver, Sarah Rajec, and participants of the Cornell/LSE Techniques of Ownership Conference for their helpful comments.

and differential compensation, drawing careful (and rule-based) distinctions between types of injured properties and types of benefited groups.

II. AVOIDING THE EXTREMES

Although the academic discourse of takings is rich and complex, presenting it as falling into two main paradigms is probably safe, even if slightly simplistic.[1] Libertarians advocate strong property rights and tough takings review of regulation, whereas their liberal opponents defend the state's ability to regulate property and seek to limit the reach of the just-compensation requirement as far as possible. In this section, I argue that both camps are misguided.

A. Against Strict Full Compensation

Libertarians argue that compensation should be required every time a taking's net impact on the landowner is disproportionate to the net impact on other property owners affected by that public action. This rule of proportionality dictates that the claimant's net burden should not be disproportionately heavy in comparison to that sustained by other beneficiaries of the public action. It disallows any changes (except, perhaps, a *de minimis* one) in the proportional economic *status quo* in the course of implementing the pertinent public project, activity, or regulation. Thus, this rule bars any public actions leading to some owners being relatively worse off due to some of their economic value being transferred to the public or to other individuals. It preserves the prevailing distribution of assets, legal rules, and wealth (although it may still "translate" people's assets or other entitlements into wealth without their consent).[2]

This strict proportionality rule is attuned to some of private property's most important social functions: shielding the individual from claims by other persons and from the power of the public authority to redefine our property, and hence our interpersonal relations. It helps to create an untouchable private sphere, which in turn facilitates personal freedom, security, and autonomy.[3] But the strict proportionality rule and the libertarian conception of property on which it is premised—Blackstone's notorious description of ownership as "sole

---

1. At least one more group of scholars, lawyer-economists, generated important insights as to the welfare implications of competing compensatory regimes. Their main lessons are integrated into the discussion below.

2. *See, e.g.*, Richard A. Epstein, TAKINGS: PRIVATE PROPERTY AND THE POWER OF EMINENT DOMAIN 4, 204–09 (1985); Richard A. Epstein, *Takings, Exclusivity, and Speech: The Legacy of* PruneYard v. Robins, 64 U. CHI. L. REV. 21, 27–28 (1997).

3. *See, e.g.*, Milton Friedman, CAPITALISM AND FREEDOM ch. 1 (1962); Randy E. Barnett, THE STRUCTURE OF LIBERTY: JUSTICE AND THE RULE OF LAW 139–42, 238 (1998).

and despotic dominion"[4]—are both normatively impoverished and analytically incoherent.

The normative difficulty derives from the indifference of this absolutist understanding of property to some important values that property can and should serve alongside its important role as a bastion of negative liberty. A commitment to these values need not, and in fact does not, entail a wholesale rejection of the protective role of property, but it does require resisting both the absolutist conception of property and its attendant strict proportionality rule.

Appreciating the role of property in promoting public welfare necessitates rejecting the Blackstonian conception of property because market failures and the physical characteristics of the resources at stake often require curtailing an owner's dominion so that ownership can properly serve the public interest.[5] A similar lesson emerges from the robust economic analysis of takings law.[6] This literature indeed shows that compensation is at times required to prevent risk-averse landowners from under-investing in their property and to create a budgetary effect that, assuming public officials are accountable for budget management, forces governments to internalize the costs of their planning decisions. These considerations are particularly pertinent to private homeowners, who are not professional investors and who have purchased a small parcel of land with their life savings, as well as to members of a marginal group with little political clout. But providing private landowners and public officials with proper incentives also implies that, in other cases, full compensation should not be granted. Where a piece of land is owned as part of a diversified investment portfolio, full compensation may lead to inefficient overinvestment, while the possibility of an uncompensated investment is likely to lead to an efficient adjustment of the landowner's investment decisions commensurate with the risk that the land will be put to public use. Similarly, landowners who are members of powerful and organized groups can use nonlegal means to force public officials to weigh their grievances properly. An indiscriminate regime of full compensation may therefore distort the officials' incentives by systematically encouraging them to impose the burden on the nonorganized public or on marginal groups, even when the

---

4. William Blackstone, COMMENTARIES, 2:*2.

5. *See* Richard A. Posner, ECONOMIC ANALYSIS OF LAW 32–39 (6th ed. 2003); Guido Calabresi & A. Douglas Melamed, *Property Rules, Liability Rules, and Inalienability: One View of the Cathedral*, 85 HARV. L. REV. 1089, 1106–10 (1972). Similarly, Harold Demsetz, in his classic defense of private property, acknowledges the costs of this regime and the need to balance these costs with benefits in order to secure welfare maximization. *See* Harold Demsetz, *Toward a Theory of Property Rights*, 57 AM. ECON. REV. 347 (1967); *see also* Terry L. Anderson & P.J. Hill, *The Evolution of Property Rights: A Study of the American West*, 18 J. L. & ECON. 163 (1975).

6. The brief analysis that follows is based on my more detailed account in Hanoch Dagan, *Takings and Distributive Justice*, 85 VA. L. REV. 741, 748–56 (1999).

best planning choice would be to place the burden on powerful or organized groups.

The absolutist conception of property and the strict proportionality takings regime are also anathema to the most attractive conceptions of membership and citizenship, which insist on integrating social responsibility into our understanding of ownership. The absolutist conception of property expresses and reinforces an alienated culture, which "underplays the significance of belonging to a community, [and] perceives our membership therein in purely instrumental terms."[7] In other words, this approach "defines our obligations *qua* citizens and *qua* community members as 'exchanges for monetizable gains,' . . . [and] thus commodifies both our citizenship and our membership in local communities."[8] To be sure, the impersonality of market relations is not inherently wrong; quite the contrary, by facilitating dealings "on an explicit, quid pro quo basis," the market defines an important "sphere of freedom from personal ties and obligations."[9] A responsible conception of property can and should appreciate these virtues of the market norms. But it should still avoid allowing these norms to override those of the other spheres of society. Property relations participate in the constitution of some of our most cooperative human interactions. Numerous property rules prescribe the rights and obligations of spouses, partners, co-owners, neighbors, and members of local communities. Imposing the competitive norms of the market on these divergent spheres and rejecting the social responsibility of ownership that is part of these ongoing mutual relationships of give and take,[10] would effectively erase these spheres of human interaction. In other words, erasing the social responsibility of ownership would undermine both the freedom-enhancing pluralism and the individuality-enhancing multiplicity that is crucial to the liberal ideal of justice.[11]

Blackstonian property and strict proportionality takings law are not only normatively disappointing; they are also suspicious on their own terms. To see why, consider the most appealing individualistic justifications of private property on which they could rest: personal liberty and personhood. These justifications typically rely on the role of ownership in providing control over the external resources that are necessary for individual autonomy[12] and over the resources

---

7. *Id.* at 771.

8. *Id.* at 772 (citing Margaret Jane Radin, CONTESTED COMMODITIES 5 (1996)).

9. Elizabeth Anderson, VALUE IN ETHICS AND ECONOMICS 145 (1993).

10. *See generally* Robert C. Ellickson, ORDER WITHOUT LAW: HOW NEIGHBORS SETTLE DISPUTES 55–56, 234–36, 274–75 (1991).

11. *See generally* Anderson, at ch.7; Don Herzog, HAPPY SLAVES: A CRITIQUE OF CONSENT THEORY 156, 166–68, 173–75 (1989); Michael Walzer, SPHERES OF JUSTICE: A DEFENSE OF PLURALISM AND EQUALITY (1983).

12. *See, e.g.*, John Rawls, POLITICAL LIBERALISM 298 (1993).

that constitute personhood.[13] Neither of these values, however, can justify the law's enforcement of the rights of property owners, if the law does not simultaneously guarantee necessary as well as constitutive resources to nonowners.[14] Likewise, private ownership cannot be justified by invoking power-spreading (decentralizing decision-making power) as a prerequisite for individual liberty,[15] without remembering that concentrations of private property (i.e., private power) may, in themselves, become "sources of dependency, manipulation, and insecurity."[16] Since the same property rights that guarantee individual liberty are also, by definition, the source of other people's duties and liabilities,[17] a credible conception of property as the guardian of liberty must always endorse the dialectic of retention and distribution. This conception finds proportionality an overly-simplistic and one-sided rule. Instead, it requires "an *ongoing* commitment to dispersal of access" and insists that we design our property system so that it dynamically ensures that "lots of people have some" property and that "pockets of illegitimately concentrated power" (i.e., property) do not reemerge.[18]

B. Against No (or Almost No) Compensation

The libertarian-recommended takings law is indeed disagreeable. But the prescriptions of some of its opponents, which seek to minimize the constitutional protection of property, are no less objectionable. Some progressive authors argue that an injury to individual property that benefits the public, even while disproportionately burdening a specific individual with the weight of public interest, is legitimate as long as it can be justified by "general, public, and ethically

---

13. *See, e.g.*, Margaret Jane Radin, *Property and Personhood*, 34 STAN. L. REV. 957 (1982). Another individualistic justification of property, which is also sometimes mistakenly presented to support the libertarian conception of ownership, is reward for labor. *See* Hanoch Dagan, *Property and the Public Domain*, 17 YALE J. L. & HUMAN. 84, 90–91(2006).

14. *See* Jeremy Waldron, *Homelessness and the* Issue *of Freedom, in* LIBERAL RIGHTS 309 (1993); Jeremy Waldron, THE RIGHT TO PRIVATE PROPERTY 377–378, 384–86, 429, 444 (1988).

15. *See* Friedman, ch. 1; Barnett, at 139–42, 238; Cass R. Sunstein, *On Property and Constitutionalism*, 14 CARDOZO L. REV. 907, 914–15 (1993).

16. *See* Frank Michelman, *Tutelary Jurisprudence and Constitutional Property, in* LIBERTY, PROPERTY, AND THE FUTURE OF CONSTITUTIONAL DEVELOPMENT 139 (Ellen Frankel Paul and Howard Dickman eds., 1990); Frank I. Michelman, *Possession vs. Distribution in the Constitutional Idea of Property*, 72 IOWA L. REV. 1319–20 (1987).

17. *See* Morris R. Cohen, *Property and Sovereignty*, 13 CORNELL L. Q. 8, 11–14 (1927); Wesley Newcomb Hohfeld, *Some Fundamental Legal Conceptions as Applied in Judicial Reasoning*, 23 YALE L.J. 16 (1913).

18. Joseph William Singer & Jack M. Beermann, *The Social Origins of Property*, 6 CAN. J. L. & JURISP. 217, 228, 242–45 (1993); *see also* Carol M. Rose, *Property as the Keystone Right?*, 71 NOTRE DAME L. REV. 329, 342–44, 347 (1996); Joseph William Singer, *Rent*, 39 B. C. L. REV. 1, 37–39 (1997).

permissible policies."[19] According to this approach, most government injuries to private property should be perceived as ordinary examples of the background risks and opportunities assumed by property owners.[20]

Gregory Alexander is probably the most prominent recent advocate of this position. Alexander criticizes my position on property and membership, which is briefly summarized in the previous section, as relying on a rather disappointing understanding of the relationship between the self and communities: one which is "contractual, strategic, and welfarist." He contrasts this view with his own favorite conception of community in which membership is constitutive, goods are shared (rather than convergent), and—maybe most fundamentally—sacrifice is normatively valuable. This last conception of community—which he terms "civic"—should serve, Alexander implies, as the normative foundation for the no- (or almost-no-) compensation approach to takings law.[21]

An ethics of sacrifice can indeed explain the "no-compensation" position. But I would be very reluctant to endorse it. Sacrifice for one's community has a rather long history, and not a very happy one. The greater good, on behalf of which calls for sacrifice are made, tends to efface individuals. As Jean Hampton has explained, selflessness is not a virtue we should celebrate. While human "saints" are often revered by those whom they beneficially serve, the subordination of their individual selves (and their own needs) from moral deliberation may well be morally blameworthy. Indirectly, self-sacrificers may be harming the very people for whom they care by teaching "the permissibility of their own exploitation by submitting to, and even supporting, their subservient role."[22] The community we should celebrate and inculcate is therefore decidedly not guided by the ethics of sacrifice and is well within the liberal tradition in which collective goods, such as communities, are important because they are good for individual human beings.

But this need not—and does not—render such communities contractual, welfarist, or strategic. The binarism, in which Alexander seems to operate, between instrumental agglomerations of autonomous individuals on the one hand, and involuntary and sacrifice-oriented communities on the other hand, is in fact false. We need not choose between these two unfortunate conceptions of

---

19. *See* C. Edwin Baker, *Property and its Relation to Constitutionally Protected Liberty*, 134 U. PA. L. REV. 741, 765 (1986).

20. *See* Frank Michelman, *The Common Law Baseline and Restitution for the Lost Commons: A Reply to Professor Epstein*, 64 U. CHI. L. REV. 57, 69 (1997).

21. *See* Gregory S. Alexander, *The Social Obligation Norm in American Property Law*, 95 CORNELL L. REV. 745 (2009). *See also* Gregory Alexander, THE GLOBAL DEBATE OVER CONSTITUTIONAL PROPERTY: LESSONS FOR AMERICAN TAKINGS JURISPRUDENCE (2006) (explaining the social obligation norm in constitutional property law).

22. Jean Hampton, *Selflessness and the Loss of Self*, *in* ALTRUISM 135, 136, 148, 161 (Ellen Frankel Paul et al. eds., 1993).

community, but can rather opt for an intermediate one, which is both constitutive and liberal. This conception is premised on the insight that communities are important human goods exactly because they are so significant to the *identities* of individual people.[23] It thus acknowledges the constitutive nature of communities and the fact that their goods are shared, rather than merely convergent. And yet, in order to qualify as a *liberal* community, members' identification with such community and their commitment to its goals should never erase their individual identity. While members are in part constituted by their participation in the community and their relationship with other members, they should be able to choose to abandon this part of their identity. Committed members of such liberal communities intermittently take up a critical perspective on the communities with which they deeply identify,[24] and at times they decide to exit the community (and that part of their identity).[25]

Furthermore, even those who agree with Alexander's normative commitments should be cautious to celebrate the no-compensation rule. Friends of this rule are quick to celebrate the possibility of subverting the economic status quo in the pursuit of worthy social causes. But they underestimate the risks latent in this option. Changes in the distribution of resources in a society implemented through law are, by definition, a result of government action. As such, they endanger property holders of all sorts, rich and poor. Moreover, both central and local governments may be corrupt despite attempts to structure them in the spirit of civic virtue. In our nonideal world, corruption of public-spiritedness can take various forms, and some of the more troubling manifestations of this phenomenon are not necessarily crude infirmities of the administrative process but more systemic and subtle problems, such as strong interest groups capturing the public authority.[26] Therefore, if we wish to make a credible claim for social solidarity and responsibility we need to remember that property owners

---

23. This insight has been recognized by many liberal thinkers. *See, e.g.*, Joseph Raz, Ethics in the Public Domain: Essays in the Morality of Law and Politics 155–74 (1994); Chaim Gans, *The Liberal Foundations of Cultural Nationalism*, 30 Can. J. Phil. 441 (2000); Avishai Margalit and Moshe Halbertal, *Liberalism and the Right to Culture*, 61 Soc. Res. 491 (1993).

24. *Cf.* Andrew Mason, Community, Solidarity and Belonging: Levels of Community and Their Normative Significance 58–59 (2000).

25. Indeed, under this conception of community the phenomenology of a decision to exit one's community is interpretive. A member contemplating exit considers the extent to which she is defined by her community, and then evaluates herself as that person. It is at this evaluative stage—"is this part of me good, or at least good enough?"—that the individual takes, and should take, center stage.

26. *See* Epstein, Takings, at 263–65; Carol M. Rose, *Ancient Constitution versus Federalist Empire: Antifederalism from the Attack on 'Monarchism' to Modern Localism*, *in* Property & Persuasion: Essays on the History, Theory, and Rhetoric of Ownership 71, 87, 90–91 (1994).

who belong to strong and organized groups will typically defend themselves even in the absence of legal protection. As we have seen, the danger of injury from government action in the absence of such protection is greater the weaker the property owner in question. Those endangered include isolated individuals as well as individuals belonging to marginal groups lacking political power.[27]

A naïve dismissal of property's protective role may thus lead to the systematic exploitation of weak property owners and to a cynical abuse of social solidarity, subverting the very aims it intends to further. In light of this disappointing conclusion, some skepticism about the disproportionate contribution to the community's well-being is appropriate, particularly when contributions are required from politically weak or economically disadvantaged landowners. Similar caution also may be warranted when the injured owner is not part of an organized interest group, and particularly if either the direct beneficiaries of the public project or the parties who successfully diverted the loss away from their own land enjoy significant political or economic power.[28]

*****

The challenge of takings law is to devise a regime that is sensitive to both property's distributive dimension and property's functions in promoting social welfare and social responsibility, without undermining the effects of ownership in protecting individuals, particularly politically weak individuals, from the power of government. This regime must beware both extremes. It must reject both the conservative approach of full (cash or in-kind) compensation "for all government regulations of property" on the one hand, and a self-defeating progressive approach, which "call[s] for eviscerating the property clause in the interest of distributive justice," on the other.[29]

Elsewhere I have suggested that the guiding principle of a takings doctrine that seeks to avoid these extremes must be long-term reciprocity. (I do not claim that reciprocity should limit the social obligation of members. Quite the contrary: in other doctrinal contexts, notably taxation—where burdens are distributed in a way that is both more nuanced and more general—a more demanding threshold may well be required.) The maxim of long-term reciprocity implies that a public authority need not pay compensation "if, and only if, the disproportionate burden

---

27. *See also* Saul Levmore, *Just Compensation and Just Politics*, 22 CONN. L. REV. 285, 305–11 (1990); Barton H. Thompson, Jr., *The Endangered Species Act: A Case Study in Takings and Incentives*, 49 STAN. L. REV. 305, 361, 366–67 (1997). The Israeli experience concerning the government's application of land expropriation laws to serve the interests of the Jewish majority at the expense of the Arab minority confirms the insight that the weak and the "other" require the protection of the law. *See, e.g.*, Alexandre (Sandy) Kedar, *The Legal Transformation of Ethnic Geography: Israeli Law and the Palestinian Landowner 1948–1967*, 33 N.Y.U. J. INT'L L. & POL. 923 (2001).

28. *See* Margaret Jane Radin, *Diagnosing the Takings Problem*, *in* REINTERPRETING PROPERTY 146, 159 (1993).

29. *See* Alexander, THE GLOBAL DEBATE, at 59.

of the public action in question is not overly extreme and is offset, or is likely in all probability to be offset, by benefits of similar magnitude to the landowner's current injury that she gains from other—past, present, or future—public actions (which harm neighboring properties)."[30] This prescription, which also guides me in the following pages, captures the subtle feature of a credible norm of social responsibility, one that is always wary of sliding into excessive (and potentially self-defeating) injury to private interest, but nonetheless rejects strict short-term accounting in order to recognize, preserve, and foster the significance of membership in a community not only as a source of mutual advantage, but also as a locus of belonging.[31]

III. RETHINKING TAKINGS

Most reconstructive efforts of takings law begin with the existing doctrine of a specific jurisdiction. Legal theorists, like other lawyers, tend to show that their favored scheme can serve as the next and better chapter of the law of the land. This is an understandable and often desirable strategy, because law is an unfolding drama that never starts from a clean slate.[32] Demonstrating the fit between a proposal and the current state of the law increases the chances of the proposal's adoption into law, meaning the probability of it making a difference in the real world. But this evolutionary strategy also involves costs. Notwithstanding the malleability of existing doctrine, starting from a given legal structure is, at least to some extent, constraining. (The constraints are not necessarily embedded in the language of the pertinent constitutional or statutory instruments, and could instead rest on underlying legal and political traditions and on the institutional context.[33]) The downside of evolutionary constructivism is that it may limit our legal imagination by obscuring possible legal architectures, only because they lack real-life precedents. This does not mean that we should always resist legal tradition; the evolutionary nature of the law is too valuable to be discarded.[34] It does mean, however, that we should occasionally suspend our respect for tradition and search for innovative ways to improve the law, looking outside the box of our doctrinal conventions for means of social advancement.

This is the approach I have adopted in this part of the chapter. Although some of my suggestions are inspired by existing bits and pieces of American, German,

---

30. Dagan, *Takings and Distributive Justice*, at 769–70.

31. *Id.* at 773.

32. This important jurisprudential insight is usually associated with Ronald Dworkin, LAW'S EMPIRE 52–53, 164–258 (1986). I trace it back to the legal realist legacy. *See* Hanoch Dagan, *The Realist Conception of Law*, 57 U. TORONTO L.J. 607, 651–59 (2007).

33. *See* Alexander, THE GLOBAL DEBATE, at 26–27.

34. *See* Dagan, *The Realist Conception of Law*, at 654–55.

and Israeli law, I will not bother to delve into the details of these legal systems.[35] Rather, I present my proposal as if it were meant for a newly established legal system. I begin with a few fundamental conceptual propositions and normative prescriptions that I can only stipulate here rather than defend, followed by the doctrinal techniques that can best implement them.

A. Foundations

The most foundational premises of the proposal below relate to my understanding of property.[36] Rather than a uniform bulwark of exclusion or a formless bundle of rights, I believe that property should be construed as it actually is in law and in life: a set of institutions, each constituted by a particular configuration of rights. More precisely: the meaning of property, the content of an owner's entitlements, varies according to the categories of social settings in which it is situated, and according to the categories of resources subject to property rights. Indeed, property institutions both construct and reflect the ideal ways of human interaction in a given category of social contexts (e.g., market, community, family) and regarding a given category of resources (e.g., land, copyright, patents).[37] Therefore, the values that property institutions serve are, at least potentially, as diverse as the values served by legal institutions at large. In particular, as already implicit in the discussion above, property institutions serve or should serve individual liberty and personhood, as well as aggregate welfare, social responsibility, and distributive justice. At least ideally, the composition of entitlements that constitute each such property institution is determined by its character and thus its underlying normative commitments, namely, its local balance of property values.

Because the two most important dimensions that distinguish property institutions from one another are the nature of the resource and the type of human interaction at hand, these two dimensions should also entail differential constitutional protection to property.

---

35. I have done so elsewhere. For American law, *see* Dagan, *Takings and Distributive Justice*. For German law, *see* Hanoch Dagan, *The Social Responsibility of Ownership*, 92 CORNELL L. REV. 1237, 1247–53 (2007). For Israeli law, *see* Hanoch Dagan, PROPERTY AT A CROSSROADS ch. 3 (2005) (in Hebrew).

36. This paragraph summarizes my extended discussion in Hanoch Dagan, *The Craft of Property*, 91 CALIF. L. REV. 1517 (2003).

37. As the text implies, I do not argue that the categories on either dimension are in any sense natural or inevitable. In fact, I assume that they are legal artifacts. But their artificiality by no means derogates from their normative significance. After all, all legal concepts and rules, including the concept of property itself, are artifacts. And, as long as we do not essentialize them in a way that obfuscates the operation of the doctrine or inhibits its normative scrutiny, their artificiality is not, in and of itself, a condemning argument. *See id.* at 1534.

1. The Nature of the Resource Consider first how the personhood value of property helps to understand the heterogeneity of property institutions and can thus provide corresponding guidelines for a truly liberal takings law. According to personhood theory, our attachment to the resources we hold is explicated and justified to the extent that those resources reflect our identity. Because society regards different resources (such as land, chattels, copyright, and patents) as variously constitutive of their possessors' identity, the law treats them differently and subjects them to different property configurations.[38]

Correspondingly, the appropriate level of the constitutional protection ensured to property should also depend on this dimension: takings law should treat constitutive property, which implicates its holder's personhood, differently from fungible property, which is wholly instrumental.[39] This should not mean that even wholly fungible property, wealth as such, should have no constitutional protection.[40] Such an extreme position is lacking on at least two counts: it ignores the simple truism that self-development also requires a degree of wealth, and it exposes all owners—rich and poor, strong and weak—to the risk of being sacrificed for the public good.[41] Therefore, instead of granting blanket immunity from constitutional scrutiny to the power to tax, a much more refined approach is required. This approach acknowledges the qualitative difference between constitutive and fungible property, and is also mindful of the unique role of tax law as the body of rules distinctly designed to redistribute from the better-off to the worse-off. This approach, however, rejects the view that perceives the power to structure and allocate tax burdens as unlimited. It founds the legitimacy of

---

38. *See* Hanoch Dagan, Unjust Enrichment: A Study of Private Law and Public Values 40–49, 63–108 (1997).

39. *See* Radin, *Diagnosing the Takings Problem*, at 153–56. *See also* Alexander, The Global Debate, at 103 ("Property interests whose function is primarily or even exclusively economic . . . receive minimal protection under German constitutional law," while interests that "implicate the owner's dignity and self-realization interests and her opportunity to practice self-governance receive strong protection"). In the U.S., recent, post-Kelo, reform proposals at the state level follow this guideline. For a collection of some examples, see Katrina Miriam Wyman, *The Measure of Just Compensation*, 41 U.C. Davis L. Rev. 239, 257 n.61 (2007). On its face, by making the content of rights dependent on the identity of their holders, this approach may put undesirable restraints on alienation. But takings are sufficiently infrequent in order to make this effect rather marginal.

40. *Contra* Alexander, The Global Debate, at 103, 127, who celebrates the German law prescription in which "the property clause does not protect wealth as such" because "private wealth-creating property interests . . . are viewed as not immediately implicating the fundamental values of human dignity and self-realization."

41. And recall that, in some contexts, this risk may be particularly real and potentially alarming to members of the unorganized public, even more so to those belonging to the weak segments of society.

current tax practice not on any kind of *a priori* immunity, but on its compliance with acceptable principles of distributive justice.[42]

2. The Social Context Property institutions also differ from one another because of the type of human relationship they help structure and regulate. This spectrum of human interactions goes from arm's-length relationships between strangers (or market transactors), through relationships between landlords and tenants, members of the same local community, neighbors, and co-owners, to intimate relationships between family members. Correspondingly, while some property institutions are structured along the lines of the Blackstonian conception of property, others (such as marital property) are dominated by a much more communitarian view of property, in which ownership is a locus of sharing. And many property institutions, governing relationships between people who are neither strangers nor intimates, lie somewhere along this spectrum from atomistic to communitarian norms.[43]

Takings law should follow suit. Rather than imposing the same demand of social responsibility in all contexts, takings law should adjust its expected level of social responsibility to the scope of the social unit benefiting from the public action at stake. Although aspiring to the coexistence of mutual advantage and belonging at the macro level of citizenship may be a worthy aim, we must concede that it is far more likely to be sustained at the micro level of our local communities, where our status as landowners also defines our membership. Thus, a distinction should be drawn between imposing constraints on private property to benefit the community to which the property owner belongs, and prescribing injurious regulations to benefit the public at large.[44] The more the constraint resembles the former type of cases, the higher the threshold of social responsibility that should be implemented (thus legitimizing the imposition of constraints or uncompensated harms as part of the meaning of ownership), and vice versa.[45] This formula is also responsive to the maxim of long-term reciprocity: the larger the scope of the benefited unit, the more attenuated the notion that its effects on the injured individual are likely to be offset in the long term.[46]

---

42. *But cf.* Eduardo Moisés Peñalver, *Regulatory Taxings*, 104 Colum. L. Rev. 2182 (2004), who argues that the almost limitless power to tax is impossible to reconcile with existing regulatory takings law, and that such incoherence calls for a narrow understanding of the Takings Clause.

43. Dagan, *The Craft of Property*, at 1559–60.

44. For the purpose of this chapter, I take the geographical divisions set by land use law as a given. Characterizing the desirable size (and other features) of a geographical community is a significant normative question of land use law as a whole, and thus beyond the scope of this chapter.

45. *See* Dagan, *Takings and Distributive Justice*, at 774–76.

46. This would be the case unless, as it is at times argued, localities are particularly vulnerable to factionalism, agency capture, and extreme majoritarianism. I tend to be

B. Technique

The main doctrinal tool for introducing these two determinative factors into the compensatory formulae of takings law is that of partial compensation.[47] Adding the option of partial compensation to the familiar binary repertoire of full or no compensation introduces a degree of flexibility that, as I demonstrate below, allows fine-tuning of the doctrine responding to the prescriptions outlined above.

Partial compensation can be applied in two ways: as a license for ad hoc judicial discretion[48] or as a technique for the promulgation (by either legislatures or high courts) of more-or-less bright line rules. I opt for the latter alternative.[49] To explain why, I need not recapitulate the vast literature on the choice between bright line rules and vague standards.[50] For my purposes, mention of three normative considerations that weigh against an ad hoc approach to takings cases will suffice.[51] The first two are rather familiar: vague standards upset predictability, and therefore undermine efficiency[52] as well as liberty.[53] The third consideration,

---

suspicious about this (quite extreme) cynicism about localism. In any event, I believe that it is normatively desirable to (try to) inculcate reciprocity especially in local settings.

47. Here I borrow from German and South-African law. *See* Alexander, The Global Debate, at 239.

48. Gregory Alexander reports that this is the way it is used by German courts and approves—even applauds—this practice. *See id.* at 4, 135, 147, 196, 217.

49. My endorsement of rules may be surprising for those who associate legal realism—which clearly guides my discussion thus far—with rule skepticism. This association, however, is mistaken. *See* Hanoch Dagan, *Restitution's Realism, in* Philosophical Foundations of Unjust Enrichment 54, 75–76 (Robert Chambers et al. eds., 2009) (explaining why a "rule-oriented realism" is not a contradiction in terms). Thus, using the two distinctions discussed above, the law (in the realist understanding of this term) can settle on a relatively stable equilibrium of rules that serve as (by definition imprecise) proxies for these underlying normative distinctions.

50. For some important accounts, see Frederick Schauer, Playing by the Rules: A Philosophical Examination of Rule-Based Decision-Making in Law and in Life (1991); Gillian K. Hadfield, *Weighing the Value of Vagueness: An Economic Perspective on Precision in the Law*, 82 Calif. L. Rev. 541 (1994); Louis Kaplow, *Rules Versus Standards: An Economic Analysis*, 42 Duke L.J. 557 (1992); Kathleen M. Sullivan, *The Supreme Court 1991 Term—Foreword: The Justices of Rules and Standards*, 106 Harv. L. Rev. 22 (1992); Jeremy Waldron, *Vagueness in Law and Language: Some Philosophical Issues*, 82 Cal. L. Rev. 509 (1994).

51. *See also* Susan Rose-Ackerman, *Against Ad-Hocery: A Comment on Michelman*, 88 Colum. L. Rev. 1697 (1988) ("[E]ven a very imperfect, but clearly articulated, formal takings doctrine is likely to be superior to open-ended balancing.").

52. The inefficiency of vague standards derives both from their adverse effects on planning ability and their excessive administrative costs. *See, e.g.*, *id.* at 1702–07.

53. By conferring discretion on officials, vague standards subject citizens to other people's authority. *See, e.g.*, Friedrich A. Hayek, The Road to Serfdom 80–81 (1944); Antonin Scalia, *The Rule of Law as a Law of Rules*, 56 U. Chi. L. Rev. 1175, 1179 (1989).

equality, may be more surprising, and is particularly important for those interested in the social responsibility of ownership.[54] Legal regimes of clear and rather simple rules[55] promote equality by reducing the (sometimes unconscious) possibility of bias in the application of officials' discretion.[56] Contexts such as land-use and planning law, in which undue influence by the rich and powerful is a real concern, underscore the importance of this virtue. Moreover, since vague standards do not self-authenticate, they require injured landowners to spend significant resources on legal advice and, therefore, tend to generate regressive outcomes.[57] The reason for this unfortunate result is that heavy dependence on legal advice creates a built-in advantage for repeat players and other strong parties; ordinary citizens and certainly members of weaker sections of society cannot afford long and expensive legal battles.[58] For all of these reasons, my proposed takings doctrine opts for using clear and quite simple rules.

*****

Table 1 below outlines my proposal for eminent domain cases, which responds to the two distinctions discussed above: the distinction between fungible property and constitutive property, and the distinction between projects that benefit

TABLE 2.1 DIFFERENTIAL COMPENSATION FOR EMINENT DOMAIN

		Identity of Beneficiary	
		Local Community	Broader Society
Type of Resource	Fungible Property	x% of fair market value	y% of fair market value
	Constitutive Property	y% of fair market value	fair market value

54. Like with liberty and efficiency, this claim is obviously limited to form. The substance of a rule may be more or less egalitarian (or friendly to liberty or efficiency). But other things being equal from a substantive point of view, clear and simple rules are, I argue, more socially progressive.

55. The requirement of simplicity is important because a thick cluster of complicated rules is subject to many of the difficulties of a vague standard: it both upsets predictability and undermines equality, because it requires a specialist to orient the uninitiated in the legal labyrinth.

56. *See, e.g.*, Sullivan, *The Supreme Court 1991 Term*, at 62.

57. *Cf.* Lawrence Lessig, *Re-crafting a Public Domain*, 18 Yale J. L. & Human. 56, 58–59 (2006) (arguing that "[u]nless the freedoms of the public domain are self-authenticating, they will be unequally distributed").

58. *See generally* Marc Galanter, *Why the "'Haves'" Come Out Ahead: Speculations on the Limits of Legal Change*, 9 Law. & Soc'y Rev. 95 (1974).

the injured landowner's local community and those that benefit the broader society or other communities.[59] It prescribes three bright line rules:

(1) When the beneficiary of the public project at hand is one's local community and the expropriated land had been held as an investment, meaning the owner held it as fungible property, compensation will be calculated as only x% (say 80%) of the fair market value.
(2) By contrast, when the land is expropriated as part of a larger (e.g., regional or state) governmental project and had previously served its owner for constitutive purposes (a home or maybe also a farm or small business), full compensation (fair market value) will be awarded.
(3) In between these two extreme categories are cases in which constitutive land is expropriated for purposes that benefit its owner's local community, and cases in which the use of fungible land benefits the broader society. These intermediate types of cases should both trigger the award of intermediate measures of recovery: y% of the fair market value where x% < y% < 100% (say 90%).

Admittedly, neither the distinction between local communities and larger governmental bodies, nor the distinction between constitutive and fungible properties, is in itself clear. But I believe that rule-conscious judges can use the rather thick body of property law that already resorts to these distinctions in order to integrate them into takings jurisprudence in a rule-based form.

Finally, notice that this proposed scheme should also prove distributionally sensitive, since it makes the targeting of owners of constitutive land (usually ordinary citizens with limited political influence) more expensive than that of owners of fungible land (typically real-estate holding corporations and wealthy individuals).[60]

*****

Takings law could employ a very similar regime for regulatory takings cases, as shown in Table 2. The basic thrust of this scheme applies the familiar diminution of value test,[61] which conditions compensation on the extent (the percentage) of the diminution of value of the property in question—for example, the extent of the loss caused by the public action relative to the preexisting value of the affected property. But unlike current (American) doctrine, my alternative

---

59. For a different suggestion of differential compensation based on the first consideration, see D. Benjamin Barros, *Home as a Legal Concept*, 46 SANTA CLARA L. REV. 255, 298 (2006).

60. For a proposal to consider each claimant's socio-economic status in prescribing the appropriate measure of compensation, see Wyman, *The Measure of Just Compensation*.

61. The diminution of value test originated in *Pennsylvania Coal Co. v. Mahon*, 260 U.S. 393, 413 (1922).

TABLE 2.2 DIFFERENTIAL THRESHOLD FOR REGULATORY TAKINGS

		Identity of Beneficiary	
		Local Community	Broader Society
Type of Resource	Fungible Property	a% of fair market value	b% of fair market value
	Constitutive Property	b% of fair market value	*De minimis*

Where a = (100–x)>b = (100–y)>*de minimis* and x and y correspond to the values in Table 1.

scheme is both rule-based and sensitive to the normative distinctions discussed above.

This scheme establishes fixed minimum thresholds of diminution in value that a regulatory taking must exceed before the government is obligated to provide compensation.[62] In correspondence to the doctrine proposed above for eminent domain cases, the threshold applied would depend on whether the type of property at issue is fungible or constitutive and on the identity of the beneficiary of the regulation, so that uncompensated harms are better tolerated when fungible rather than constitutive properties are at stake and when public action results from the work of local rather than larger government bodies. Thus, the thresholds would be set, relative to the fair market value of the property, at a%, b%, and *de minimis* (0%), where a=(100–x) and b=(100–y). Finally, the reference point for measuring the percentage of the claimant's loss in this proposed doctrine is the value of the parcel as a whole[63] and, in the event that the claimant owns other parcels within the relevant local community, the total value of these holdings.[64]

If, as I think it should, this doctrine remains aligned with that of eminent domain, and assuming that the figures I mentioned above are adopted, then *a* here should represent 20% and *b* should represent 10%.

This scheme too is distributionally sensitive,[65] because a given loss of absolute dollar value resulting from a specific public need may be very substantial

62. If the diminution in value from a regulatory taking is below the appropriate threshold, the government is not obligated to compensate the property owner. If, by contrast, the diminution in value surpasses the threshold, the government must provide compensation for the entire diminution in value.

63. In this scheme, then, a strategy of "conceptual severance," be it horizontal, vertical, or functional, is disallowed. For a critique of conceptual severance, see, for example, Alexander, The Global Debate, at 78–80.

64. For this refinement, *see* Dagan, *Takings and Distributive Justice*, at 783.

65. Although, as always happens when clear rules serve as proxies for underlying normative commitments, sensitivity will not necessarily be found. Specifically, the effect

if imposed on an inexpensive parcel and much less so if imposed on a more costly one.[66] Employing this version of the diminution of value test will therefore (at least at the margin) discourage the public authority from choosing inexpensive (and usually small) parcels. Instead, all things being equal from the planning perspective, this test will encourage the public authority to impose the required burden on landowners of more costly (and usually larger) parcels. Insofar as owners of inexpensive parcels are generally less well-off than owners of more costly ones, this bright line rule will in all likelihood lead to distributionally desirable results.

IV. CONCLUDING REMARKS

Property is a complex and heterogeneous legal construct, which regulates a wide range of human relationships. This heterogeneity explains why the institutions of property bear only a family resemblance to each other. Property law, in its wisdom, has always tailored different configurations of entitlements to different property institutions so that they fit both the social context and the nature of the resource at stake. In this way, each property institution is, at least ideally, designed according to the balance between property values best suited to it.

This conspicuous characteristic of property is not echoed in takings law, which may explain why this important doctrine has so long been struggling for coherence with so little success. Implanting the wisdom of property law into takings law requires a rather radical reshaping of its doctrines. But the exercise is worthy because only in this way can we break away from both the normatively disappointing blueprint advocated by the right and its analytically self-defeating counterpart celebrated by the left.

---

described will not always apply because the physical configuration of the parcels may also influence the diminution of their value in the event that public action affects them.

66. This will be true whenever the required injury is fixed, irrespective of the injured parcel's value.

3. HOW PROPERTY NORMS CONSTRUCT THE EXTERNALITIES OF OWNERSHIP

JOSEPH WILLIAM SINGER*

I. INTRODUCTION

Every morning since 9/11, Donald Lamp has hung an American flag outside his condominium balcony in Omaha, Nebraska.[1] Like many Americans, he wanted to express his solidarity with his fellow countrymen and his strong support for the values that Americans hold dear. But his understandable display of patriotism was met with an unexpected response. The condominium association ordered him to take the flag down; it violated a condominium rule prohibiting external adornments such as wind chimes, banners, and flags. This decision became national news, partly because Lamp is the father-in-law of United States Supreme Court Justice Clarence Thomas, and partly because of popular outrage at the idea that one's neighbors could have the power to prevent an owner from flying an American flag from the balcony of one's home at a time when the United States was under attack from foreign enemies. Indeed, in 2006 the Congress of the United States passed a federal law protecting the right of home owners to display the American flag—a law that expressly makes unenforceable any condominium rule or restrictive covenant to the contrary.[2]

---

* Bussey Professor of Law, Harvard Law School. Thanks and affection go to Martha Minow, Mira Singer, Greg Alexander, Ed Baker, Eduardo Peñalver, Jed Purdy, Jim Ryan, Mike Seidman, Laura Underkuffler.

1. Associated Press, *Apartment dweller, managers clash over flag display*, June 6, 2004, http://www.firstamendmentcenter.org/news.aspx?id=13469; *see also* Tony Mauro, *An unwelcome mat for free speech*, Aug. 18, 2004, USA TODAY, at 13A; Eric Olson, *Father-in-Law of High Court Justice Defies Rule, Flies Flag*, May 29, 2004, ST. LOUIS POST-DISPATCH, at 6.

2. *Freedom to Display the American Flag Act of 2005*, Pub. L. 109-243 (July 24, 2006), *U.S. Statutes at Large* 120: 572, codified at U.S. Code 4 § 5 note. The statute provides, at § 3:

> A condominium association, cooperative association, or residential real estate management association may not adopt or enforce any policy, or enter into any agreement, that would restrict or prevent a member of the association from displaying the flag of the United States on residential property within the association with respect to which such member has a separate ownership interest or a right to exclusive possession or use.

Donald Lamp believed he had a right to fly an American flag from his own home and the Congress of the United States agreed with him. "A man's house is his castle," said Sir Edward Coke, and many Americans embrace that view with a vengeance.[3] From Lamp's perspective, although his neighbors were clearly *interested* in regulating his use of his land, their interests were *not legitimate*. If Lamp is right, we should not only not defer to their preferences, we should not count them at all. Rather, we should judge their preferences as out of bounds: they had no business telling him not to fly an American flag on his own balcony. On this view, we can say that his property use was what John Stuart Mill would have called a "self-regarding act."[4] His actions on his land did not harm others in any tangible way and his neighbors therefore have no legitimate interest in stopping him from doing as he wished on his own property. At the same time, we must acknowledge that the neighbors did indeed *feel harmed* by Lamp's actions. If we define an externality as an effect on others caused by our actions, then Lamp's use of his property caused a negative externality as to his neighbors. But not all externalities merit our attention; some have no normative weight. They may have no moral relevance because the interests asserted are illegitimate either in general or in the particular social context in question. If this is so, then they should have no legal relevance either. If the neighbors' interests in preventing Lamp from flying the flag are illegitimate, then they have no legal relevance. If that is so, then we should not balance the neighbors' interests against those of Lamp; rather, the neighbors' interests simply do not count at all in any comparison of the costs and benefits of alternative rules of law.

Economists use the term *externality* in an ambiguous fashion. One possible meaning is any effect (positive or negative) on others resulting from one's actions. If one adopts a stance of complete neutrality with respect to human interests, then analysts should count all externalities of any kind, no matter how morally repugnant. But a different meaning of externality is any effect (positive or negative) that has moral significance and to which the law should pay attention.[5] The theory underlying much contemporary efficiency analysis is that the law should maximize satisfaction of human preferences, whatever they happen to be. But in the actual analysis employed by real economists (and certainly by judges and other lawmakers), we do not count all preferences in determining the costs and benefits of alternative legal rules. In fact, we do rule some preferences as out of bounds. Congress arguably passed the Freedom to Display the American

---

Section 4 of the statute contains an exception for "any reasonable restriction pertaining to the time, place, or manner of displaying the flag of the United States necessary to protect a substantial interest of the condominium association, cooperative association, or residential real estate management association."

3. Sir Edward Coke, THIRD INSTITUTE OF THE LAWS OF ENGLAND 162 (1644).

4. John Stuart Mill, ON LIBERTY (Gertrude Himmelfarb ed., Penguin Books, 1974) (1859).

5. These are obviously not the same. Some moral claims are not enforced by law.

Flag Act of 2005, not because it thought Lamp's interest in flying the flag outweighed his neighbors' interests in the esthetic appearance of their properties but because if thought the neighbors had no legitimate interest in stopping any American from flying the American flag.

If Lamp's actions have no legally relevant effects on others, then he should be able to do as he pleases on his own land. He is the lord of his own castle. This *castle* or *ownership* conception of property views legally imposed restrictions on the ability to act freely on one's own land as limitations on the rights of the owner and presumptively illegitimate.[6] From this perspective, the federal statute protecting the right to display the American flag outside one's home was a *deregulatory* law that restored the freedom of owners to use their property as they see fit without meddlesome interference by their neighbors or by the community at large.[7] From the standpoint of both Lamp and the U.S. Congress, flying the flag from one's home causes no externalities at all, regardless of what the neighbors might say.

Lamp's neighbors did not see it that way. They bought units in a condominium partly so that they could collectively regulate the external appearance of the property, as well as the use of individual units. From the neighbors' point of view, Lamp's act in flying the flag was anything but a self-regarding act; it was a kind of nuisance—an unreasonable interference with the use and enjoyment of neighboring property. By flying the flag, he interfered with his neighbors' bargained-for property rights, depreciating both the value of their investments in their homes and the setting in which their homes were located. From the neighbors' point of view, Lamp simply did not *own* the right to fly a flag from his balcony; by buying property subject to a condominium declaration, he had impliedly agreed to be bound by rules adopted by his neighbors. By flying the flag, he not only exceeded the scope of his own property rights but invaded the property rights of others. The harm that he caused to them was not only real but it was one that the law should take into account.

In contrast to the *castle* or *ownership* conception of property, we might call this the *good neighbor* or *environmental* conception of property. This view conceptualizes property rights as *socially situated*.[8] The view that the use of one's land often affects the legitimate interests of neighbors (and thus may be limited to the extent necessary to protect those legitimate interests) is associated with a conception of property rights as *overlapping* or *imbricated*.[9] Physical borders between owners

---

6. Joseph William Singer, *The Ownership Society and Takings of Property: Castles, Investments, and Just Obligations*, 30 HARV. ENVTL. L. REV. 309, 314–22 (2006).

7. On the complex relation between property and freedom, *see* Jedediah Purdy, *A Freedom-Promoting Approach to Property: A Renewed Tradition for New Debates*, 72 U. CHI. L. REV. 1237 (2005).

8. *See* Singer, *Ownership Society*, at 322–25, 328–38.

9. *See* Joseph William Singer, ENTITLEMENT: THE PARADOXES OF PROPERTY (2000).

may define the space within which owners are presumptively free to act, but those borders do not define the scope of the owner's freedom—nor of the owner's property rights. This view takes for granted that owners have *obligations* as well as rights and that one purpose of property law is to regulate property use so as to protect the security of neighboring owners and society as a whole.[10] From this perspective, the federal statute protecting Lamp's right to display the American flag gave Lamp the right to harm his neighbors and to deprive them of their bargained-for right to control the external appearance of his home. The harm he caused not only interfered with their legitimate interests but infringed on their property rights. The neighbors believed that the harm Lamp caused was one the law should recognize and their bargained-for right to control the appearance of his property was a property right that the law should allow people to create. From their standpoint, Congress authorized him to impose an externality on them.

How do we choose between the *castle* conception and the *environmental* conception of property? Must we choose? In fact, both conceptions are important to the structure of property as a social and legal institution, and both have a hold on us.[11] When we are imagining the owner exercising his property rights, the castle conception looms large in our minds; others have no claim to take from the owner what is his, and we start from the assumption that owners are free to use what they own for their own purposes and in their own way. We do not view the ordinary uses of property as causing externalities. On the other hand, when property use affects others—and they complain about those effects—we need to consider whether their complaints are legitimate. We know that owners are not generally entitled to cause harm to others. When the exercise of a property right causes harm to a legitimate interest, we are confronted with an externality; in such a case, the environmental conception looms large.

But now we reach the heart of the matter. When we say that an exercise of a property right causes externalities, what we mean is that the exercise of the right causes external effects that the law will recognize as normatively (and hence legally) relevant. If legally relevant effects are present, then we need either to enjoin the property owner from committing the harm or we need to give reasons to the persons who suffer those harms to justify allowing the actor to harm them. If, however, we believe the harms are not legally relevant, then we might find ourselves saying that the property use causes no externalities despite the fact that harm is present. It turns out that economists, like everyone else, make judgments about what harms should count in determining the costs of alternative rules of law. If that is so, then when we talk about externalities, we are talking, not about all external effects of our actions, but morally and legally relevant

10. *See* Singer, *Ownership Society*, at 322–25, 328–38.
11. *See also id.* (describing three models of property).

effects, i.e., effects we should include in any comparison of the costs and benefits of alternative rules of law.

How then do we decide when property rights cause negative externalities? What harms will the law recognize? Was Lamp harming his neighbors by flying the flag on his balcony, or were they harming him when they made him take it down? Or was this a case of legitimate interests on both sides, which could only be resolved by choosing to avoid the more serious harm? How do we conceptualize the harms to which owners and the legal system must attend? When is an act of ownership within the scope of the owner's domain, and when does it cross the boundary to invade the domain of others? Which harms must the law account for and which may it legitimately ignore? How do we distinguish the *inside* and the *outside* of property?

In Part 2, I will explain that the identification of legally relevant harm involves three different inquiries, including (1) deciding whether an actor is exercising a property right; (2) determining who owns the property right; and (3) determining whether the exercise of the right harms legitimate, legally relevant interests.

In Part 3, I will present a brief intellectual history of externalities to explain the significance of the theory of self-regarding acts and the legal realist critique of that theory. We are left with a historical muddle because we are the heirs of two opposed traditions—one that assumes that many exercises of property concern the owner alone and another that views all exercises of property rights as potentially affecting others and thus imposing externalities on them.

Because we cannot determine who is harming whom without determining whether someone is exercising a property entitlement in the first place, Part 4 will explain how property norms construct our understanding of ownership and our intuitions about who is the owner of a particular entitlement. In Part 5, I will explain how property norms construct our understanding of externalities by defining when an owner has exceeded the scope of her property rights by imposing legally relevant harm on others. In conclusion, I will reflect on the ways that property norms both reveal and obscure the presence of externalities.

II. EXTERNALITIES, HARMS, AND NORMS

Externalities are effects on others not directly involved in a transaction or act. How do we determine which externalities we should pay attention to and worry about? How do we identify legally relevant effects? This may involve three separate inquiries. First, is the actor exercising a "property" right? This inquiry matters because the legal system grants owners presumptive control over the resources they own; this means that the exercise of the entitlement does not, *ab initio*, invade the rights of others or cause any harms to which they have a right to complain. I am presumptively not causing an externality by sleeping in my own bed, although I would be if I slept in my neighbor's bed against his will. The fact that

I own the bed (it is my property) gives a *prima facie* reason not to view my use of it as causing harm to others. More problematically, a homeless person may need a place to sleep, but if he demands to sleep in my empty guestroom, the courts will protect my right to exclude him no matter how desperate his need. In the United States (unlike South Africa, for example), the courts do not balance his interests against my own. Moreover, I do not even have to give a reason to exclude him; the inquiry ends when it is determined that I own the house. My exclusion *in fact* harms him (and thus causes an externality broadly considered), but our current legal regime does not recognize my actions as creating a *legally relevant* harm (and thus may not cause an externality to which we should attend). I am not the legal cause of his homelessness even though I am, in fact, depriving him of a bed that he needs. If we believe I have a right to sleep in my bed (because it is my property) and that the homeless person has no legitimate claim to sleep in my bed or exclude me from my bed, then we could say that my exercise of my property rights causes no externalities at all; there are no legally relevant negative effects of my choice to use my own property for my own purposes. Conversely, if a homeless person tried to sleep on my property against my will, he would not be exercising a property right under U.S. law and he would be infringing on my right to exclude him; in so doing, he would be imposing an externality on me by interfering with my legally relevant interests.

Second, we may know that the law defines an entitlement as a property right, but not be sure who owns the entitlement. We cannot determine who is imposing an externality on whom if we do not know who owns the entitlement in question. In Donald Lamp's case, does condominium ownership entail the right to fly the flag on one's own balcony, or does it entail the right to prevent other unit owners from flying the flag? If Lamp owns the right to fly the flag, he has a plausible claim that he is both legally and morally entitled to do so, and any complaints about his exercise of his property rights are misplaced. If this is so, his neighbors' interference with his use of his property invades his property rights. If an externality is a harm to a legitimate, legally protected interest, then we have here a paradigm case of an externality. Conversely, if the neighbors own the right to control the external appearance of the building, then Lamp's violation of the rules invades their property rights and we have an externality going the other way.

A third, logically distinct question is whether the exercise of a property entitlement imposes legally relevant harm to the legitimate interests of others. This might seem to be an easy question; if we define externalities broadly to encompass all possible external effects, then we would argue that all interests count equally and we should make no judgments of any kind about what preferences are worthy of attention by lawmakers. This is the philosophical approach taken by some legal realists and by some contemporary law and economics scholars. But it is not the approach taken by most people; nor is it the approach taken by most judges. Indeed, if we focus on property rights, it becomes clear that many interests are excluded from our moral calculations. The desire to steal someone else's property is not one we weigh in the balance; it is illegitimate and of no consequence. That means that our conception of property is intimately linked to our conception of legally relevant harm.

For example, Lamp may own the right to fly the flag, but he may have waived that right by buying property governed by a condominium association. Conversely, even if the condominium association has the power to regulate the use and appearance of units (it owns this entitlement), it may not have the legitimate power to limit the free speech of the residents. In either case, the question is whether the exercise of the property right harms the legitimate interests of others, and this question depends on a prior determination that those interests are legitimate in the context of the case we are examining.

This raises a potential circularity problem. In a case like that of Lamp and his neighbors, we have property rights on both sides. In such cases, a decision either way would seem to impose an externality because one owner will be entitled to exercise his rights at the expense of the other. If we decide that Lamp owns the right to fly the flag, then he is asking to be left alone and the neighbors are imposing an externality on him; if we decide the neighbors own the right to force him to take the flag down, then they are exercising their property rights and Lamp is imposing an externality on them. We seem to need to define property rights in order to figure out who is imposing an externality and who is engaging in a self-regarding act. But we also seem to need to determine who is engaged in legitimate, self-regarding behavior to figure out how to assign property rights. Which comes first: property rights or externalities? If property rights come first, then we can view an exercise of a property right as a self-regarding act; because owners are entitled to exercise their rights, others who seek to limit their freedoms have no legitimate interest in doing so. If externalities come first, then we must consider all effects our actions have on others, balance competing interests, and define property after engaging in a balancing exercise. The only way to escape this circularity loop is to make a normative judgment about whose interests are legitimate and, if there are legitimate interests on both sides, to consider carefully which interests should be given priorty when they clash.

Libertarians approach these issues by adopting some version of the castle model of property as an organizing paradigm. They start from an image of the rights of the owner. Because they generally have expansive views of property rights, they are likely to identify any claim to control valued resources as a property right deserving strong legal protection. And because they seek to limit state interference with the powers of the owner, libertarians are almost always ready to view the exercise of a "property right" as a self-regarding act. This means that they are likely to define externalities narrowly. If an owner is exercising a property right, then the complaints of others are presumptively illegitimate. This stance does not necessarily decide what to do in Lamp's case. One libertarian view is that owners have the right to fly the flag from their own homes, while another is that owners have the right to create the condominium form of ownership and bind themselves to rules chosen by the homeowners' association. The point is that, whichever way we go, once we have decided who "owns" the entitlement, it becomes hard to see the complaints of the other side as legitimate. Nonowners may covet the property of their neighbors, but they have no right to it, and those owners are not generally thought to be causing harm to others by the mere choice not to give up what they own.

Conversely, both economists and legal realists view legal rights as protection of individual interests that may clash and thus must be balanced against each other. They are therefore much less likely to view entitlements as indefeasible "property rights." Because they may purport to eschew moral judgments about the legitimacy of interests, they are likely to view almost all exercises of rights as entitlements that may impose externalities on others. They are therefore more likely to begin from a skeptical stance, taking the entitlement in question and placing it on the table assuming it belongs to no one. To whom should it belong? They assume the environmental conception of property; adopting this approach, they define property rights by reference to externalities rather than defining externalities by reference to property rights. We identify all the external effects, add up the costs and benefits of assigning the entitlement to Lamp and the costs and benefits of assigning it to the neighbors, and allocate the property right in a manner that best promotes the welfare of all.

Most people however—including most judges—are in the muddled middle; both images have intuitive appeal, depending on the context. Sometimes we are moved by the castle image and identify one person as the owner entitled to exercise her rights. In so doing, we may view the complaints of others as unjustified; they have no legitimate claim to limit the property rights of the owner. But at other times, we recognize that the exercise of a property right often affects the legitimate interests of others, and we are more ready to adopt a skeptical stance about the allocation or limitation of property rights to the extent necessary to protect those legitimate interests.

In fact, we do make normative judgments about which interests are legitimate and which harms are relevant in particular social contexts. All private property systems authorize owners to impose harms on others, but all such systems also limit the ability of owners to cause harm. To draw the line between freedom and security, we not only balance competing interests but reflect on the relevance, strength, and cogency of those interests and harms in particular contexts. We do this based partly on implicit and explicit normative considerations and partly on our intuitions about the rights of "owners." Based on those normative reflections, we reach considered judgments about the legitimacy of claims and the significance of harms. Competing conceptions of property may influence our deliberations, but they may also help express our considered judgments about appropriate social relationships. Remember the Freedom to Display the American Flag Act: it views the right to fly the flag an an inalienable property right and, to come to that conclusion, one must believe that the neighbors' interests in stopping

Donald Lamp from flying the flag are *per se* illegitimate and entitled to no legal weight.

Property norms are standards that help allocate and define the legitimate interests of persons with respect to control of valued resources. More fundamentally, property norms shape our understanding of the *meaning* of property rights and the *legitimate contours of social relationships.* Neither lawmakers nor ordinary persons in their daily life view all interests as legitimate and worthy of defense. Nor do we value all interests equally. Rather, we judge certain interests to be illegitimate *per se* and other interests to be legitimate but unworthy of legal protection. And we often judge interests to be legitimate only in particular social settings or in the context of particular social relationships. Consider that you are free to choose your friends on the basis of race or religion but you are not free to choose your customers in your restaurant on these bases. When interests conflict, we are not indifferent to *qualitative* distinctions among them. Built into our moral consciousness, our way of life, and our legal system are judgments about the *appropriateness* of claims of entitlement and the *legitimacy* of claims of harm.

Sometimes these moral judgments are well-known and accessible to us and, as such, may reflect what Charles Taylor has called "strong evaluations"[12] and Mark Timmons has called "evaluative assertions."[13] These evaluative assertions may take the form of *moral demands*—claims we feel entitled to make on each other. As such, they express *human values.* They may, however, take the form of *narratives* that shape the way we view human relationships, interests, needs, and desires. Sometimes, however, norms may be so deeply embedded in our way of understanding the world that they serve as unconscious assumptions. Charles Taylor

12. Charles Taylor, SOURCES OF THE SELF 4 (1989) ("[M]oral issues [involve] what I have called elsewhere 'strong evaluations,' that is, they involve discriminations of right or wrong, better or worse, higher or lower, which are not rendered valid by our own desires, inclinations, or choices, but rather stand independent of these and offer standards by which they can be judged.").

13. Mark Timmons, MORALITY WITHOUT FOUNDATIONS: A DEFENSE OF ETHICAL CONTEXTUALISM 129 (1999) ("Evaluative assertions, including moral assertions (in their primary usage), do not describe the world or purport to describe it, but play a fundamentally different sort of role in human discourse—broadly speaking, an action-guiding role. Since moral statements make genuine assertions, they are truth-apt; that is, truth and falsity are properly predicated of them."); *see id.* 145–46 ("First, moral statements typically effect a *demand,* of those to whom the statement is addressed, to behave in ways that conform to the moral stance being asserted. Second, they typically signal the speaker's readiness to back the moral stance being asserted with *non-subjective reasons,* in other words, reasons that do not appeal to matters of individual taste, personal preference, or the like. Third, they typically *challenge* the listener, insofar as he adopts some conflicting moral stance, to provide non-subjective reasons in support of that stance and against the speaker's own stance.").

has called these fundamental assumptions "social imaginaries"[14] or "background understandings" that inform our understanding of social life. Importantly for law, they shape our understanding of the legal institutions of a free and democratic society—one of which institutions is the institution of private property.[15] As Taylor has suggested, we will not understand property law or the institution of property unless we *articulate* these background understandings and bring to consciousness the strong evaluations underlying them.[16]

Property norms are essential components of both private and public governance. After all, classical liberalism identifies the protection of both persons and property as two of the core functions of government. However, these twin goals come into conflict when the existence or exercise of a property right results in harm to others. Yet it can be argued that recognition of any property right necessarily harms others by excluding them from resources they may need for human life or desire for their own purposes. How then do we determine when an exercise of ownership is legitimately viewed as a "self-regarding act" that does not affect the legitimate interests of others (and thus does not involve any legally relevant negative externalities) and when such an exercise does harm legitimate interests and thus becomes an appropriate candidate for regulation? Property norms help answer this question by orienting us in a moral universe through background understandings that define legitimate interests that deserve legal protection. Norms orient us, first, by telling us who is an "owner" and who is a "nonowner" with regard to any particular entitlement in a particular resource, and second, by telling owners when they are obligated to take into account the effects of their actions on others and when they are entitled to think of their own interests alone. In so doing, property norms define which externalities we as a society must pay attention to, worry about, and seek (if possible) to prevent.

III. A BRIEF INTELLECTUAL HISTORY OF EXTERNALITIES

Liberalism starts with the idea that each individual is of infinite and equal importance and that a central aspect of human dignity is the power to live life as one chooses on one's own terms. This idea represented a radical break with the

---

14. *See* Charles Taylor, MODERN SOCIAL IMAGINARIES (2004).

15. *See* Joseph William Singer, *Things that We Would Like to Take for Granted: Minimum Standards for the Legal Framework of a Free and Democratic Society*, 2 HARV. L. & POL'Y REV. 139 (2008).

16. Taylor, SOURCES OF THE SELF, 8–11; *see id.* 34 (arguing that "articulation" involves "try[ing] to increase our understanding of what is implicit in our moral and evaluative language"); *see id.* 41 (discussing the need to "explore the background pictures which underlie our moral intuitions"); *see also* Charles Taylor, *Leading a Life*, *in* INCOMMENSURABILITY, INCOMPARABILITY, AND PRACTICAL REASON 170 (Ruth Chang ed., 1997).

normative world that existed in ancient and medieval times.[17] The older view saw the world as possessing an inherent structure supported by nature and God, with human beings occupying a particular place in that structure. Natural law shaped the obligations of individuals and fixed their place in the social world. If anything, this created a jurisprudence of obligation rather than one of right. Plato saw the good as timeless and believed that if human beings thought clearly, we could learn what was good for us; once we knew what was good for us, we would know what to do and how to live. Aristotle believed reason would tell us the nature of human beings and enable us to fulfill our potential by living virtuous lives through exercising appropriate judgment. The Jewish tradition embodied in the Torah and the Talmud developed norms of conduct based on a covenant with God that ordered human life so as to follow God's commandments, to do what is good in God's eyes, and to participate in the creation and the healing of a broken world.[18] St. Augustine and St. Thomas Aquinas developed Christian notions of an orderly universe with inherent notions of right and wrong that would give guidance to human beings in how to live.[19] All these traditions see an inherent order in the universe, founded in nature or God, with knowable content as to what constitutes a good human life.

Liberalism changed all that. Most clearly presented by Thomas Hobbes and John Locke, liberalism put the individual at the center.[20] Liberals developed the idea that individuals had the inherent natural right to act in a self-interested manner, as long as they did not harm others or interfere with the ability of others to similarly pursue their own, freely chosen ends. Of course, one must remember that belief in God was still strong at the time they wrote, and this tempers the invitation to act in a self-interested manner. Hobbes, in particular, assumed that fear of heaven would substantially constrain the monarch from acting in a tyrannical manner.[21] Religious obligation would necessarily limit harmful acts even if those acts were not illegal under civil law.

For this new theory to work, one had to believe that natural law gave human beings reason that made us capable of discerning the limits on freedom necessary to protect the rights of others. On one view, the culmination of this theory came with John Stuart Mill's theory of self-regarding acts. In his essay, *On Liberty*,

---

17. *See generally* Taylor, SOURCES OF THE SELF.

18. *See* Jonathan Sacks, TO HEAL A FRACTURED WORLD: THE ETHICS OF RESPONSIBILITY (2005).

19. *See* Thomas Aquinas, SELECTED POLITICAL WRITINGS (A. P. D'Entrèves ed., J. G. Dawson trans., Oxford, 1974); THE POLITICAL WRITINGS OF ST. AUGUSTINE (Henry Paolucci ed., Gateway ed. 1962).

20. *See* Thomas Hobbes, LEVIATHAN (C. B. MacPherson ed., Penguin Books, 1976) (1651); John Locke, THE SECOND TREATISE OF GOVERNMENT (Thomas P. Peardon ed., Bobbs-Merrill ed. 1952) (1690).

21. *See* Hobbes, 409–626 ("Of a Christian Common-wealth"); *see id.* 627–715 ("Of the Kingdome of Darknesse").

Mill argued that individuals should be free to act as they please as long as their actions do not affect others.[22] Once their actions do affect others, then it becomes open to question whether to regulate (meaning limit or prohibit) the other-regarding conduct that is experienced by the victims as harmful. Our freedom of action must be limited to protect the security of others. This theory nicely reconciles the invitation to act in a self-interested manner with the reality that we do not live alone and that our actions may interfere with the similar ability of others to seek their own ends in their own way. This view was adopted by analytical jurists like John Austin to justify both the rule of law in general and the common law in particular.[23]

Over time, however, this legitimating theory began to break down. Over the course of the nineteenth century in the United States, property law was modernized to decrease common law regulations of land use that had previously been in effect. Nuisance law became narrower. The abolition of the fee tail—although clearly a regulatory limitation on freedom of contract—was conceptualized as freeing current owners to control their property as they saw fit, allowing them to sell the land, to move elsewhere, to develop it without worry about the desires or wants of future generations. The move from monopolistic franchises to general incorporation statutes and from secure protection of prior investors to increased economic competition suggested a movement in the direction of freeing individuals to commit observable harms on others. Economic competition, in particular, was associated with dynamic property rather than static landed estates or monopolies, and it rested on the ability to put others out of business or entice their customers away.[24]

As both law and morals changed, it became more evident to jurists and scholars that the legal system allowed a great deal of *damnum absque injuria*—damage without legal redress. Indeed, Edward Weeks wrote a remarkable treatise on the subject in the tort field, explaining all the ways one was entitled to harm others without being subject to legal penalty—in effect, an "anti-torts" book.[25] This led the analytical jurists, such as Henry Terry, John Salmond, and Wesley Newcomb Hohfeld, to redefine legal liberties. No longer was liberty the freedom to engage in self-regarding acts; rather, liberty entailed the freedom to impose harms on others.[26]

---

22. *See* Mill, On Liberty.

23. Joseph William Singer, *The Legal Rights Debate in Analytical Jurisprudence from Bentham to Hohfeld*, 1982 Wis. L. Rev. 975, 1009–12 (1982).

24. *See* Morton J. Horwitz, The Transformation of American Law 1780–860 (1977).

25. Edward Weeks, The Doctrine of Damnum Absque Injuria Considered in its Relation to the Law of Torts (1879), discussed in Singer, *Legal Rights Debate*, at 1026–34.

26. *See* Singer, *Legal Rights Debate*.

The legal realists, spurred on by the views of Oliver Wendell Holmes, Jr.,[27] adopted Hohfeld's construction of the problem, by asserting that it was a policy question whether the law should or should not prevent one person from harming the interests of another.[28] The theory of self-regarding acts can only work to reconcile the interest in freedom of action with the interest in security if one can identify in an objective manner what acts affect others and what acts do not. Once the jurists began to eschew moral judgment about which effects on others are legitimate and which are not, they moved to the language of balancing interests. This had an especially profound effect in property law because Hohfeld defined property as a bundle of rights, none of which entailed the others; it was a policy question how the rights would get divided up. Before Hohfeld, we could define the exercise of a property right as a self-regarding act; that is what it means to own the right. After Hohfeld, we could no longer define acts as self-regarding by reference to property rights; in fact, the exercise of a property right by definition affected others by making them vulnerable to effects of one's actions. That meant that the legal system might well limit one's free use of one's property to protect the security of others. The fact that one owned property did not necessarily mean that a particular set of rights went along with ownership.

Both the Progressives and the legal process theorists picked up on this change by arguing that the courts should let the legislatures balance interests. But this solution could not solve actual cases because judges still had to decide in common law cases which interest would prevail when both parties argued that an action affected their interests. Efficiency theorists responded in the 1960s by using their version of utilitarian normative theory, arguing that the courts should defer to consumer preferences, whatever they happen to be, to measure the strength of those preferences by market measures (dollar amounts), and seek to maximize social wealth.[29] This skeptical approach to moral judgments makes it even harder to distinguish self-regarding from other-regarding acts. Any claim to interfere with an interest claimed by someone else appears as an externality to an economist like Ronald Coase.[30] The factory that is polluting the neighborhood may be causing externalities on home owners, but according to Coase, the homeowners' claim that the factory is not free to harm their property by polluting imposes an externality on the factory by limiting the factory owner's freedom to use its own land. If each is imposing an externality on the other (or claiming a right to do so), then the distinction between self-regarding and other-regarding acts falls away.

Or does it? Try as the economists might to argue that the imposition of pollution on homeowners is morally and legally equivalent to the homeowners'

27. *See* Oliver Wendell Holmes, Jr., *Privilege, Malice, and Intent*, 8 Harv. L. Rev. 1 (1894).
28. *See* Singer, *Legal Rights Debate*.
29. *See generally* Steven Shavell, Foundations of Economic Analysis of Law (2004).
30. Ronald Coase, *The Problem of Social Cost*, 3 J. L. & Econ. 1 (1960).

desire to limit the factory's polluting activity, there is something in us that wants to rebel and not to see the actions as equivalent. It remains true, in other words, that many people do not view the homeowners as imposing a legally relevant harm on the factory when they ask the factory to stop hurting them and their property. It is as if an assailant were to complain that my chin got in the way of his fist, that we should be agnostic about his power to beat me up, and that we should leave it to the jury to determine whether I deserved to be beaten up. While the factory owner may have a legitimate interest in running his business, he does not have a legitimate interest in polluting neighboring land. If the exercise of the right of homeownership entails the right to live safely in one's home, then there is a tendency to judge the homeowners as having a morally superior claim to that of the factory. Indeed, one might even view them as claiming that their exercise of their property rights is legitimately viewed as a self-regarding act. Like Greta Garbo, they merely want to be let alone.

In my own work, I have argued that although the legal realists and economists tried to make the claim that we should flatten all interests and view them as either equally valid or equally suspect, they could not remove the cultural power of ownership norms.[31] They could not erase the idea that when you hit me, you have done something wrong; you have imposed an externality on me. The fact that I was standing in the way of your fist does not constitute a harm I was imposing on you; while it is true your fist would have caused no harm if I were not standing in the way, it is a distortion of our moral understanding of the situation to equate my chin with your fist.

As a social, legal, and normative practice, property entails judgments about interests. Our cultural norms support the idea that the exercise of a "property right" is presumptively a self-regarding act; indeed, *one might say this is the very meaning of property*. The social meaning of property, combined with our typical ("normal") property arrangements, creates strong assumptions on our part about who is the "owner," what rights the owner has, and which rights prevail when ownership rights clash with each other. A "norm" may be what is typical or it may describe what we believe we have a right to expect. Either way, our conceptualization of property rights powerfully affects our understanding of when an externality is present and when an action should be viewed as legitimately self-regarding. And those conceptions are powerfully influenced by both conscious and unconscious norms.

IV. HOW NORMS CONSTRUCT OWNERSHIP

Property norms shape our understanding of externalities most fundamentally by orienting us in the normative world through defining who is the *owner* of

31. *See* Singer, ENTITLEMENT.

a particular entitlement. As Laura Underkuffler explains, the idea of property suggests that owners have full (and, I would add, *rightful*) powers over what they own. The identification of something as *property* and someone as the *owner* creates a strong presumption that, in any dispute about the property, the "owner" will prevail.[32] More than that, we may even presume that the owner is the only one with any legitimate claim to control the property. Any claims by "nonowners" are, by definition, claims to limit the rights of the owner, thereby causing harm to a legally protected interest. Conversely, the "owner" is, by definition, exercising her rights when she acts within the borders of her own property; however much others may seek to control what she does on her own land, they have no legitimate business in doing so. That means their interests in doing so will not count or be considered in determining the applicable rules of law governing the allocation or regulation of property rights. More abstractly, the ownership idea means that one is presumably engaged in a self-regarding act if she is *exercising her lawful property rights;* ownership of land furnishes a schema for this idea because it rests on the idea of boundaries surrounding a space devoted to one's own control. The idea of ownership, therefore, is a powerful cultural tool that encompasses one of the most important ways that we, as a society, define when someone is and is not imposing an externality on someone else.

Recall the case of Donald Lamp. His view of the matter was that he had bought a condominium and that, when condominiums were brought into the United States as a legal form in the 1960s, their innovative feature was that one could actually *own* and not merely *rent* an apartment in a building. This means that the "condo" is no different from a single family home; it is, in short, his castle. On this view, limitations on the rights of owners are encumbrances that should be presumptively invalid. Indeed, the legal idea of the "fee simple absolute" rests on the ways in which property ownership is different from feudal holdings. A fee simple owner has no lord, owes no periodic duties or fealty to a superior; the fee owner is the lord of his own castle. On this view of ownership, the neighbors were busybodies interfering with Lamp's property rights. Seeing Lamp as the owner leads us to see the condominium association as imposing externalities on him.

The neighbors, of course, see it differently: *they* were the owners here, not Lamp. Although Lamp was flying the flag physically on "his own" balcony, he did not "own" the right to do so.[33] On the contrary, his deed at the time he bought the unit was impressed with restrictive covenants under which he promised to comply with rules of the condominium association. For that reason, his neighbors *owned*

---

32. *See id.*

33. I say "arguably" because the RESTATEMENT (THIRD) OF PROPERTY (SERVITUDES), published in 2000, suggests that covenants should not run with the land if they violate fundamental interests in freedom of speech. *See* RESTATEMENT (THIRD) OF PROPERTY (SERVITUDES) § 3.1 cmt. h (2000).

the benefit of those covenants and had the right to impose restrictions on external decorations of the units. His act of flying the flag was an intrusion on the ownership rights of his neighbors.

We can see the implications of conceptions of ownership by looking at the *limits* to the rights created by Congress in the Freedom to Display the American Flag Act. Congress clearly did not believe it was interfering with property rights when it prohibited enforcement of covenants limiting display of the flag; rather, it viewed the right to fly an American flag on one's own property to be an *inalienable right*. But this right applies only to invalidate restrictions imposed by a "condominium association, cooperative association, or residential real estate management association" and, even then, only protects the interests of "members" of those "associations" who have "a separate ownership interest or a right to exclusive possession or use."[34] Although there is some ambiguity in this language, it appears not to grant rights to residential tenants who are prevented from flying the American flag by a covenant in a lease. Why might this be so?

Perhaps Congress simply did not think about tenants. The more likely answer is that Congress likely views *landlords* as the "owners" of the property; *tenants* are denied the rights granted to condo owners because they are seen as temporary guests—in other words, as *nonowners*. If this interpretation is correct, then the right to fly the flag belongs, not to the tenant, but to the landlord. A tenant who sought to violate a lease covenant against flying a flag would be viewed as infringing on the retained property rights of the landlord. This popular conception of tenants as less than "owners" is not shared by many property law professors who are steeped in the history of property law and know that leaseholds have technical names, such as "term of years" and "periodic tenancies" and that these were traditionally thought of as "estates in land." It is thus not uncommon to hear property lawyers talk about "owning" a "lease." And if this sounds odd, recall that in a number of states in the eastern part of the United States, mortgages take the form of granting title to the land to the lending institution. Rather than an individual buying land and becoming the owner, while granting the bank a "lien" on the property, in states like Massachusetts, the bank takes "title" to the land while the so-called homeowner takes merely an "equity of redemption." Yet despite this legal arrangement, we routinely talk about homeowners in Massachusetts, even when they are still paying off their mortgages to the bank that actually has title to their land. It would be perfectly logically to argue that tenants, like condominium owners, should have the right to fly the American flag outside their own homes. Yet the Congress of the United States refused to extend this right to tenants; arguably, it did not consider them to be "owners" at all. Thus property norms may explain why Congress viewed Donald Lamp's flag

---

34. U.S. Code 4 (2006), § 5 note.

flying as a self-regarding act while the same act undertaken by a tenant against the wishes of the landlord would be viewed as imposing an externality.

Thus, norms of ownership, and not just the law, identify who is and who is not an "owner." For another example, consider the law of servitudes. Real covenants serve an ambiguous role in property law. The older view was that they were encumbrances that limited the presumptively absolute rights of owners. They were thus viewed with suspicion. If it was ambiguous whether a seller intended to create a covenant, the law ruled against finding the limitation. The older image is that of aggregated rights in the current owner. The common law limited the number of negative easements that could be created and prevented enforcement of covenants that did not "touch and concern" the land; under that test, because it is not clear how flying a flag "touches and concerns" the dominant estate, a covenant preventing flag flying might have been held not to run with the land, freeing Lamp from the restriction altogether. This construction of property rights had its origins in doctrines designed to concentrate powers over property in current owners as a way to avoid the re-creation of feudalism. Granting individuals full powers over their own land allows them to control their own lives, to move from one place to another, to sell their land and buy other land, and to develop it as they see fit.

The more modern view goes the other way. Current property law in the United States emphasizes freedom of contract. This is especially evident in the Restatement (Third) of Property (Servitudes), adopted by the American Law Institute in 2000, and in the increasing number of states that have abolished the rule against perpetuities. Owners are *prima facie* allowed to create whatever servitudes they like. However, this increasing contractual freedom to disaggregate property rights and create new bundles of rights is limited by increasing regulation through both common law and statute. The Restatement (Third), for example, provides that covenants will be void if they violate public policy; the Restatement grants wide discretion to courts to determine what that means, advising them only that a variety of fundamental values may be implicated by covenants. For the purpose of thinking about our case of the American flag, one of those values is freedom of speech.[35]

This means that we have a conflict between two images of ownership. The older view emphasizes the full powers of the owner while the modern view is based on the notion of freedom of contract whereby owners may disaggregate property rights as they see fit, creating the packages of rights that please them.

When I ask my students whether the Freedom to Display the American Flag Act protects property rights or attacks them, their answer depends on how they conceptualize real covenants. If they understand covenants as property rights, they are apt to find the law to be an attack on property; the law limits the freedom

35. RESTATEMENT (THIRD) OF PROPERTY (SERVITUDES) § 3.1 cmt. h (2000).

to create particular packages of rights and takes away vested rights created under prior conveyances. If they understand covenants as merely contract rights, they apply the theory of efficient breach they are taught in their contracts class; they remember that contracts are normally enforced by damages rather than injunctive relief, that there is a duty to mitigate damages, and that this often makes damages low. The law of contract enforcement thereby often encourages contracting parties to discard their contractual obligations, break their promises, pay damages if needed, and go on about their business.[36] If we couple this dim view of contract obligations to a capacious understanding of the rights of fee simple owners of land, then my students are apt to view the statute as a restoration of the rights of owners to control their own land without undue limitations imposed by busybody neighbors. If every person's house is his or her castle, then this federal law restores dignity, power, autonomy, *and property rights* to individuals. In contrast, if they see covenants as property interests, they are likely to see the statute as congressional meddling in private property arrangements; after all, unlike the doctrine of "efficient breach," they have been taught that "efficient theft" is an oxymoron.

The distinction between efficient breach of contract and efficient theft shows that assumptions about the nature of property rights and the nature of a free and democratic society in which they are situated *orients* us in developing understandings of both property rights and regulatory laws and the relation between them. If the condo rule against flag flying is seen as an intrusion on the inherent rights of the owner, then the regulatory statute restores property rights and prevents the neighbors from imposing externalities on the individual owner who wants to fly the flag. If, on the other hand, the right to control neighboring property is a legitimate entitlement accompanying condominium ownership, then it is the dissident who seeks to fly the flag in violation of a collectively adopted rule who is imposing externalities on his neighbors. In that case, the federal statute redistributes property rights from covenant beneficiaries to scofflaws.

V. HOW NORMS CONSTRUCT EXTERNALITIES

I have argued that property norms identify presumptive "owners" of entitlements. Because owners are entitled to do what they want with their own property, the identification of an entitlement as a "property right" creates a presumption that the exercise of that right by the "owner" is a self-regarding act. But I have also noted that property rights are far from absolute, and that the exercise of those rights may well be deemed to invade the legitimate interests of others. Here

36. But for a view of the compatibility of the idea of efficient breach with the moral basis of promising, see Charles Fried, *The Convergence of Contract and Promise*, 120 Harv. L. Rev. F. 1 (2007).

again, norms operate by distinguishing legitimate from illegitimate interests, or more precisely between legally relevant and legally irrelevant interests.

In our American flag case, the law gives individuals the power to create the condominium form of ownership with the power in the owners' association to regulate the use and appearance of individual units. When Lamp bought his apartment, he therefore arguably waived the right to complain about such regulatory rules imposed by his neighbors. On this view, his complaint about a rule restricting his ability to fly the American flag is without foundation. He does not own the right to fly the flag, and a rule prohibiting him from doing do does not invade any legitimate interests of his. The condominium association has imposed no externality on him.

He has one ace up his sleeve, however: he may claim that the rule in question impinges on his fundamental right to free speech. A law imposed by the town preventing him from flying the flag would certainly violate the First Amendment.[37] Although condominium rules regulating the external appearance of the property are legitimate in general, they may be illegitimate if they infringe on interests in engaging in legitimate political speech. The *character* of the interest invaded by the condominium rule may justify a conclusion that the rule causes a legally relevant externality. Indeed, the Restatement (Third) of Property (Servitudes) explains that a homeowners' association rule may violate public policy if it interferes with interests in free speech.[38] If a legally relevant externality is present, then we reach the further question of how to resolve the conflict between the presumptively legitimate exercise of the neighbors' property rights and the legitimate complaint that exercise of those rights infringes on an individual's legitimate interests in freedom of speech.

Nonowners often have interests recognized by the legal system even when a property owner is exercising his property rights if the owner acts in a manner that affects them. In the famous case of *State v. Shack*,[39] the Supreme Court of New Jersey ruled that a farm owner could not keep a doctor and lawyer off his farm when they were entering to provide medical and legal services to migrant farmworkers who were living and working there. The farm owner argued that they were trespassing by entering land of another without the owner's consent. He argued that he was the owner of the land and that one of the central rights of ownership is the right to exclude nonowners from one's land and to condition rights of entry on terms chosen by the owner. Moreover, the workers' employment and housing contracts did not give them the right to receive such visitors. Since the owner had not waived his right to exclude by agreement either with his

---

37. *City of Ladue v. Gilleo*, 512 U.S. 43 (1994).

38. RESTATEMENT (THIRD) OF PROPERTY (SERVITUDES) § 3.1 cmt.h (2000). *See, e.g.*, Fla. Stat. § 718.123 (making unenforceable any condominium rule that interferes with freedom of assembly in common areas of the condominium).

39. 277 A.2d 369 (N.J. 1971).

workers or the service providers, they had no legal right to enter his property against his will. If we go by background norms of ownership, the farmer should have won hands down; after all, he is the one we would identify as the "owner" of the land. The doctor and lawyer are intruding on his land; the farmer did nothing to them. As the owner, he has the right to exclude or admit others to his land and his exercise of that right, *one way or the other*, is the paradigm case of a self-regarding act. In contrast, trespass is a paradigm case of harm to an existing property right. Under this construction, we know who is asking to be left alone (and thus not causing any externalities) and who is causing harm (a legally relevant negative externality).

But things are not so simple. The court ruled against the owner, accepting the argument of the doctor and lawyer that real property owners are not entitled to prevent service workers funded by the federal government from getting access to workers living on the owner's land. The right to receive government assistance may, for example, prevent the owner from excluding the police who enter property to help nonowners who happen to be on the land. The right to exclude is limited by public policy; ownership rights (even exclusionary rights) are not absolute. That is especially true when an owner has alienated some of his rights to others. It is a firm rule that tenants have the right to receive visitors in their apartments, regardless of what the lease contract may say. This right is so well accepted that few precedents establish it. It is assumed that the transfer of possessory rights gives the tenant the ability to create a home and that it is a necessary part of that right to form human relationships with friends and neighbors and to receive family members as guests. According to the New Jersey Supreme Court, migrant farmworkers housed in baracks have the same rights—regardless of what the contract says. The farmer may be the owner of the land but by entering a contract that allows his workers to live on his land, he parts with some of his ownership rights, and it is the workers, not the farmer, who have the right to receive or turn away guests. This result may seem jarring only because the workers do not have the status of "tenants" but are merely licensees; but the fact that one has to work to understand the farmworkers as possessing rights in the land proves the power of the ownership conception operating here. Reconceptualizing the case as akin to a landlord barring his tenants from receiving guests recasts the situation as one in which the landlord is causing harm to the tenant, effectively depriving the tenant of bargained-for property rights.

But suppose we conclude that the farmworkers merely have licenses to be on the farmer's land and that their employment contracts give them no right to receive visitors in the barracks. When you invite friends to dinner, this does not give them the right to bring others along without your consent. In that case, the farmer retains the right to exclude the doctor and the lawyer, and the workers cannot claim that their legitimate interests have been harmed by his innocent act of excluding nonowners from, what, after all, is his own land. But the court did not see it that way.

In a famous sentence, Chief Justice Weintraub wrote: "Property rights serve human values. They are recognized to that end, *and are limited by it*."[40] Whether a claimed property entitlement can be recognized depends on the *values underlying the claim* and the *context* in which the claim is asserted. Here the farmer would assert an interest in the ability to operate his business as he sees fit, to engage in mutually advantageous employment contracts, the freedom to exercise autonomy and to choose the character of his associations with others. He will also assert interests in freedom of contract and social interests in economic efficiency. The farmer did not force the workers to work for him. They chose to do so, and it would deny the farmer dignity if the court tried to control the terms on which he chooses to employ others on his own property. Protecting the owner's free control of his own land and his own business and freedom of all the parties to contract on mutually beneficial terms is the way to treat each person with equal concern and respect, while governmental regulation of property and contract fails to treat individuals as self-governing persons in charge of their own fates. As Professor Alan Schwartz argues, individuals have the right to "do the best they can for themselves, given their circumstances."[41] It is a fundamental assault both on freedom and on human dignity to dictate the course of someone's life or to impose the terms of one's associations with others by regulating contracts, thereby depriving individuals of the power to make their own choices, suffer from their own mistakes, and chart the course of their own destiny.

In contrast, the defendants in *Shack* focused on the reasons why people have the right to receive visitors in their homes. The farmworkers have the same interests in freedom of association as their employer, and while he does have interests in excluding others from his land and running his business as he sees fit, they have strong interests in developing what the New Jersey Supreme Court called "associations customary among our citizens" as well as receiving government aid designed to ensure basic human needs.[42] And in a remarkable phrase, the court explains that, although the farmer is the acknowledged owner of the land, "we find it unthinkable that the farmer-employer can assert a right to isolate the migrant worker in any respect significant for the worker's well-being."[43] Preventing individuals from receiving visitors in their homes or having their basic needs met denies them "dignity" and treats them as if they did not deserve to be treated as human beings.[44] Thus, the court concludes that the farmer's interests are *not legitimate* when they cause the *kinds of harms* implicated in this case. If that is so, then the farmer's simple act of ownership—excluding

---

40. *State v. Shack*, 277 A.2d 369, 372 (emphasis added).

41. Alan Schwartz, *Justice and the Law of Contracts: A Case for the Traditional Approach*, 9 HARV. J. L. & PUB. POL'Y REV. 110, 114–15 (1986).

42. *Shack*, 277 A.2d at 374.

43. *Id.*

44. *Id.*

nonowners from his land—becomes something far different from a self-regarding act; it causes legally relevant harm to others, and not only that, but it imposes a particular kind of externality that one should not be entitled to impose on others and therefore exceeds the rights of the owner.

VI. CONCLUSIONS

Consider the current subprime mortgage foreclosure crisis. Congress is currently debating whether to amend the bankruptcy law to allow the courts to rewrite the terms of subprime mortgage loans—in particular by reducing the amount of principal owed. Why is Congress thinking of doing this? The answer is that allowing millions of foreclosures to happen will have devastating effects on the national (and the international) economy. Foreclosures do not only affect the ousted homeowner; they affect others as well. A neighborhood spotted with foreclosed homes lowers the property values of all properties in the neighborhood, and the ensuing dilapidation of abandoned properties that are not maintained by banks poses a harsh barrier to economic reconstruction.[45] The externalities of the practice of subprime lending are evident for all to see. The practice of securitization of bad loans that cannot be valued by any living person makes fixing the problem a veritable nightmare. What we have here are packages of property rights created to promote the interests of the immediate parties that have wrecked the world economy. The negative externalities of these loans are both obvious and enormous. Yet despite this, it remains politically controversial to subject mortgages to revision by the bankruptcy courts. Why is that?

The banking industry argues that this will decrease incentives for banks to give such loans in the future, resulting in fewer loans at higher interest rates, hurting both potential homebuyers and the general public.[46] For others, the problem is that applying bankruptcy law to mortgages granted in the past could be understood as taking property without just compensation.[47] Homeowners have no legitimate interest in stealing the property in someone else's bank account to pay off their mortgage, so why does Congress have the power to give them the right to take from the bank the bank's right to full repayment of

---

45. Alex Kotlowitz, *All Boarded Up*, N.Y. TIMES MAGAZINE, Mar. 10, 2009, http://www.nytimes.com/2009/03/08/magazine/08Foreclosure-t.html?_r=1&scp=2&sq=cleveland&st=cse.

46. Jim Puzzanghera, *Bankruptcy law may be modified: Measure could give judges more power to modify primary home mortgages*, CHICAGO TRIBUNE, Mar. 11, 2009, http://www.chicagotribune.com/business/chi-090225-bankruptcy,0,6222482.story.

47. *See* Randy Picker, *Government's Promise: Taking Away Property?* U. CHI. LAW SCHOOL FACULTY BLOG (Jan. 20, 2009) http://uchicagolaw.typepad.com/faculty/2009/01/governments-promise-taking-away-property.html (suggesting this worry but expressing no clear view on the matter).

the loan? What is striking about this argument is that it assumes that the contract between the parties (and the property rights they created) cannot be interpreted as imposing harm on others. The bank and the borrower had a right under existing law to make the contract they made and to change the terms of the arrangements now without compensation would take vested rights. This kind of argument rests on the identification of the bank's interest as a property right and the exercise of that right as a self-regarding act. Treating the bank's interests this way obscures the existence of externalities by taking our attention away from the fact that the banks that engaged in these practices caused harm to the financial markets and the world economy; it may not be inaccurate to say that they caused a severe economic recession. If rewriting the terms of the arrangements would mitigate some of that harm, then it may be that the bank never owned the right to inflict those externalities on the world community in the first place. And if that is so, then it is not the bankruptcy bill that would impose externalities on the bank but the bank (with the cooperation of the borrower) that imposed externalities on the rest of us—externalities the bankruptcy bill seeks to lessen by redefining the property rights of the lender. From the bank's perspective, they merely gave out loans to people who wanted them; from the perspective of the rest of us suffering from a recession caused by those loans, the mortgage industry engaged in anything but self-regarding acts.

Property norms both reveal and obscure the presence of externalities. Property norms reveal externalities, first, by allocating property rights and classifying certain kinds of actions as invasions of those rights. Property norms may also reveal externalities by identifying legally relevant interests that deserve protection even if they do not rise to the level of property rights. Conversely, property norms may obscure externalities in several ways. They may do so, first, by defining particular entitlements to be core aspects of "ownership." The exercise of those entitlements may sometimes be conceptualized as self-regarding acts. In so doing, they may obscure the fact that exercising those entitlements has real effects on others. Property norms may also obscure externalities by defining certain interests as illegitimate and unworthy of legal protection, thereby converting what one might think was a harmful action into a self-regarding act. When norms function in these ways, and we view an action as a self-regarding act, externalities magically vanish. On the other hand, when externalities are present, property norms help us identify the values underlying competing interests, the social contexts in which those values legitimately operate, and the relative strength of the conflicting values. Judgments of these kinds do not merely rest on quantitative comparisons of costs and benefits but on qualitative judgments about the contours of a free and democratic society that treats each person with equal concern and respect.

4. PROPERTY AND MARGINALITY

A. J. VAN DER WALT*

I. INTRODUCTION

In this chapter, I reflect on a shifting but nevertheless enduring characteristic of property in modern Western legal culture, namely its tendency to focus on (and justify its outcomes with reference to) what I will describe as the logic of centrality. My first hypothesis is that lawyers, owners, and users of property habitually and unreflectively accept that property institutions naturally assume a central place in society and that property—as an organizing concept—similarly assumes a central role in law and legal theory. The logic of centrality thus relies on unreflective intellectual habits. My second hypothesis is that these habits and the property practices they support (described as "governance" elsewhere in this volume) inhibit much-needed social and legal transformation in that they condemn certain persons to the margins of society and of the law, either by design or by default.

In what follows, I briefly survey efforts to undermine or escape from the hold that centrality logic continues to exercise over property thinking. For purposes of the discussion I use "property" in its widest sense, referring not only to the legal institution of formally recognized and protected ownership and other rights in property,[1] but also to the unequal distribution of property as a social

---

* B Jur et Art, Honns (BA) (Philosophy), LLB, LLD (Potchefstroom), LLM (Witwatersrand). Professor, Law Faculty, Stellenbosch University; South African Research Chair in Property Law (hosted by Stellenbosch University, funded by the Department of Science and Technology and administered by the National Research Foundation). Research for a larger project on property theory, of which this paper forms part, was made possible by financial assistance from the National Research Foundation (NRF, grant number GUN 2050532) and Stellenbosch University. The views set out in the article are those of the author and should not be attributed to any of these institutions. Thanks to Greg Alexander, Eduardo Peñalver, and Alain Pottage for advice and comments, to Elmien du Plessis for research assistance and to Johan van der Walt, Henk Botha, Karin van Marle, and Wessel le Roux for a standing debate over many years that gave shape to some of the ideas in this paper. I take responsibility for remaining errors and misconceptions.

1. Although some aspects of the problems I consider are specific to the narrower notion of ownership, I will mostly refer to the wider notion of property without reflecting on the differences between them.

phenomenon and to property as an organizing concept in legal doctrine and in legal and social theory.

I describe centrality as a quality of property to indicate that property, understood in terms of the logic of centrality, occupies a central position in and thereby exercises important functions in the social and legal system. On the one hand, centrality assumes that property is central to the human condition and hence to societal organization. The notion of centrality links the power that follows from the presence of property to essential human qualities and values such as desert, human flourishing, or utility. The dominating role that centrality assigns to property in upholding and safeguarding these qualities and values explains and justifies the otherwise startling inequalities that follow from the unequal distribution of property. Although society no longer treats marginal social and economic positions such as poverty and dependence with the same disdain and condescension as in the nineteenth century, these conditions still carry some stigma of physical, mental, or moral weakness or shortcoming, just as the central position of having property is still associated with personal, social, and moral superiority. Even when members of society sympathize with the status of not having property and requiring state or social support as the unavoidable and personally unblameworthy outcome of natural disaster or irresistible social, economic, or political force, its description in terms of emergency, dire straits, or desperate circumstances still tends to confirm the normality of property and the abnormality of need, poverty, and marginality.[2]

Accepting or confirming the centrality of property, even indirectly, tends to confirm a certain hierarchical ordering between having property, which centralists consider normal, and not having property, which centralists consider extraordinary. Assignment of having property to the center and not having property to the margins of normality justifies the unequal distribution of property and power in society, not only when the lack of property results from the personal shortcomings of the have-nots but also when society accepts it more sympathetically as the result of some natural or social disaster that upset the normal course of events. Ownership or property famously acts as a fence that protects the individual against outside threats; this protective function of property and the central role that it plays in recognizing and upholding certain social, economic, and legal patterns of privilege depends for its rhetorical power and its legal efficacy upon the presence of property on one side of the conflict as much as on its absence on the other. In what follows, I argue that even the critical, poststructuralist theories that deny the liberal link between moral desert and property and

---

2. I use the notion of "normality condition" in the sense developed by Rosemary Coombe; see *"Same as It Ever Was": Rethinking the Politics of Legal Interpretation*, 34 McGill L.J. 603 (1989). Gregory S. Alexander probably had something similar to my thesis in this paragraph in mind when he wrote *The Concept of Property in Private and Constitutional Law: The Ideology of the Scientific Turn in Legal Analysis*, 82 Colum. L. Rev. 1545 (1982).

that advocate social redefinition and significant redistribution of property tend to group property, power, and normality versus poverty, weakness, and abnormality in a hierarchical configuration. This configuration in turn positions the first group in the center and the second on the margins of society and the law, thereby failing to unsettle the assumed "normality condition" of liberal tradition.

In addition, centrality means that property is the key to the system of property rights (and, by extension, to a large part of the system of rights as a whole)—having ownership (or other rights) in property triggers a whole series of legal entitlements and privileges, just as its absence implies exclusion from those entitlements and privileges. Thus, property is central to the system in that the presence of property equals and justifies recognition and protection of social, economic, and legal autonomy and power, whereas absence of property self-evidently translates into and justifies the continued existence of social, economic, and legal weakness, vulnerability, and dependence. The centrality of property in the system of rights means that the presence or absence of property decides cases—in this sense, property is central in that the outcome of legal disputes depends upon the mere presence (or absence) of property. In this (particularly doctrinal) perspective, having property (and enjoying the privileges and powers resulting from it) is sometimes a self-evident result that follows logically and inevitably upon satisfying certain technical legal acquisition requirements, whereas not-having property (and the absence of these privileges and powers) follows naturally and inevitably from not having complied with those requirements. Once the requirements have been met, property simply "is there"; if not, it simply is not. Even more importantly, legal implications and results inexorably follow from that "simple" ontological "fact."

In addition to the aspects mentioned above, the notion of centrality also signifies that property fulfils an organizing role in legal thinking. In this role, property embodies the organizing framework or paradigm for all rights in the sense that the presence of a (particularly exclusionary) right is generally the central fact that triggers a whole series of doctrinally linked and legally conclusive results. The qualities that centrality associates with having property have a ripple effect in other areas of law; property becomes a kind of model–right that influences the way in which we think and argue about rights and law in general. The well documented and widely known boundary-like or fence-like role of property is the best example of the powerful influence of property on legal rhetoric.[3]

3. See particularly Henk Botha *Metaphoric Reasoning and Transformative Constitutionalism*, 2002 Journal of SA Law: 612–27; 2003 Journal of SA Law: 20–36 (specifically on the power of "container" rhetoric); Carol Rose, Property and Persuasion: Essays on the History, Theory, and Rhetoric of Property (1994) (rhetoric of property and specifically the power of fence or boundary rhetoric); Pierre Schlag, *Rights in the Postmodern Condition*, *in* Legal Rights: Historical and Philosophical Perspectives 263–304

Perceptive and history-sensitive readers would have identified the centrality logic described above as a reflection of nineteenth-century Formalist thinking and might counter that this kind of thinking has become irrelevant or ineffectual. Similarly, one could argue that the rather one-dimensional Lockean or utilitarian justification for private property inherent in the centrality thesis is outdated. Of course these observations are accurate, but my argument is that centrality remains a problem in legal thinking—generally, not just in property—although we started moving away from it at least a hundred years ago, because the centrality logic has become embedded in the law so deeply that Realist and other critiques of Formalism have not displaced it completely. Even though the theoretical underpinnings of Formalism were seriously shaken by Realism and by post-Realist thinking in the United States, variants of Formalist thinking remain, especially in civilian systems where Realism was less influential. Even in post-Realist circles, utilitarian analysis (including law and economics) continues to follow the aesthetics of centrality thinking, merely replacing the crude liberal justification of private property on the basis of desert with the subtler distributive logic of utilitarian or efficiency calculus that still regards having property as normal and central to the social and legal system. Property theory based on the notion of human flourishing—still a significant and influential school of thinking, even in postliberal circles—is also clearly still embedded in centrality logic. We may all be Realists now, but liberalism is alive and kicking in subtler, newer forms of exclusionary logic.

Similarly, while Marxian and poststructuralist critique has to a certain degree displaced this centrality logic, centrality retains a hold on legal thinking through the stabilizing influence of doctrine and legal culture—practices and traditions that other contributions to this volume describe as governance. Post-Realist, Marxian, and poststructuralist critique may have been influential in social and legal theory, but it has not managed to displace deep-seated doctrine and tradition in Western legal culture, at least not to a significant extent, with the result that vestiges of liberal and Formalist understanding remain entrenched in the dark nooks and crannies of legal culture. If anything, Marxian and poststructuralist theory underlined the ways in which legal tradition is shaped by and embedded in social, economic, or linguistic structures or practices of governance, as the introductory chapter describes them. The closer one gets to the "mere" administration of the law, the longer the shadow of liberal legal culture appears. My argument is that this shadow is still shaped very strongly by centrality thinking, in terms of which having property is normal and central to the social and legal system, while not having property is extraordinary and therefore relegated to the margins of the law and of society.

(Austin Sarat & Thomas R. Kearns eds., 1997) (particularly on the "analytical aesthetic" of legal thinking).

All this is not to deny that the hold of centrality thinking on legal consciousness has been and is under constant pressure, especially in poststructuralist and postmodern legal theory. It is only through the force of inertia that centrality thinking has withstood this pressure against it. When Oliver Wendell Holmes gave his famous lecture on "The Path of the Law"[4] on January 8, 1897, he already indicated a double decentering of and in the law; first, a shift of the law to the margins of our focus, and second, a shift of our focus to the margins of the law.[5] Holmes was remarkably perceptive, but my argument in what follows is that the first of the decenterings that Holmes predicted has had much more direct effect in law than the second. Moreover, the success of the first has backfired on us to a certain extent because what originally looked like a significant decentering of law eventually involved merely shifting the focus of scientific endeavour from Formalist to utilitarian or economic positivism, without changing the underlying aesthetic of centrality thinking. I cannot attempt a full analysis here, but it is useful to consider a few striking moments in the struggle against centrality thinking in property law.

II. HOLMES AND DECENTERING IN LEGAL THINKING

The first decentering predicted by Holmes involves a shift away from "pure legal analysis" toward empirical and economic analysis of the law: "For the rational study of the law the black-letter man may be the man of the present, but the man of the future is the man of statistics and the master of economics."[6] This shift away from formal doctrinal reasoning based on abstract legal axioms illustrated the growing impatience with metaphysics and formalism[7] and the increased

4. Oliver Wendell Holmes, *The Path of the Law*, 10 HARV. L. REV. 457 (1897); repr. 110 HARV. L. REV. 991–1009 (1997).

5. There is a certain sympathy between these two decenterings of law and what Allan Hutchinson describes as the two "mutually supportive" fronts on which Critical Legal Studies has operated, namely the "external" and "internal" fronts respectively: Allan C. Hutchinson, introduction to CRITICAL LEGAL STUDIES, 1–11, at 3–6 (Allan C. Hutchinson ed., 1989).

6. Holmes, *The Path of the Law*, at 1001.

7. In *The Path of the Law*, Holmes explained his preference for an empiricist rather than the formal mathematical model of science: "The danger of which I speak is . . . the notion that a given system, ours, for instance, can be worked out like mathematics from some general axioms of conduct." Holmes, *The Path of the Law*, at 993, 998. A striking illustration of the decentering of law in Realism is Felix Cohen, *Transcendental Nonsense and the Functional Approach*, 35 COLUM. L. REV. 809–49 (1935). In Critical Legal Studies, an important legacy of this decentering is the indeterminacy thesis and the notion of reification. *See, e.g.*, Allan C. Hutchinson, introduction to CRITICAL LEGAL STUDIES, 1–11, at 4; David Kairys, introduction to THE POLITICS OF LAW: A PROGRESSIVE CRITIQUE, (David Kairys ed., 3d ed. 1998), 1–20, at 4.

emphasis on empiricism that would eventually inform the Realists' critique of classical legal reasoning. (I use the term "classical legal reasoning" to refer to American Formalism, but it equally applies to the continental European version of Formalism, namely German Pandectism, which influenced the development of modern Dutch and South African law more directly.)[8] The decentering of legal science predicted by Holmes meant that "The Law" would lose its central position in legal consciousness as our focus moved toward empirical, inductive, and statistical methodologies adopted from other antimetaphysical disciplines in favour at the time, such as sociology and economics.[9] The path of the law that Holmes described logically had to move toward a point where the law, in its classical guise as a formal system of rules based on abstract axioms and held together by formal logic, would become marginal in the scientific or intellectual analysis of law as a social and economic institution. As we know, this decentering of law as a science has indeed taken place to a very large degree, although the economic, social, or interpretive principles upon which so much of legal thinking was subsequently based often resulted in a new formalism that is vulnerable to the same criticism that Holmes and the Realists raised against classical legal thinking. The first move of modernism away from metaphysics and "transcendental nonsense" therefore did not really succeed in decentering scientific thinking; it merely replaced deductive with inductive formalism and shifted the law's reliance for truth and certainty from metaphysical to empirical foundations.

Between 1950 and 1970, scientific thinking experienced a further and much more dramatic and incisive decentering, sometimes described as the "linguistic turn," because of unexpected outcomes of the very same empirical and experimental methodology that the Realists and their contemporaries embraced so enthusiastically. The linguistic or interpretive turn in the social and human sciences, based on observation of the mutual dependency of language and thinking and the impossibility of describing the outside world objectively from a neutral

---

8. Johan W. G. van der Walt, LAW AND SACRIFICE: TOWARDS A POST-APARTHEID THEORY OF LAW 2 (2005), points out that American Realism's critique of Formalism was influenced by von Jhering's critique of German Pandectism, as indicated by extensive references in Felix Cohen, *Transcendental Nonsense*, to Rudolf von Jhering, *Im juristischen Begriffshimmel*, in SCHERZ UND ERNST IN DER JURISPRUDENZ (1909). See Gary Minda, POSTMODERN LEGAL MOVEMENTS: LAW AND JURISPRUDENCE AT CENTURY'S END 13–23 (1995), on American Formalism; Franz Wieacker, PRIVATRECHTSGESCHICHTE DER NEUZEIT, 430–58 (2nd ed. 1967), on German Pandectism. See Henk Botha, *Democracy and Rights: Constitutional Interpretation in a Postrealist World*, 63 THRHR 561, 563–67 (2000), on the implications of postrealist tendencies in constitutional law; *cf.* Andre J. van der Walt, *Ownership and Personal Freedom: Subjectivism in Bernhard Windscheid's Theory of Ownership*, 56 THRHR 569, 589 (1993) on the effects of Pandectism in private law.

9. What Holmes could not foresee was that this decentering of law would, much later, extend even further to methodologies adopted from disciplines that were not grounded in empiricism, such as literary criticism and aesthetics.

Archimedes point, was influenced by developments in the natural sciences, particularly the realization that even the most stringent scientific experiment and observation were subject to limitations deriving from the observer's double or biased position. In sociolinguistics, the same principle is known as the "(language) observer's paradox," referring to the researcher's double role as participant in the conversation(s) that she uses as data and as a posteriori observer or interpreter of the same data.[10] This development need not detain us here, but social scientists like William Labov and Clifford Geertz gave us even stronger reason than Holmes did to accept that formal, abstract reasoning and even empirical, experimental scientific reasoning cannot be the source of truth and certainty. Legal reactions to and acceptance of the linguistic turn and associated post-Realist sensibilities vary, and of course pockets of Formalism and abstract or positivist legal reasoning survived the onslaught of modernity, but by and large these developments have decentered our scientific techniques, at least to a degree. Not surprisingly, legal theory shaped by the linguistic turn has so far had remarkably little direct effect on legal doctrine, and hence its effect in displacing centrality thinking was negligible. For the most part, legal doctrine remains firmly locked into centrality logic informed either by Formalism or by some sort of economic or utilitarian calculus. For my purposes, it is not necessary to dwell on Holmes's first decentering and the resulting shifts in legal method—suffice it to say that it anticipated a fundamental critique of legal Formalism without really displacing it with a less centrality-focused approach.

I am more interested in the second decentering within the law that Holmes described, whereby our attention shifts from the center to the margins of the law as an institution of social ordering: "If you want to know the law and nothing else, you must look at it as a bad man, who cares only for the material consequences which such knowledge enables him to predict."[11] On this score, we have not followed Holmes as enthusiastically, trained as we are in law to focus on the holders of rights, the essential, the principle, the normal case. Because of its provocative style and unusual representation of what the law is about, Holmes's

---

10. The term "observer's paradox" is from William Labov, LANGUAGE IN THE INNER CITY: STUDIES IN THE BLACK ENGLISH VERNACULAR (1972). I am indebted to Christa van der Walt for this information. See further in this regard Coombe, *Same as It Ever Was,* at 606, with reference to Paul Feyerabend, AGAINST METHOD: OUTLINE OF AN ANARCHISTIC THEORY OF KNOWLEDGE (1978) and Thomas Kuhn, THE STRUCTURE OF SCIENTIFIC REVOLUTIONS (1962). The link between poststructuralist developments in the social sciences and earlier developments in the natural sciences has been related to legal methodology in the South African context before by Daniel P. Visser, *The Legal Historian as Subversive or: Killing the Capitoline Geese, in* ESSAYS ON THE HISTORY OF LAW, 1–31, especially at 11, 14 (Daniel P. Visser ed., 1989). The information in this note was taken from Andre J. van der Walt, *Legal History, Legal Culture and Transformation in a Constitutional Democracy,* 12 FUNDAMINA 21 n.56 (2006).

11. Holmes, *Path of the Law,* at 993.

"bad man" image was destined to attract criticism from the mainstream, although much of its critical sting was lost in that this decentering was soon interpreted as nothing more radical than an attention-grabbing illustration of the pragmatism that Holmes was advocating in describing the law as nothing more complicated than prediction of outcomes.[12] When focusing on the pragmatist roots of the "bad man" example it is easy to forget that Holmes's example can also be interpreted as propagating a rather revolutionary legal technique that involves shifting the focus of the law away from the "normal" case and onto the marginal, the outlier. Apart from pragmatism, the example presaged a more general decentering of the subject of law, a shift that would become more visible indirectly in some of the most influential work of the Realists (especially their interest in poverty and welfare issues),[13] although its philosophical implications would only really become clear much later, under the auspices of postmodernism.[14] Legal doctrine, with its focus on principles and norms, obviously does not work well on the margins, and hence this kind of decentering has had preciously little effect on doctrinal thinking. As could be expected, doctrinalists avoid the margins.

With the "bad man" example, Holmes shifted our focus away from the center and toward the margins of the law, where the law does not feature as guarantor of the rights of the upright citizen, the property-owning and contract-concluding entrepreneur, the WASP family man, or the owner of forty acres and a mule.

---

12. In *The Path of the Law*, 994, Holmes explained that law was about prediction of outcomes, something that the "bad man" is more aware of than anybody else: "prophecies of what the courts will do in fact, and nothing more pretentious, are what I mean by the law." The law-as-prediction aspect of the "bad man" example epitomized Holmes's pragmatism. John P. Diggins, THE PROMISE OF PRAGMATISM, 342–59 (1994), points out that Holmes was a pragmatist, although he personally thought that most pragmatists "lacked tough-mindedness and allowed sentiment to do the work of thought."

13. *See, e.g.*, William Simon, *The Invention and Reinvention of Welfare Rights*, 44 MD. L. REV. 1 (1985); William Simon, *Rights and Redistribution in the Welfare System*, 38 STAN. L. REV. 1431 (1986); Lucy A. Williams, *Welfare and Legal Entitlements: The Social Roots of Poverty*, *in* THE POLITICS OF LAW: A PROGRESSIVE CRITIQUE, 569–90 (David Kairys, ed., 3d ed. 1998). However, critical theorists did not simply accept the Realist critique unquestioningly. See, e.g., Gregory S. Alexander, *The Concept of Property in Private and Constitutional Law*, at 1599 for a significant critical assessment of the "scientific turn" that accompanied the shift of focus to poverty and welfare issues in Realist thinking.

14. The theoretical potential of the decentering of the subject that Holmes anticipated was unveiled by Emmanuel Lévinas, TOTALITY AND INFINITY: AN ESSAY ON EXTERIORITY (1969), pointing out that traditional Western notions of knowledge proceed from the presence and identity of the self and thus reduce "the Other" to that identity. Lévinas steered postmodern legal theory further along the "path of the law" anticipated by Holmes's "bad man" example when he insisted upon the priority of confrontation with the Other. I am indebted to Wessel le Roux and Karin van Marle, *Postmodernism(s) and the Law*, *in* JURISPRUDENCE, 354–81, at 368 (Christopher Roederer & Darrel Moellendorf, eds., 2004), for this explanation of Lévinas.

Here, the legal cast is made up of an unfamiliar and often rather unsavory bunch that do not normally feature prominently (or at all) in legal discourse, at least not as far as principles are concerned: criminals, outlaws, the homeless, the sick, the poor, the elderly, the immigrant, the ex-slave, the handicapped, women, and whoever else is vulnerable and weak or unusual and ill-fitting in the face of the law. The law has always found it difficult to deal with representatives of this group, mostly because they "normally" encounter the law only in conflict with ownership and other vested rights (fugitive slaves, trespassers, squatters, intruders, and encroachers) or by demanding exceptional treatment founded not in law but in moral obligation and compassion (the poor, the homeless, the hungry, the unemployed, the sick, and the disabled). On the margins where these groups feature, the law mostly shines in its absence, its shortcomings, its inability to include, to safeguard, and to protect those who do not themselves occupy central positions in law because of their status or possessions. The "bad man" example shifted our attention away from the strong and powerful who are most likely to influence the making and enforcement of law toward those who have least influence on the law and who mostly experience it from a position of exclusion, poverty, weakness, vulnerability, and suffering.[15] Traditionally, the law knew only two ways in which to deal with these marginal groups: first, prescribing and enforcing rules that govern their (mostly unlawful) interaction with the property rights of the privileged; second, ignoring them completely for being marginal and hence irrelevant to the business of rules and principles.

The two decenterings that Holmes anticipated can be related, in one way or another, to most debates and developments in legal thinking since the Realists. Without arguing the merits or otherwise of changes that Holmes or Realism brought about, I will simply accept, for purposes of this chapter, that in the post-Realist world decentering is at least always on the table, not only in the first but also in the second meaning alluded to before. On that basis, I will highlight a particular implication of post-Realist decentering in law, namely that in the margins, the law inevitably acquires a liminal quality, as Ruti Teitel described it. Teitel describes law in transition as both settled and unsettled, restrained and restraining, historically and politically contingent, partial, provisional, limited, and symbolic in nature, and best understood in its liminal quality as law "in between regimes." Teitel uses the term "liminal" to refer to the forward-looking

15. The most striking illustration of the resulting decentering of the legal subject in Realism is Robert L. Hale, *Coercion and Distribution in a Supposedly Non-Coercive State*, 38 POL. SCIENCE Q. 470, 494 (1923), pointing out the effect and role of power and coercion in a legal regime supposedly based on equality and liberty. In Critical Legal Studies, a significant legacy of this decentering is the development of Critical Race Theory and Critical Feminist Theory, which further developed the critique of mainstream legal theory from the perspective of the marginal legal subject. *See, e.g.*, Patricia J. Williams, THE ALCHEMY OF RACE AND RIGHTS (1991).

and backward-looking quality of transitional law that renders it separate from its predecessor but also informed by prior injustice in forming a notion of what is just.[16] As I understand it, this liminal quality of law, in as far as we recognize it, means that we are compelled to work on and deal with the limits, the margins, the fringes of the law, and whomever or whatever we find there. We cannot simply accept (as classical legal thinking did) that law is about the essential, the central, or the normal, and we cannot simply ignore the margins of the law and those who feature on them.[17]

Inevitably, this requires recognition of the somewhat unusual and disturbing notion that property law is not exclusively or even primarily about owners and holders of rights, but about those who do not own property and whose lives are shaped and affected by the property holdings of others; those who are required to respect property and who are owned as or through property. On the margins, property law is deeply concerned with absence of property; no-property; not-property.[18] In the terminology of contemporary legal theory, the best context within which to discuss ownership is not condominium development or ownership of valuable urban air space, but ownership as it appears in its absence, in confrontation with poverty, slavery, or unlawful occupation—property in the margins.[19]

---

16. Ruti G. Teitel, TRANSITIONAL LAW at 6–7, 196, 215, 220 (2000). When Johan W. G. van der Walt, LAW AND SACRIFICE: TOWARDS A POST-APARTHEID THEORY OF LAW (2005), refers to the understanding of law as sacrifice, he has something similar in mind, particularly in so far as his analysis focuses on the blurring of the boundaries of law (at 5); on the destructive effect of presence and representation in law (at 8, 24); and on plurality and its decentering effects (at 8–11). See also Coombe, *Same as It Ever Was*, at 652 for a critical analysis of the notion of "normality" in law; see further Andre J. van der Walt, *Modernity, Normality, and Meaning: The Struggle between Progress and Stability and the Politics of Interpretation*, 11 STELLENBOSCH L. REV. 21–49; 226–43 (2000).

17. *See* Gerrit E. van Maanen, *Balanceren op de Grens van de Rechtsorde (Balancing on the Margins of the Legal Order)*, 8 RECHT & KRITIEK 467, 469 (1982): "Met andere woorden ik veronderstel een mogelijkheid tot grensverlegging binnen de rechtsorde, bijvoorbeeld veranderingen in het denken over het eigendomsbegrip. [. . .] Of je het nu leuk vindt of niet, je bevindt je *in* deze rechtsorde. Je kunt hooguit proberen de grenzen te verleggen door te balanceren op de grens van de rechtsorde. Maar je kunt er niet uit." (In other words, I presuppose the possibility of a certain shifting of boundaries within the legal order, for example, changing thinking about ownership. Whether you like it or not, you find yourself within this legal order. You can at most try and shift the boundaries by balancing on the margins of the legal order, but you cannot escape from it.).

18. According to Hohfeldian analysis. *See* Wesley Hohfeld, *Some Fundamental Legal Conceptions as Applied in Judicial Reasoning*, 23 YALE L.J. 16–59 (1913); *Fundamental Legal Conceptions as Applied in Legal Reasoning*, 26 YALE L.J. 710–70 (1917).

19. This insight was first brought home to me, quite forcefully, some years ago when I read Robert Cover's outstanding book on slavery and realized that it was about property as much as slavery: Robert M. Cover, JUSTICE ACCUSED: ANTISLAVERY AND THE JUDICIAL

III. NOTICING THE MARGINS

Although Holmes's second decentering had little effect in legal doctrine, theorists noticed it, and, accordingly, the marginality thinking that it inspired reverberates in several subsequent developments in property theory. Progressive theorists reacted to the decentering that Holmes's "bad man" example predicted by questioning the very notion of rights, one of the strongest centripetal forces in law. Under the influence of Marxian thinking, the critique of rights initially gravitated toward what became known as needs-based theory,[20] focusing legal analysis on the needs of weak and marginalized people instead of on the rights of the rich and powerful. These theories emphasized the obligations that accompany and are implicated by property, instead of simply relying on the entitlements and power enjoyed in terms of it. The obligations of ownership, in particular, were said to include social responsibility in the sense of not using property antisocially or irresponsibly, but also ethical obligations in the sense of making allowances for the needs of the poor, the socially weak, and those who are in need of support and care.[21] In a wider context, this line of thinking coincided nicely with arguments to the effect that ownership entails rights as well as obligations and, more particularly, that it brings with it a certain social and environmental responsibility—ownership as absolute dominion was replaced by ownership as stewardship; absolute ownership was replaced by ownership that is subject to stringent legal restrictions and ethical obligations.

Needs-based theories met with strong criticism: liberals claimed that they misrepresented rights talk;[22] activists on the left said that they ignored the strategic benefits of rights-talk for racial minorities and women[23] and that they

---

PROCESS (1975); for my reaction, see Andre J. van der Walt, *Rendition/Eviction: A Post-Apartheid Reflection*, 15 LAW & CRITIQUE 321–44 (2005).

20. The original antirights essay was Mark Tushnet, *An Essay on Rights*, 62 TEX. L. REV. 1363–1403 (1984). A more nuanced early needs-based analysis based on constitutional notions of self-government is Frank I. Michelman, *The Supreme Court 1968 Term—Foreword: On Protecting the Poor through the Fourteenth Amendment*, 83 HARV. L. REV. 7–59 (1969). On Michelman's theory of social justice, see Andre J. van der Walt, *A South African Reading of Frank Michelman's Theory of Social Justice*, 19 SA PUBLIC LAW, 253–307 (2004).

21. For a much later exploration of needs discourse in the South African constitutional context, see Danie Brand, The *Politics of Need Interpretation and the Adjudication of Socio-Economic Rights Claims in South Africa, in* THEORIES OF SOCIAL AND ECONOMIC JUSTICE, 17–36 (Andre J. van der Walt ed., 2005); Sandra Liebenberg, *Needs, Rights and Transformation: Adjudicating Social Rights*, 17 STELLENBOSCH L. REV. 5–36 (2006).

22. Jeremy Waldron, *Rights and Needs: The Myth of Disjunction, in* LEGAL RIGHTS: HISTORICAL AND PHILOSOPHICAL PERSPECTIVES, 87–109 (Austin Sarat and Thomas R. Kearns eds., 1997).

23. *See, e.g.*, Kimberle Crenshaw, *A Black Feminist Critique of Antidiscrimination Law and Politics, in* THE POLITICS OF LAW: A PROGRESSIVE CRITIQUE, 356–80 (David Kairys ed.,

reflected and helped to entrench a paternalistic and insulting attitude toward poverty and the poor.[24] In the postmodernist version of Holmes's second kind of decentering, one could say that the needs-based theories tend to approach poverty and need as marginal positions from the central position of self-presence, taking the sufficiency of the self as the standard by which "the Other" is characterized as needy and marginalized. On the positive side, the needs-based approach to social justice shifted the focus from the "normal" subject of the law, who enjoys rights and therefore is empowered by law, to those on the margins, who have no rights and are powerless because they do not qualify for the rights-defined syllogism of legal power. By actively engaging in theoretical analysis and practical lawyering in support of workers, the homeless, receivers of state welfare, and other marginalized groups in society, needs-based theories succeeded in shifting the attention of lawyers, lay people, and policy-makers alike toward the fringes of society. That in itself was a laudable and worthwhile exercise, but it did not succeed in dislodging the rights-based centring of law. Needs-based discourse retained an air of exceptionalism; social justice appeared as something that ethical and responsible property owners had to do in addition to enjoying their powerful and privileged position. Responsibility qualified the notion of ownership but did not affect its centrality.

A second, related shift that contributed to the decentering of property was the critical tendency to emphasize the social origins (and hence contingency) of property as a social artifact.[25] The idea that a property regime protects individual holdings while at the same time exposing them to (even severe) limitation has become trite in the wake of Hohfeldian rights theory and acceptance of the notion that property rights are accompanied by certain obligations, particularly the social responsibility not to use property in an antisocial way. Almost regardless of the exact phraseology of specific property clauses, most theorists and courts now accept that properly authorized, constitutionally justifiable, and lawfully implemented exercises of the police power and the power of eminent domain are not in conflict with the state's duty to protect property.[26] Initially, this theoretical shift in constitutional law merely acknowledged that limitations of property are justified when they protect public health and safety.

3d ed. 1998); Patricia J. Williams, *Alchemical Notes: Reconstructing Ideals from Deconstructed Rights*, 22 HARV. C.R.-C.L. L. REV. 401 (1987).

24. Thomas Ross, *The Rhetoric of Poverty: Their Immorality, Our Helplessness*, 79 GEO. L.J. 1499–1547 (1991); *see also* Gregory S. Alexander, *Socio-Economic Rights in American Perspective: The Tradition of Anti-Paternalism in American Constitutional Thought, in* THEORIES OF SOCIAL AND ECONOMIC JUSTICE, 6–16 (Andre J. van der Walt ed., 2005).

25. Joseph W. Singer & Jack M. Beerman, *The Social Origins of Property*, 6 CAN. J. OF LAW & JUR. 217–48 (1993).

26. See, for example, Andre J. van der Walt, CONSTITUTIONAL PROPERTY LAW, 132–37 (2005), regarding the police-power principle.

Subsequently, the social origins theories extended the decentering to instances where the limitations are specifically designed to accommodate the particular needs and circumstances of nonowner groups and individuals; considerations that are traditionally relegated to the margins of the law for being irrelevant.[27] By focusing on the paradox that property simultaneously protects individual security and privilege and serves (or at least has to take account of) the public good, social origins theories established that property is not only inherently limited by social obligations, but that those obligations could extend beyond the requirements of public health and safety to embrace the (even conflicting) interests (and needs) of others.[28] Theorists thinking along similar lines, but inspired by a more radical Hohfeldian departure from liberal rights theory, produced a version of rights theory that still functions within the discourse of rights but places stronger emphasis on social relationships and care.[29]

---

27. In *Brisley v. Drotsky*, 2002 (4) SA 1 (SCA) paras [42]–[46], the South African Supreme Court of Appeal decided that sec. 26(3) of the constitution (nobody shall be evicted from their home without a court order, and a court shall only grant an eviction order having considered all the circumstances) did not grant the courts the discretion to deprive a landowner of an eviction order based on the personal circumstances of the occupier and her family; in the absence of explicit statutory provisions, the personal circumstances of the occupier are not "relevant circumstances," and an eviction order is granted purely with reference to proof of ownership and possession (the classic requirements).

28. The theoretical basis in CLS is Duncan Kennedy's notion of the fundamental contradiction. *See* Duncan Kennedy, *Form and Substance in Private Law Adjudication*, 89 HARV. L. REV. 1685–1778, 1713–24 (1976) ("sense of contradiction"). *Compare* Duncan Kennedy, *The Structure of Blackstone's* Commentaries, 28 BUFF. L. REV. 209, 211–13 (1979) (notion of the fundamental contradiction), *with* Peter Gabel & Duncan Kennedy, *Roll Over Beethoven*, 36 STAN. L. REV. 1, 15–16 (1984) (abandoning the fundamental contradiction). On the paradoxical nature of property, which relates to the notion of a fundamental contradiction but is not necessarily identical to it, see Gregory S. Alexander, COMMODITY AND PROPRIETY—COMPETING VISIONS OF PROPERTY IN AMERICAN LEGAL THOUGHT 1776–1970 (1997); Robert W. Gordon, *Paradoxical Property, in* EARLY MODERN CONCEPTIONS OF PROPERTY, 95–110 (John Brewer & Susan Staves eds., 1996); Joseph W. Singer, ENTITLEMENT: THE PARADOXES OF PROPERTY (2000). The most consistently worked out theoretical notion of property that attempts to "internalize" the paradox was worked out (not in CLS terms) by Laura Underkuffler. *See* Laura S. Underkuffler, THE IDEA OF PROPERTY: ITS MEANING AND POWER (2003); Laura S. Underkuffler-Freund, *Takings and the Nature of Property*, 9 CAN. J. LAW & JUR. 161–205 (1996); Laura S. Underkuffler, *On Property: An Essay*, 100 YALE L.J. 127 (1990).

29. Jennifer Nedelsky, *Reconceiving Rights as Relationship*, 1 REV. CONST. STUDIES 1–26 (1993) proposed the theory of rights as relationship; an idea that ultimately relies on Realist thinking and that goes beyond Tushnet's rights critique in that it redefines rights instead of abandoning rights discourse for needs discourse. For strong property-related work in the same vein, see Joseph W. Singer, THE EDGES OF THE FIELD: LESSONS ON THE OBLIGATIONS OF OWNERSHIP (2000); see most recently Joseph W. Singer, *After the Flood: Equality and Humanity in Property Relations*, 52 LOY. L. REV. 243–343 (2006).

The decentering of legal focus based on social justice considerations even enjoys some support in constitutional law—provisions that explicitly prescribe or justify social justice limitations of property are uncommon in constitutional property clauses, but they do occur and policy-makers have given them effect. The Constitution of Ireland 1937 states in Article 43.2.1° that, in civil society, the principles of social justice ought to regulate property rights.[30] Policy-makers have employed these principles to justify statutory limitations of property designed to bring about greater equity in property relations, for instance by allowing certain tenants to purchase the fee simple interest from their landlords at a fixed price.[31] The German Basic Law also provides that property entails obligations and that its exercise and enjoyment should serve the public interest.[32] Once again, German policy-makers have employed this provision to justify limitations of property aimed at promoting social justice, for example by restricting the rights of landowners in favor of security of tenancy or limiting the rights of shareholders to promote the interests of employees.[33] The South African Constitution contains several provisions, both inside[34] and outside[35] the property clause that explicitly promote social welfare and justice.[36] In each of these cases,

---

30. Art. 43.2.1°: "The State recognizes, however, that the exercise of the rights mentioned in the foregoing provisions of this Article ought, in civil society, to be regulated by the principles of social justice." The Directive Principles of Social Policy in Article 45 require the State to promote social justice, ensure a fair distribution of essential commodities and safeguard the economic interests of the weaker sections of society. The Directive Principles have a limited effect in adjudication because they are not open for judicial pronouncement or application. It is not entirely clear what the Courts may consider or decide with reference to the Directive Principles, but a constitutional challenge to legislation cannot be based upon them: Gerry Hogan and Gerry Whyte, KELLY: THE IRISH CONSTITUTION, 2085 (4th ed. 2003).

31. *See John E. Shirley v. A.O. Gorman* [2006] IEHC 27.

32. Art. 14.2: "Property entails obligations [imposes duties]. Its use should also serve the public interest." Art. 14.1 stipulates that the laws determine the content and limits of property rights.

33. *Respectively BVerfGE* 89, 1 [1993] (*Besitzrecht des Mieters*); *BVerfGE* 50, 290 [1979] (*Mitbestimmung*).

34. Sec. 25(4)(a): "[T]he public interest includes the nation's commitment to land reform, and to reforms to bring about equitable access to all South Africa's natural resources"; *see further* sec. 25(5)–(9), authorizing various aspects of land reform.

35. Sec. 26 (right of access to housing), specifically 26(3) (restricting the right to obtain an eviction order); sec. 24 (environment), sec. 27 (health care, food, water, and social security), sec. 28(1)(c) (children's right to basic nutrition, shelter, basic health care services, and social services).

36. Each of these provisions has authorized legislation that must give effect to it. In the case of sec. 25(5)–(9), the most important legislation regulates restitution of property dispossessed under apartheid in terms of sec. 25(7), promotes greater and more equitable access to land in terms of sec. 25(5) and improves the security of tenure of those whose security of tenure is legally insecure because of apartheid laws or practices: sec. 25(6).

the constitution goes further than simply recognizing the post-Realist truth that property is limited and that lawful exercises of the police power and power of eminent domain are therefore "inherent" to constitutional protection of property, adding that property implies social responsibility toward the needs of others, which means that individual property interests might justifiably be subjected to the promotion of social justice and the needs of others.

In addition to constitutional obligations, social justice legislation has been promulgated in a number of countries to limit the rights of property holders by subjecting them, in one way or another, to restrictions prescribed by the personal needs or circumstances of nonowners. Examples can be multiplied: in many instances, they bear a family resemblance. For the moment I will merely refer to section 26(3) of the South African Constitution 1996,[37] a provision that plays an important role in reversing the apartheid legacy of forced removals and preventing it from recurring, as well as the various land reform laws in which the antieviction principle has been fleshed out for different circumstances.[38]

Other laws regulate the provision of housing and social services. The most striking new laws, for purposes of this chapter, are the National Water Act 36 of 1998 and the Mineral and Petroleum Resources Development Act 28 of 2002, both of which abolished existing property regimes with regard to specified categories of property that are particularly sensitive in the larger scheme of national social justice values (water and mineral resources respectively) and replaced them with closely regulated licensing schemes in terms of which previously existing individual property rights had to be reapplied for and reawarded in a significantly more precarious form. Important case law that reflects the same attitude includes *Government of the Republic of South Africa v. Grootboom*, 2001 (1) SA 46 (CC) (state housing policies that merely establish a waiting list and do not provide special remedies for those in extreme housing needs are not reasonable and do not satisfy the requirements of section 26(1)); *President of the Republic of South Africa and Another v. Modderklip Boerdery (Pty) Ltd (Agri SA and Others,* Amici Curiae), 2005 (5) SA 3 (CC) (weakening the landowner's right to evict temporarily so as not to render people homeless, while at the same time pressuring the state to provide access to housing and to compensate the landowner for his losses); *Jaftha v. Schoeman; Van Rooyen v. Stoltz*, 2005 (2) SA 140 (CC) (established statutory principles regarding attachment and sale in execution of poor people's homes for minor and extraneous debts must be authorized by court order, having taken into consideration all circumstances, including the justifiability of eviction); *Port Elizabeth Municipality v. Various Occupiers*, 2005 (1) SA 217 (CC) (property rights in terms of sec. 25 and occupiers' rights in terms of sec. 26 must be weighed up against each other in a fair manner to reach an equitable balance).

37. Sec. 26(3): "No one may be evicted from their home, or have their home demolished, without an order of court made after considering all the relevant circumstances. No legislation may permit arbitrary evictions."

38. *See* Andre J. van der Walt, *Exclusivity of Ownership, Security of Tenure, and Eviction Orders: A Model to Evaluate South African Land-Reform Legislation*, 2002 JOURNAL FOR SA LAW: 254; *cf.* Andre J. van der Walt, *Exclusivity of Ownership, Security of Tenure, and Eviction Orders: A Critical Evaluation of Recent Case Law*, 18 S.A. JOURNAL ON HUMAN RIGHTS 371 (2002).

In the Prevention of Illegal Eviction from and Unlawful Occupation of Land Act 18 of 1998, a law intended to prevent arbitrary eviction of specifically unlawful occupiers of land, section 4 states that a court should only allow eviction of occupiers who have been in occupation for longer than six months after having considered all the relevant circumstances, including the needs of elderly persons, children, disabled persons, and households headed by women. The Act takes the decentering anticipated by Holmes's "bad man" example a step further by subjecting a landowner's normal right to have unlawful occupiers evicted to considerations that bear no relation to and are completely out of the control of the landowner, namely the personal circumstances and needs of persons who are in fact trespassing on the owner's land. Property rights, and especially ownership of land, are thereby subjected to the needs and the personal circumstances of people who "normally" feature only in the margins of the classical legal picture of eviction—an effect that runs directly against the trend of classic centrality logic.[39] Similar examples occur in English, Dutch, and German legislation that allows certain tenants to strengthen their tenancy or to renew or prolong it after termination or that protects the tenants (or their families once the primary tenant dies) against summary eviction.[40]

The combined result of developments described so far is that the focus of legal thinking has shifted away from rights and those who hold and enjoy rights, toward individuals and groups who do not have rights (or strong rights) because of their marginal social, economic, or legal-political position. To a large degree this shift has concentrated legal focus on the needs of the weak and vulnerable, with the result that contextual social justice issues have started to penetrate traditional property discourse. However, beneficial as this decentering process is for property law in general, it is nevertheless a limited process that does not really amount to a shift to the margins. As long as the shift assumes the form of a more or less condescending nod toward the needs of the not-rich, not-propertied, not-powerful, it remains inspired by the self-centered autonomy of the traditional paradigm—having property, being rich, and being powerful still determine the norm against which the shortcomings of the have-nots are measured.

The problem with decentering the focus of property law on the basis of its social origins or its foundation in relationship is that the decentering remains focused too strongly on the social need to care for others, especially others in dire straits, as an exceptional (but ethical) reaction to exceptional needs. The propertied

---

39. See Singer, Entitlement, at 1–5, on the "normal" property picture where the right of the property owner is central; *cf.* Gregory S. Alexander, *Critical Land Law*, *in* Land Law: Themes and Perspectives, 55–56 (Susan Bright & John Dewar eds., 1998).

40. I do not rehearse the examples here, but I discuss and analyze them in various chapters of Property in the Margins (2009). Lorna Fox, Conceptualising Home: Theories, Laws and Policies (2007), recently analyzed some examples in English law that relate to the unusual organizing concept of "home" (as opposed to "property").

Self remains the norm; the have-not Other the exception. The process of caring for those in need does no more than remind the rich and powerful that they have a duty of conscience not to forget the needs of the less privileged. In this sense, decentering is no more than a side mirror that reminds the driver of the legal bus of the presence, somewhere on the edges of his vision, of moral duty and social obligation toward those who have been less fortunate, less determined, or perhaps less gifted. This danger is particularly worrying with reference to needs-based theories that focus on poverty and the survival needs of the poor or those who find themselves in dire emergencies. Of course it is important to recognize the social responsibilities of ownership and the obligation to assist people in emergency and other socially and economically extreme circumstances of need, and some of my colleagues have already developed a strong and varied literature on the legal aspects of those responsibilities.[41] However, for present purposes, I am interested in a different aspect—in the next section I argue that marginality manifests itself in other ways that also deserve attention if we are to avoid simply adding concern for the poor to mainstream ownership thinking as an afterthought. In this sense, property lawyers have certainly noticed the margins since Holmes postulated his "bad man" example, but we have not mastered the art of balancing on the very edge of the legal order yet.

IV. EXPLORING THE MARGINS

My first hypothesis above was that we habitually and unreflectively assign the quality of centrality to property because we accept that property institutions naturally assume a central place in society and that property—as an organizing concept—assumes a central role in law and legal theory. My second hypothesis was that the logic of centrality relies on unreflective intellectual habits and that these habits and the property practices they support inhibit much-needed social and legal transformation.

In the sections above I argued, in support of these hypotheses, that a number of decentering theories and developments over the last century have questioned and critiqued the centrality of property without dislodging it from its strongly embedded position in Western legal culture. Relying on the classic article by Karl Klare,[42] I have argued elsewhere that the entrenched central position of property

41. Just on the South African literature, see Danie Brand, *The Politics of Need Interpretation and the Adjudication of Socio-Economic Rights Claims in South Africa, in* Theories of Social and Economic Justice, 17–36 (Andre J. van der Walt ed., 2005); Sandra Liebenberg, *Needs, Rights and Transformation: Adjudicating Social Rights*, 17 Stellenbosch L. Rev. 5 (2006).

42. Karl Klare, *Legal Culture and Transformative Constitutionalism*, S.A. Journal on Human Rights 14 (1998): 146–88.

in Western culture is frustrating much-needed and justified legal and social reforms[43]—I will not repeat that argument here. The remaining question for purposes of this contribution is, how do we conceptualize marginality or no-property as an organizing principle that is relevant to property law and theory in a wider context and more forcefully than ethical or social concern for the weak and the poor? How do we conceptualize marginality in property or, stated differently, how do we balance on the very edge of property law?

Understood as any position that falls outside of the central focus, the "same as it ever was"[44] of mainstream property dogma, marginality involves legal positions not characterized or dominated by the presence of rights, possessions, privilege, and power. Developing a theory of property that takes the persons in those positions and their interests and circumstances seriously means, at the very least, that we have to try and think away the power and the centrality of rights, entitlements, and privileges and to imagine a legal order not dominated by the hierarchies built on the distinction between their presence or absence. In one of its recent decisions, the South African Constitutional Court signalled the importance for social and legal transformation of breaking loose from the hierarchies embedded in legal tradition:[45]

> In sum, the Constitution imposes new obligations on the courts concerning rights relating to property not previously recognized by the common law. It counterposes to the normal ownership rights of possession, use and occupation, a new and equally relevant right not arbitrarily to be deprived of a home. The expectations that ordinarily go with title could clash head-on with the genuine despair of people in dire need of accommodation. The judicial function in these circumstances is not to establish a hierarchical arrangement between the different interests involved, privileging in an abstract and mechanical way the rights of ownership over the right not to be dispossessed of a home, or vice versa. Rather it is to balance out and reconcile the opposed claims in as just a manner as possible taking account of all the interests involved and the specific factors relevant in each particular case.

The Court does rely on needs analysis in its reference to "people in dire need of accommodation," but the explanation of the "new obligations" imposed on courts by the constitution is nevertheless interesting for the way in which it genuinely attempts to break away from a centrality logic that is simply dominated and

---

43. Andre J. van der Walt, *Property Theory and the Transformation of Property Law, in* MODERN STUDIES IN PROPERTY LAW, 361–80 (E. Cooke ed., 2005); Andre J. van der Walt, *Legal History, Legal Culture and Transformation in a Constitutional Democracy*, 12 FUNDAMINA 1–47 (2006).

44. With apologies to Rosemary Coombe, see Coombe, *Same as It Ever Was.*

45. *Port Elizabeth Municipality v. Various Occupiers*, 2005 (1) SA 217 (CC) par 23, per Sachs, J. for the Court (references omitted).

determined by abstract and hierarchical thinking, privileging either ownership over "home interests" or vice versa. In other words, the Court makes it clear that the new obligation imposed by the constitution does not allow courts to simply follow the logic of central ownership, but neither does it allow them to simply follow the logic of need and emergency. In this way it might be possible to account for marginality in property law without simply reducing marginality to poverty, need, and weakness—in other words, the mere absence of property or the conceptual counterpoint of property.

The decision of the Constitutional Court also makes it clear that an effort to account for marginality does not imply ignoring or simply overriding or undermining ownership or property rights. Property law is not possible without attention, at some level, for property rights and the power that they entail; my quest is not to ignore property rights or ownership or even necessarily to weaken their legal power, but to imagine a perspective on property that includes, in a meaningful way, the interests of those who are not "normally" considered part of the property elite, without automatically reducing them to the status of weakness and dependency. In this perspective, marginality is not limited to poverty, need, or even necessarily the absence of property—at least in some cases, marginality and absence of property indicate surprisingly strong positions that deserve more focused and serious attention from legal theory.

What I have in mind with this effort to theorize marginality more fruitfully in property law is illustrated by a powerful story from the most recent work of Afrikaans novelist Eben Venter, entitled *Trencherman*.[46] When Marlouw, the principal character, revisits his erstwhile family farm in the Eastern Cape to convince the only remaining white family member to leave, he finds that the former workers who now own the farm are living in part of the former homestead, but they do not sit in the chairs or sleep in the beds left in the house when the white family left. This curious state of affairs reflects the general unease with which the former workers occupy their new position as owners of the farm—they obviously are not entirely at ease in the position of the white family whom they once served as laborers. In a sense, they remain marginalized even now that they own the farm. Koert, the only white family member left on the farm, could be seen as a metaphor for the lingering presence of the white family—hence the desire of the remaining former farm workers in the latter stages of the novel to exorcise the past by killing him and burning down the part of the house he occupied, with the remains of the family's furniture and possessions stacked in it.

While it is no doubt possible to attach other readings to the novel, my reading allows us to see the former workers' unease in their new position and their failure to sit on the former white owners' chairs or sleep in their beds as a refusal to simply take over the former white owners' position and to continue in it as if nothing much has happened. By extension, this could be seen as a refusal to be

46. Eben Venter, TRENCHERMAN (Lukes Stubbs trans. Tafelberg 2008).

satisfied with a specific kind of transformation, where the previously oppressed cling to their marginalized position rather than simply take the place of the former oppressors. In it, I see a refusal to accept an impoverished transformation that simply replaces white owners with Black owners without ever critically questioning the justifiability and legitimacy of their roles in the established social and political hierarchies. In this perspective, being marginal is not a weak position at all—it is a powerful refusal to continue the "normal" trajectory of an inherently unjust tradition by simply stepping into the shoes of the former oppressors. Marginality becomes a powerful symbol of real transformation.[47] In the final section below, I attempt to trace possible implications of this view of marginality for property law.

V. CONCLUSIONS

The focus of marginality affects our thinking about the foundations of law and our method of legal reasoning. The wider implications of Holmes's "master of economics" argument and of the linguistic turn already eroded traditional foundational thinking in law to a large extent.[48] What I have in mind here implies having greater patience with marginal and alternative methodologies borrowed from linguistic theory or aesthetics; it also builds on the decentering brought about by Realism in that it requires paying more attention to facts and unique circumstances and relying less on abstract principles and doctrine. To a certain extent, this shift has already taken place in legal thinking as a result of Realism and post-Realist legal critiques. However, marginality thinking should go further—it also implies acceptance that marginality has its own logic in that it will tend to look for the paradox and the contradiction rather than for broad theory and grand narrative, for diversity rather than uniformity, for dissent rather than consensus, for conflict and chaos rather than consent and order. In other words, it directs our attention to fault lines and disputes or historical breakdowns rather than concentrating on or searching for the golden thread of continuity. In a very real sense, a marginality perspective requires us to make a fundamental switch in what we regard as important or central in law. One example illustrates the point.

In a recent article, South African law professor Susan Scott concluded that (despite academic discourse to the contrary) recent cases in neighbor law do

---

47. These paragraphs and the story about Venter's novel as an illustration of refusal was inspired by and used more extensively in another context, namely as a contribution to a session entitled "Refusals, Transitions, and Postapartheid Law," organized by Karin van Marle, at the Law and Society Conference, Berlin, July 25–28, 2007.

48. See further in this regard, Peter Fitzpatrick, MODERNISM AND THE GROUNDS OF LAW (2001).

not deviate from the traditional emphasis on the absoluteness of ownership.[49] As far as it goes, her analysis supports this conclusion, but the result of her study was predisposed by her focus on the "normal science" of reasonableness analysis in cases of nuisance and encroachment. In the area of neighbor law, legal development often requires nothing more than small, incremental adaptations to clarify or expand upon the well-settled doctrinal explanation of the reasonableness standard by which neighboring landowners' rights are balanced against each other. In balancing the rights of subjects who are equally privileged and powerful—as neighbors in privileged "white" residential neighborhoods mostly are in South Africa—the issue is merely to establish the optimal balance, in any given case, between the roughly equal but competing rights of roughly equal parties. In the majority of cases it does not have any bearing on political conflicts about land, because both parties involved in neighbor disputes would normally have been favored rather than marginalized by apartheid land law.[50] In that sense Scott's project, at least as far as she explains it as an investigation into changing concepts of landownership, was theoretically misconstrued from the outset. In order to get a theoretically interesting perspective on changes in landownership in South Africa, it is necessary to take into account land relations that were marginalized by colonialism and apartheid. Scott missed the point about changes in landownership because she chose to gloss over the one area where neighbor law does hold some interest for a marginal analysis of property, namely "nuisance caused by squatters," where the rights of landowners conflict with the no-rights position of individuals and groups who have been marginalized by apartheid politics and who occupy land unlawfully, in the process creating a "public nuisance" for owners of neighboring land in formally established residential areas. The debate about this conflict shades over into instances where the government is establishing new (and often so-called "informal") townships, inevitably occupied mostly by poor residents, close to or in the vicinity of established, privileged (white) residential areas. Scott's analysis highlights the futility of discussing transformation issues in terms of the traditional concepts and logic of property law and with exclusive reference to conflicts between equally privileged and powerful beneficiaries of apartheid land law. Formulated differently, it is true but also meaningless to state that, judged strictly between the privileged

---

49. Susan Scott, *Recent Developments in Case Law Regarding Neighbour Law and its Influence on the Concept of Ownership*, 16 STELLENBOSCH L. REV. 351–52 (2005).

50. The point is illustrated nicely in a recent newspaper article: Bongani Mthethwa, *The Sand-Castle Wars*, SA SUNDAY TIMES, September 2, 2007, at 5, relates the story of bitter infighting between super-rich (almost exclusively white) residents of "the plush sea-facing millionaire's row of Lower La Lucia," where owners of beachfront properties are allegedly "stealing" each other's sand from sand dunes between the properties and the beach in an effort to bolster the defences of their houses against storm erosion and flooding.

neighboring landowners in former white areas, nothing much has changed in post-apartheid property law.

A second implication of marginality thinking in property theory is that it should focus our attention much more on the social position, economic status, and personal circumstances of the parties involved in property relations or disputes and less on their legal status or established property rights. Of course, this is exactly what Holmes and the Realists have urged us to do all along, but I want to push the point further. Marginal people such as criminals (Holmes's "bad men"), outlaws, the homeless, the weak, the poor, the elderly, and the handicapped often have no rights and therefore they cannot enter the dogmatic syllogism to compete in a classic legal battle about property. The interests that they do have might either not be recognized by law or, if they are recognized, might be protected weakly because these interests enjoy lower status than mainstream rights. The result is that we do not recognize or "see" the rights that they do have. A focus on the margins, therefore, should involve more than just having sympathy or greater understanding for them because of their social context; it should include developing an eye for the power and status of their position in the margin. Recent property literature suggests that there is an increasing interest in the property status and the possible protection of people who occupy land unlawfully, whether for economic, political, or social reasons, indicating a shift toward marginal interests in property law. Lorna Fox pointed out that the "home" interest of residential tenants or defaulting debtors is enormously important to them even if it is not always recognized or protected as strongly by the law as the investment interests of the landlord or the creditor.[51] My aim is to strengthen the impulse of that shift. An example from Irish case law reminds us of this point.

Mainstream lawyers who focus too strongly on the golden thread of continuity in legal and social history often deny or forget that marginal property interests have, historically speaking, in certain instances become dominant property rights in the mainstream and vice versa, because of social, economic, and political changes and developments. By reminding property lawyers of these often denied or forgotten events it becomes possible or easier to imagine or accept similar changes again, even though they might appear impossible or even unthinkable in

51. *See* Fox, Conceptualising Home. See further on socio-political squatters in the Netherlands and Germany, Andre J. van der Walt, *De Onrechtmatige Bezetting van Leegstaande Woningen en het Eigendomsbegrip: Een Vergelijkende Analyse van het Conflict tussen de Privaat Eigendom van Onroerende Goed en Dakloosheid*, 17 Recht en Kritiek, 329–59 (1991); Freek Bruinsma, *Ongehoorzaam in en buiten de Rechtsorde*, 125–28 Nederlands Juristenblad (1983); Peter H. Bakker Schut, Ties Prakken, & Theo de Roos, *Politiek Protest in de Rechtszaal*, 10 Recht & Kritiek 33–62 (1984). For a very interesting recent analysis of "property outlaws," see Eduardo M. Peñalver and Sonia K. Katyal, *Property Outlaws*, 155 U. Pa. L. Rev. 1095–1186 (2007).

the everyday slog of property practice. However, these shifts still occur. The decision of the High Court of Ireland in the case of *Shirley v. Gorman*,[52] which dealt with the Landlord and Tenant (Amendment) Act 1984,[53] confirmed that interventionist social legislation can reverse the roles of landowners and tenants—which, for historical reasons, are tied to broad social, political, and economic changes—without the state acquiring the land compulsorily. The Act provides a price-fixing mechanism to determine the purchase price in instances where tenants who qualify under the broad scheme of the Act can acquire the fee simple interest held by their landlords by paying the landlord a prescribed percentage of the current value of the lease (as defined in the Act). The Court held that the broad scheme of the Act was justified by principles of social policy and that tenants who were not necessarily poor could also benefit from it, since the aim was to eradicate ancient remnants of "pyramid" landlord interests in land and not purely to benefit poor tenants. Although different jurisdictions have abolished feudal land relations at different times and in varying ways, this case reminds us that similar reversals have taken place in the past, both in English law[54] and in civil law (processes in postfeudal Dutch law where ownership "shifted" from feudal landlords to vassals by force of social and economic changes)[55] and that it is again featuring in the postcolonial era; on the one hand to get rid of detrimental remains of outdated tribal land holdings (land condemnation [expropriation] scheme whereby title in real property could be taken from lessors and transferred to lessees in order to reduce the concentration of landownership in a small number of hands)[56] and on the other to eradicate the legacy of discriminatory apartheid land law.[57] A stronger focus on the margins of property and on the fault lines and breakdowns in historical continuity enables us to notice and remember these marginal but very

---

52. *John E. Shirley v. A.O. Gorman* [2006] IEHC 27.

53. Information here was taken from Andre J. van der Walt, *The Protection of Private Property under the Irish Constitution: A Comparative and Theoretical Perspective* (The Irish Constitution: Governance and Values, 398, 405 (Eoin Carolan & Oran Doyle eds., 2008)).

54. *Cf. James v. United Kingdom* [1986] 8 EHRR 123.

55. *See* Willem van Iterson, *Beschouwingen over Rolverwisseling of Eigendomsverschuiving*, in Verslagen en Mededelingen van de Vereniging tot Uitgave van het Oud-Vaderlands Recht, 13 n.3, 407–66 (1971).

56. See the U.S. decision in *Hawaii Housing Authority v. Midkiff*, 467 U.S. 229 (1984), dealing with the Hawaii Land Reform Act of 1967.

57. The restitution procedures provided for in the Restitution of Land Rights Act 22 of 1994 (return of land dispossessed under discriminatory laws and practices) and the tenure reform processes foreseen in the Land Reform (Labour Tenants) Act 3 of 1996 (upgrading security of tenure of labor tenants and creating the possibility of their purchasing the land) are most instructive. These laws are authorized by the 1996 constitution in sec. 25(7) and 25(6), respectively.

important changes in legal status and, by remembering them, we are able to imagine their recurrence in the future.

Furthermore, marginal property analysis must inevitably be aware that property rules and practices are vague and contested rather than clear and consensual. It therefore requires awareness of dissent and contention rather than just focusing on apparent consensus. An example is the point that Stephen Schnably made with regard to the supposed virtues of the private family home as a locus where property enables the fostering of personhood: when viewed from a more critical perspective, the suburban family home is not just a heartwarming textbook example of all that is good and necessary about private property; it is also a contested space that entrenches and hides inequality, such as gender oppression, racial and class inequality and exclusion, bad town planning favoring the economic domination of the white middle class and others.[58] Because critical awareness of marginality requires awareness of the existence and effects of social or political disputes, hierarchies that privilege rights over marginal interests may often look normal or unproblematic.[59] Marginal property interests often resemble or are even recognized as rights, but when assessed against their socio-political background, they are weak and marginal because they do not fit into the mainstream hierarchy of rights, dominated by ownership. A good example is the residential permits granted to Blacks in urban white areas during apartheid. Only political sensitivity will reveal the marginality and the fault line inherent in this land interest of the politically marginalized victims of apartheid.[60] The position of modern travelers and urban squatters in situations dominated by urban decay and social unrest may resemble some of the postapartheid security of tenure problems in interesting ways. In this context, it will no doubt be useful to approach analysis of their property status from the perspective of what Johan van der Walt describes as "alterity" and plurality, which means that we cannot afford to see the hegemony of the normal, the everyday, or the mass consensus as a norm; we have to leave room for otherness, for difference.[61]

In the same spirit, we should realize that marginality does not necessarily imply weakness. In his inaugural lecture, Paul Cilliers argued convincingly, from the perspective of complexity theory that relative positions do not necessarily have to be weak positions.[62] In this regard, I would particularly like to focus our

58. Stephen Schnably, *Property and Pragmatism: A Critique of Radin's Theory of Property and Personhood*, 45 Stan. L. Rev. 347–407 (1993), in response to Margaret J. Radin, *Property and Personhood*, 34 Stan. L. Rev. 957–1015 (1982).

59. See to the same effect, Coombe, *Same as It Ever Was*.

60. *Cf.* Andre J. van der Walt, *Property Rights and Hierarchies of Power: An Evaluation of Land Reform Policy in South Africa*, 64 Koers 259–94 (1999).

61. Johan W. G. Van Der Walt, Law and Sacrifice: Towards a Post-Apartheid Theory of Law 11–17 (2005).

62. Paul Cilliers, "Do Modest Positions Have to be Weak? A View from Complexity," a version of which was also published as Paul Cilliers, *Complexity, Deconstruction and*

attention on marginal property positions that are founded on direct rejection of or confrontation with the dominant property regime. I like the term "property outlaws" that Eduardo Peñalver and Sonia Katyal coined,[63] referring as it does to the fact that no-property positions are sometimes founded in the quite powerful action of political activists, squatters, and land invaders who later become folk heroes and national idols because they opposed and rejected social, legal, and political structures or traditions. Apart from the examples that Peñalver and Katyal discussed, the Western European politically inspired urban squatting movement of the 1980s is another forceful and instructive case in point. Refusal to abide in the conventional property structures and roles of mainstream society could therefore be an indicator of marginal property positions that deserve special attention from property theorists.

A marginal perspective on property further requires that more attention be given to marginal aspects of property law and to marginal fields in property law. Instead of focusing first and foremost on property (security) and contract (exchange), we should look at landlord and tenant law and squatting law, where the primary focus is not the position and the rights of the owner-landlord but the status and legal position of marginal people such as tenants and squatters. To put it coarsely: sometimes we should forget about the big property developments and focus our attention on the squatter huts and slave cottages that also represent powerful and significant property loci. During apartheid, the South African property syllabus never included apartheid legislation: that was seen as politics best left to the politicians. As a consequence, property law was always typically the white law of the business district and the suburbs, never the struggle law of the forcibly evacuated Black townships or the rural areas destroyed by migrant labor and political neglect. This situation is changing, not only in South African but elsewhere as well, as more and more journal articles and books focus on marginal property interests and positions. However, property lawyers might also have to pay increasing attention to what was traditionally regarded as marginal issues in property law, such as environmental law, confiscation and forfeiture of property in terms of crime prevention legislation, social and economic regulation of the development and use of land, and patrolling the margins of supposedly established and accepted distinctions such as the private/public divide and the ownership/use rights hierarchy. What is the role or the doctrinal function of these concepts, distinctions, institutions, rules, and practices in upholding and entrenching the property regime? That is, how can they be used to undermine that regime and imagine an alternative that is less dominated and predisposed by its legacy of inequality, hierarchy, privilege, and power?

Relativism, 22 Theory Culture Society, 255–67 (2005) (also available online at http://tcs.sagepub.com/cgi/content/abstract/22/5/255, visited September 4, 2007).

63. Eduardo M. Peñalver & Sonia K. Katyal, *Property Outlaws*.

5. FACTS ON THE GROUND

NOMI MAYA STOLZENBERG

> Walk into the Domino's Pizza outlet in French Hill and make the following statement: "This neighborhood is a settlement. It is illegal according to International Law and must be dismantled in the event of a peace settlement between Israelis and Palestinians." Even if made in perfect Hebrew, the statement would most likely be met with confused stares and laughter. Make this same statement about French Hill to Palestinian Jerusalemites from the nearby village of Issawiya and it will most likely result in the same response. The only difference will be the acknowledgment that the Jerusalem neighborhood was built on land from the village. These reactions attest to the effectiveness of the Israeli strategy of creating facts on the ground as a method of holding territory acquired by war.[1]

What is being described here? On the most literal level, this passage, taken from a report put out by PASSIA, a Palestinian think tank, is describing the neighborhood of French Hill, a place, a space, a physical, geographical area in the northeast corner of Jerusalem that is part of the physical and social geography of Israel/Palestine. On a less physical level, the passage is describing a practice, a social practice, a "strategy" or "method," known as "creating facts on the ground." Also conveyed in this passage is a remarkable array of effects seen to issue from this practice: profound alterations and transformations in the fabric of social existence that somehow result from "creating facts on the ground." These include internal psychological effects (the "confused stares and laughter" signifying the cognitive and emotional states of disbelief that greet the supposedly absurd proposition that French Hill is a "settlement"), in addition to outward social and economic effects, that is, *changes* that have occurred in the objective demographic situation and in the distribution of land.

The most direct, tangible, and widely noted result of the practices called "creating facts on the ground" is that property changes hands. As the PASSIA report explains, the acquisition of the territory that is now French Hill was an outcome of the 1967 war between Israel and its Arab neighbors (Jordan, Syria, and Egypt), as were the subsequent transfers of property from Palestinians to Jews that took place not only in the Jerusalem neighborhood of French Hill but in many other parts of the land of Israel/Palestine. With regard to the particular

1. Allison B. Hodgkins, Israeli Settlement Policy in Jerusalem: Facts on the Ground, 27.

case of French Hill, the 1967 war was crucial. The attacks and counterattacks that culminated in the 1967 war ended with Israel in possession of four geographic areas that had been under the control of Syria, Egypt, and Jordan since the end of the first Arab-Israeli conflict in 1948. These territories included the Golan Heights (formerly under the control of Syria), the Sinai Peninsula and the Gaza strip (controlled by Egypt), and the expanse of land that extends from the eastern half of Jerusalem through the Judean desert up to the Jordan River. This is the territory widely known as the West Bank,[2] an area that was originally slated to be part of a newly created Arab state under the United Nation's partition plan for Palestine,[3] but which fell under Jordanian control immediately after the establishment of the Jewish state and the ensuing 1948 war.

It was here, in the occupied territories of the West Bank and Gaza, that the concept of "creating of facts on the ground" gained wide currency. One commentator after another has used the term to describe the Israeli settlement policy that emerged soon after the 1967 war as, overriding internal objections, the Labor Government set about establishing the legal and political apparatus that would, over the next forty years, support the creation of over three hundred settlements, inhabited by almost four hundred thousand Jews, in Gaza, the West Bank, and East Jerusalem. "Facts on the ground" has been the term of choice both for proponents of the radical settler movement, which has been the leading force in establishing Jewish strongholds in the occupied territories, and for critics of Israeli settlement policy, who use the term to issue dire warnings about the impact of the settlements on the peace process and their injurious effects on the local population. Countless journalistic reports and white papers have been produced in which the term appears as a kind of policy jargon, summarizing the techniques and aims of the radical settler movement and of the government policies supporting them in a few pithy words.

But "facts on the ground" is not a technical term. It is not a legal concept (though it bears more than a passing resemblance to the legal doctrines of adverse possession and prescription, which enshrine the maxim that "possession is nine tenths of the law"), and it is certainly not a scientific term. Far from a technical concept, "facts on the ground" is simply a highly evocative colloquial phrase that has gained popularity in this and other contexts because it seems to capture something obvious but elusive and hard to put into words. It is, in essence, a metaphor, albeit one that succeeds precisely because it seems to be so literal. Especially when applied to the *de facto* possession of property, the phrase, "facts on the ground," seems to be referring to concrete facts that are literally on, or

---

2. The place names, like all facts and issues in this area, are disputed. Supporters of the religious settler movement dispute the West Bank appellation and call the area Judea and Samaria.

3. *See* Charles D. Smith, Palestine and the Arab-Israeli Conflict: A History with Documents, 190–195 (2001).

of, the ground. It is only on further reflection that we realize that the term is referring not just to physical facts of geography and possession of a particular piece of land, but to the myriad psychological and social effects unleashed by these facts, in addition to the complex processes whereby these facts were "created."

Indeed, "facts on the ground" is so evocative a term, and seems so aptly to describe the nature of the Jewish settlements in the occupied territories, that it sometimes seems as if it had been invented just to describe them. But the usage of the term long predates its application to the Zionist settler movement, and it continues to be employed to refer to a wide variety of phenomena in a wide variety of contexts. Which raises the question: what is the similarity between these diverse phenomena? What, if anything, do Israeli settlements have in common with other things that have been described as "facts on the ground"? And what do the circumstances of their creation have in common?

Answering these questions requires having some sense of what the terms, "facts on the ground," "creating facts on the ground," "establishing facts on the ground," *mean*. But, evocative as all of these terms are, and as intuitive as they seem to be, their meaning is actually deeply obscure. Not only do these terms fail to disclose what the defining features are that distinguish "facts on the ground" from other land settlement and real estate development projects and all the other facts and empirical states of affairs that we never call by that term. They also are frustratingly vague and ambiguous with regard to the all-important question of how, by whom, or by what, they are created. The idea that they *are* created, through some sort of human action or social process, rather than just appearing as naturally occurring facts, is built in to the very terms. Words like "creating" or "establishing" are clearly meant to imply human agency. Indeed, the idea that facts on the ground are human artifacts is so central to the concept that we tend to infer the existence of a human agent, deliberately bringing about the facts at issue, even when we don't use verbs like "create" or "establish," and opt instead for the shorter usage ("facts on the ground") without any modifying verb. All of this forms a striking contrast to the more commonplace view that facts are "not made, but found."

Yet, at the same time that the idea of a human agent is built into the concept, the precise identity of that agent, its nature, its methods, and, most importantly, its responsibility for the acts it commits (and the unfolding consequences of those actions), are rarely adequately specified. The passage quoted at the beginning of this chapter is typical in this regard. We learn (as if we didn't know already) that the practice of creating facts on the ground is an "Israeli strategy." But what, or whom, precisely does "Israeli" refer to? The Israeli state? The government? The Israeli people? The Jewish people on whose behalf the country was ostensibly established, and in whose name the settlement project is carried out (despite the protestations of many Jews)? Should we point our finger at the private individuals who promote and fund the settlements without themselves going to live there? What about the many settlers who moved to the occupied territories because of economic incentives, lured by government housing subsidies, with little awareness that the developments they were being offered a chance to live in were anything other than ordinary suburban developments at a bargain price, and little commitment to the ideological tenets of the settler movement? In the final analysis, is it the government or private actors who bear responsibility for establishing the settlements—or both? Is every settler equally responsible, or do we need to distinguish between the ideologues and the moderates, the leaders and the followers, the violent and the nonviolent, the grownups and the children who were born on the settlements or brought there without their consent?

Anyone with any knowledge of the complexities of the settlement process, and the divisions of opinion within the Israeli public (and the Israeli government), knows that these are not simple questions to answer. That does not necessarily negate the responsibility of the state—or of the "Israeli people" or the "Jewish people" at large—if one finds it meaningful to speak of such collective entities bearing collective responsibility. But it does mean that it is necessary to stake out a view on such issues as collective responsibility, and to match that view with a grasp of the facts regarding who did what, when, and where, and with what intention, before one can arrive at any sound conclusions about responsibility and agency.

In other words, it requires attending to the normative dimension of facts on the ground. Facts on the ground have both normative *effects* and human *causes* that give rise to claims (or charges) of moral responsibility. As already noted, facts on the ground are not just physical, because the physical aspects of facts on the ground—the facts of geography, demography, and physical possession of land—embody and engender myriad psychological, economic, and social transformations. That the simple physical act of occupying property or territory can bring about all of these inward and outward, psychological and social, empirical consequences is by itself remarkable. But observable empirical realities are not the only kinds of consequences brought into being through the creation of facts on the ground. There is also a host of less tangible but equally powerful *normative* consequences that issue from the practice of establishing facts on the ground—political consequences (such as the alteration of territorial boundaries, the expansion of a sovereign nation's jurisdiction, and even the establishment of new sovereign entities), and moral consequences as well.

These normative consequences bear on the questions of human agency and responsibility raised above, since the question of moral responsibility for the creation of facts on the ground is naturally tied to the question of what the responsible agent is responsible *for*. But if the usage of the concept of facts on the ground is frustratingly vague regarding the important question of who, or what, the morally responsible agent or agency is, it likewise tends to cloud the issue of how facts on the ground generate their normative consequences, and what, precisely, those normative consequences are. Both the normative inputs (the agents and their methods) and the normative outputs (the political and moral force that facts on the ground somehow acquire) are deeply obscure. The metaphorical phrases we use to describe them give expression to our intuitive recognition that there *are* such normative inputs and outputs, but they rarely illuminate the specific processes whereby facts on the ground acquire their normative power or clarify the nature of the normative power that they acquire. These are the deep mysteries buried in the heart of the concept of creating the facts on the ground.

On one level there is nothing surprising or mysterious about the normative consequences generated by facts on the ground. The social and economic changes effected by facts the ground, such as land redistribution and changes in the demographic and cultural character of a particular area, are almost always morally and politically controversial, giving rise to charges of unjust dispossession and other wrongful acts and consequences. It is precisely because there are prior occupants of the land or resource in question, and contestation over its ownership, that resort is made to the unorthodox methods of acquiring resources characterized as establishing facts on the ground in the first place. The very reason that phrases like "facts on the ground" were coined is that we need a way of distinguishing these methods from the standard methods of land acquisition and demographic movement. The methods of staking out possession that are used to establish facts on the ground constitute a deviation from the normal, sanctioned, legitimate methods of acquisition. Presumably, they are resorted to because the usual methods of acquiring or establishing ownership are unavailable—or unavailing. And perhaps there are good justifications for engaging in such deviant practices in some circumstances.[4] But whenever the rules defining the orthodox methods of land transfer are violated, it is natural that charges will be made on behalf of the people who have *lost* the resource (who have literally and figuratively *lost ground*) against the people who brought this about and took possession of the resource—claims that hold the latter to be morally responsible, or *guilty*, if the circumstances of the transfer are deemed to be in violation of fundamental moral principles.

These claims, and the counterclaims made in defense of the legitimacy of the land transfers described as facts of ground, are obviously normative in nature, and there is nothing surprising or mystifying about them. But the normative dimension of facts on the ground goes beyond the positions that are taken in the political debates that rage about the legality and morality of Israeli settlement practices (or about the morality and legality of *any* practice characterized as creating facts on the ground). It's not just that facts on the ground and the practices that generate them are adjudged to be immoral or illegal (or, contrariwise, perfectly in accordance with the relevant standards of judgment). Israel's critics and its

---

4. *See* Eduardo Peñalver & Sonia Katyal, Property Outlaws (2010).

would-be defenders both take positions about the conformity of Israeli settlement policy with standards of morality and international and domestic law. But these judgments, be they positive or negative, are what we might call second-order normative effects of the practice of establishing facts on the ground. By that I mean they are judgments *about* the practice's *first-order effects*, which include, in addition to their observable psychological, social, economic, and political consequences, *normative* effects—political and/or moral effects that exist independently of the moral and political judgments that we make about them.

These first-order normative effects consist specifically in the pressure exerted by facts on the ground on the resolution of the disputes that routinely arise about whether they should be preserved, that is, whether the people who have taken *de facto* possession have a *de jure* legal or a moral right to keep it. The recognition that *de facto* possession has a strong tendency to ripen into *de jure* possession, or at least into some kind of social acceptance of the legitimacy of the current occupants' occupation, is part of what we *mean* by facts on the ground. Everyone understands the power of the status quo not only to perpetuate itself but also to legitimate itself. We recognize that practical reality has a kind of normative power or force that affects the outcomes of disputes, biasing the outcome in favor of the established status quo and, hence, against a restoration of the status quo ante. It is our intuitive appreciation of this normative pressure generated by "reality"—by facts on the ground—that leads people to offer phrases such as "fait accompli," "accomplished facts," and "irreversible facts" as synonyms or glosses on "facts on the ground." These phrases convey our appreciation of the pressure or resistance to reversing the established status quo that is generated by the status quo's sheer existence. All of these formulations reflect our sense that the actions necessary to reverse the facts on the ground are difficult if not impossible to undertake—not because they are physically impossible, but because they are somehow, for reasons that have yet to be explained, socially, psychologically, politically, and, arguably, even morally, impossible to undertake.

This is the basic "first order" normative effect of facts on the ground. It is not just a random or accidental consequence of the establishment of facts on the ground, but rather, an expected and, very often (although not always), a deliberately intended result. Thus, the radical religious settler movements that have, since the 1970s, been the most zealous proponents of establishing Jewish settlements in the occupied territories, have established them with the deliberate aim of making them "irreversible facts," i.e., realities that will have to be accommodated if and when a resolution of the final status of the territories ever takes place (and which, in the meanwhile, shape the political situation to their advantage).[5] So, too, government policy supporting the radical settler movements was formulated with the deliberate aim of having the settlements eventually become annexed to

5. Whether it is to *Israel*'s advantage is highly debatable.

the Israeli state. Alternatively, the settlements have been conceived as bargaining chips, leverage to be used in future negotiations, with the expectation of extracting an eventual concession to a land swap. Thus, as outlined in a U.S. Government report on the "umbrella municipality plan" for Jerusalem and its environs:

> Insofar as planning and construction is concerned, the relevant Jewish settlements in the West Bank will be functionally detached from the authority of the Civil Administration (the Military Commander) and, in essence, will come under the direct control of civilian Israeli authority. In terms of planning and construction, these settlements will be empirically indistinguishable from those towns and cities in Israel proper. . . . Until now, and even after Oslo, there has been a clear, binary distinction between Israel proper (the rule of Israeli Law) and the West Bank (despite all discounts, Military Rule). The proposed umbrella municipality plan blurs this distinction, rendering the "green line" meaningless, even as a term of reference. . . . The term "Greater Jerusalem" has to date been a rather amorphous, and not terribly binding, declaration of intent. After this proposal the same term will constitute a geographically and ethnically defined entity, clearly expressed in legally defined borders, in which [Israeli] civilian control is exerted over territories previously deemed "occupied."[6]

Behind this vision of the umbrella municipality, behind the settlers' vision of a Greater Israel, behind all of these government and settler visions is the common goal of creating communities that "couldn't" be uprooted.

With this aim in mind, the policy adopted by the government early on was to create settlements with a civilian rather than a military character. In this regard at least, government policy was perfectly in harmony with the radical settler movement. The standard procedure adopted was first to establish a settlement as an army outpost, under cover of the laws of belligerent occupation, which restrict the taking of property and building of settlements by an occupying military force to military encampments serving legitimate security purposes. Legally, such "military outposts" are temporary, since by law the property expropriated for their establishment has to be returned to its owners once the "military necessity" that justified its taking has ended. But the settlers of such outposts, and the military and civilian authorities that oversaw their establishment, operated with the tacit understanding that these "temporary military outposts" established for "military security purposes" would soon be converted into multipurpose communities of a civilian and hence more permanent character. Thus, hundreds of settlements that began as supposed security outposts were very quickly transformed into densely populated residential communities, where families raise children, and members of the community establish schools and synagogues, run

---

6. Excerpts from a U.S. State Department analysis quoted in FACTS ON THE GROUND, 86.

stores and businesses, have homes and all of the accoutrements of ordinary life—precisely what international law seems intended to prohibit.

The dramatic consequences of this covert policy are vividly described in the PASSIA report:

> Numbers alone cannot express how the landscape of occupied territory has changed. East of Jerusalem, the apartment buildings of Ma'aleh Adumim rise starkly from the desolate slopes leading down toward the Dead Sea. The settlement that [a radical settler] sought to establish surreptitiously as a "work camp" has grown into a bedroom community of thirty-one thousand people, the single largest Israeli community in the West Bank (excluding East Jerusalem). North of Jerusalem, a highway built to serve the settlements runs through the hill country, bypassing Ramallah and other Palestinian towns and villages. On the way to Ofrah, now a gated exurb of over two thousand people, the road passes settlement after settlement—Adam, Kohav Ya'akov, Psagot—carpets of houses with red-tile roofs on the hilltops overlooking Palestinian towns and villages. On the hills stand "outposts," the newest wave of settlements, clumps of mobile homes lacking official approval but established with the active assistance of government agencies, often on privately owned Palestinian land.[7]

This description reveals the dynamic heart of facts on the ground: the passage from an initial stage of exceptionality to a later stage of seeming normality, and with that, a kind of normativity or legitimacy—or at least a very strong pressure to be accepted as legitimate. The settlements, as described above, start off as "exceptional" both in a legal sense and a sociological sense, and end up normalized, or de-exceptionalized, again in both legal and sociological terms. Insofar as their legal status is concerned, the settlements are, at the start, either flatly in contravention of the laws governing occupied territories—"illegal," as many would have it—or, alternatively, as their defenders would have it, they conform to and are governed by the exceptions to the prevailing legal prohibitions on expropriation and settlement in the occupied territories provided for (and limited to) cases of "military necessity." Either way, their status is that of a legal exception, that is, an exception to the laws that (are supposed to) generally prevail.

In a sociological sense, as well, the settlements are in their initial stage exceptional, insofar as the initial *character* of the settlements is military (or pioneering), rather than civilian (and established), without any of the infrastructure of normal life, e.g., roads, buildings, businesses, schools, permanent structures, etc. Perhaps the sharpest indication of the transition to ordinary civilian life is the presence of women and children and the prominence of childrearing as an activity, which clearly signals a shift away from military purposes, at least as they

7. Facts on the Ground.

are commonly defined. Tellingly, the settlements lose their exceptional sociological character and their exceptional legal status at the same time. Or, more precisely, they acquire a normative character by the second sociological stage that either "supersedes"[8] their initially illegal or legally exceptional character, or, if a change in legal status isn't fully accomplished, at least challenges that extra-legal character with a competing, potentially overriding norm.

This, indeed, is the core idea of the concept of facts on the ground: the conversion of a *de facto* reality into a *de jure* reality, either a newly and fully legalized state of affairs, or if not that, then a state of affairs that nevertheless cannot be undone—"cannot" not in the sense of a physical necessity, but, rather, in the sense of a normative necessity—because the social costs of doing so are unacceptable. When we say that facts on the ground "cannot" be undone, we do not mean that they "cannot" be undone in a literal sense. (Of course they *can* be undone; all it takes is physical force, as the pullout from Gaza boldly demonstrated). Rather, "cannot" is a normative term, referring to political or moral "impossibilities." This is both the core idea and the basic mystery of facts on the ground.

It is true that the changes introduced into the normative landscape are not always dispositive—they can be, and sometimes are, offset by competing political or moral considerations, considerations that demand a restoration of the status quo ante or the establishment of a new, presumably more just or politically acceptable arrangement. In the face of countervailing moral and political imperatives, some militating in favor of a preservation of the current status quo, others militating against it, it is never preordained which side will win out. We might, as we say, "refuse to accept reality," recognizing the superior force of the moral principles or political considerations that dictate tearing down the facts on the ground. But the fact is, societies are notably reluctant to tear down established facts on the ground, an indication of the normative as well as the practical hold that they have on us. And even when it is determined that countervailing normative concerns outweigh the normative claims that facts on the ground generate, facts on the ground are still exerting their normative force, even if that force hasn't prevailed over the forces that demand their destruction.

To resort to a different metaphor, it is as if facts on the ground generate a kind of invisible force field, a normative force field that can only be penetrated with great effort and at a high (perhaps an "impossibly high") moral/political cost. And this is perhaps the most radical transformation of all: above and beyond the changes effected externally by the possession of land (in the allocation of land and resources, the "exchange" of populations, the redefinition of territorial borders,

---

8. The allusion is to Waldron's theory of supersession. *See* Jeremy Waldron, *Settlement, Return, and the Supersession Thesis*, 5 THEORETICAL INQUIRIES IN LAW 237 (2004). For a lucid critique of Waldron's supersession thesis, see Chaim Gans, *The Palestinian Right of Return and the Justice of Zionism, in* ISRAEL AND THE PALESTINIAN REFUGEES, 256–293 (Eyal Benvenisti, Chaim Gans, and Sari Hanafi eds., 2007).

and establishment of new political jurisdictions) and in addition to the changes effected internally (in people's feelings and beliefs about what's possible in the future and what happened in the past), this normative force field cloaks all of these changes in empirical reality with a kind of moral or political force. This is why we are so often sympathetic to claims put forth on the part of current occupants who claim the right to be protected from dispossession (or at least a right to compensation in the event of being dispossessed) even when we think they acquired their occupancy through a wrongful act. Such rights claims, and the deference they are widely given, reflect the widely shared sense that there are either political reasons or reasons of principle not to undertake to "reverse the facts."

An important distinction is being finessed here between reasons of principle and pragmatic calculations of *realpolitik*, which might support the conclusion that the facts on the ground should not be disturbed. The point here is that, however the distinction between moral and pragmatic considerations is resolved (or not resolved), the existence of some combination of considerations counseling against the dismantlement of facts on the ground—some kind of "normative force field"—emerges as yet another by-product of the physical fact of possession. That force field does not emerge overnight. It takes time for facts to acquire their normative power, and the strength of that power grows over time. Recognizing this point, the PASSIA report emphasizes the signs of the passage of time in its description of French Hill as an example of the "effectiveness of the Israeli strategy of creating facts on the ground." Thus, the report continues:

> Established in 1968, the 30-year-old settlement is an accomplished fact. Parents that have raised children in French Hill now have their grandchildren living just around the corner. It is inconceivable that any of these residents would see themselves as settlers in an impermanent settlement project. Its weathered buildings and well-worn strip malls are testament to the neighborhood's permanence. . . . [N]ot even the most idealistic of Palestinian negotiators would ever dream of French Hill being dismantled as part of a final status agreement.[9]

Vividly conveyed here is not only the importance of time to the construction of facts on the ground and their endowment with normative power, but also the particular kinds of things that transpire over time, which generate that normative endowment. This nutshell portrait of life in French Hill also shows how the external social, internal psychological, and intangible normative effects all intertwine, forming a skein of perceptions and self-perceptions, beliefs about the past and attachments to the present, memories, false memories, and, above all, *a sense of normality*, all of which conspire to make a reversal of the status quo "inconceivable."

---

9. FACTS ON THE GROUND, 41.

The psychological dimension of that "inconceivability" is crucial. Three psychological phenomena, in particular—collective memory, attachment, and adaptation, the psychological counterpart to *normalization*—play particularly important roles in constituting this "skein" and the normative force field that it holds together. Perhaps the most obvious psychological force at work in the construction of facts on the ground is collective memory. As described by students of the phenomenon, collective memory refers to "the subjective use of the past to sustain a vision of individual or collective identity."[10] Unlike "scientific" historical scholarship or "critical history," which attempts to establish "objective knowledge of what actually happened in the past"[11] and seeks to prevent present-day interests from distorting our understanding of the past, collective memory is frankly "presentist," shaping and reshaping our understanding of what happened in the past (and its importance) in the service of present-day needs and understandings. Above all, collective memory serves "a *group's* consciousness,"[12] at once reflecting and constructing a people's sense of its identity. Such a process of reconstructing the past to construct and conform to a group's sense of identity clearly lies behind the "inconceivability" of the residents "see[ing] themselves" as settlers.[13] It is not that the residents have necessarily forgotten that the area now known as French Hill was conquered in the 1967 war. Any Israeli schoolchild knows *that.* Nor is the point that no one in French Hill knows, or would accept, the fine points of international law, according to which this historical fact of military conquest means that French Hill is technically a settlement in occupied territory subject to international law (in particular, the laws governing military occupations). What *has* been forgotten, or, if not literally forgotten, then conveniently suppressed, is the fact that the land on which French Hill was developed was expropriated from the Arab village of Issiwaya, in violation of the laws governing military occupations. To be sure, some residents of French Hill know this fact, and are aware of the international law perspective, according to which French Hill is an illegal settlement on occupied territory; some of them concur with that perspective and others dispute it. But those individual judgments do not represent the collective memory of the community. Most of the residents (and fellow-citizens of Jerusalem and Israel) simply do not concern themselves with such matters, at least not most of the time. Instead, they go about the business of their daily lives, without giving the legal—or illegal—origins of French Hill much thought. After all, there is no visible trace of the original Arab owners or of the Arab village of which this area used to be a part to

---

10. Elisheva Carlebach, John M. Efron & David N. Myers, eds., JEWISH HISTORY AND JEWISH MEMORY: ESSAYS IN HONOR OF YOSEF HAYIM YERUSHALMI, xiii.

11. *Id.*

12. David N. Myers, RE-INVENTING THE JEWISH PAST: EUROPEAN JEWISH INTELLECTUALS AND THE ZIONIST RETURN TO HISTORY, 31 (1995).

13. FACTS ON THE GROUND, 41.

serve as a reminder. Instead, all of the visible markers of the community's past—its "weathered buildings and well-worn strip malls" and, most especially, its "grandchildren living just around the corner"—lend the impression that French Hill originated as an ordinary residential development. They foster a "memory" of the community's origins from which the history of land expropriation and unwilling transfer from the original Arab owners of the properties is conveniently erased.

This is a textbook example of how the mechanisms of collective memory operate. In contradistinction to critical historical scholarship, which looks behind the always potentially misleading visual cues of the present, collective memory takes its cues from the visible, external, physical surroundings[14] in a reflexive process that simultaneously imbues the present-day facts on the ground with meaning (including historical meaning) while being shaped by those same external facts. In the case of French Hill, the surface features of the community make its historical origins and status under international law "inconceivable" because they make the community *look like* any other (Jewish) neighborhood in Jerusalem—and not like a stereotypical settlement. As the U.S. government report on the Jerusalem "umbrella plan" stated (referring to nearby communities outside the city), such surface features "blur[] the distinction" between "Israel proper" and the West Bank, "rendering the 'green line' meaningless."[15] The real feat accomplished in French Hill, through the mechanism of collective memory, is that, since its founding, the area has been radically transformed yet, at the same time, normalized, rendered utterly ordinary.

This blurring of the "binary distinction" between the two sides of the Green Line, between "Israel proper" and the West Bank, legal and illegal settlements, civilian law and military rule subject to the international law of belligerent occupation, is the stated aim of the policy of establishing facts on the ground. The whole idea is to make settlements seem so much like ordinary places where ordinary people live and civilian law applies that the thought that they *are* settlements, whose dismantlement is required under international law, becomes unthinkable. This is the cognitive work accomplished through the processes of collective memory. It is a familiar time-bound phenomenon. As time passes, our memories fade, allowing newly constructed memories, which take their cue from the visible visual and cultural character of a community, rather than from any invisible legal line, to crowd in. The role of collective memory is thus revealed to be a critically important causative factor in endowing facts on the ground with their normative power.

It is in this regard that the concept of facts on the ground is more than a little reminiscent of the legal doctrines of adverse possession and prescription.

---

14. For a particularly evocative description of this process, see Meron Benvinisti, Sacred Landscape: Buried History of the Holy Land Since 1948 (1995).

15. Facts on the Ground 86.

Adverse possession and prescription are legal doctrines that enshrine the maxim that "possession is nine tenths of the law." As counterintuitive and even shocking as it sounds, this ancient maxim forms the basis of a number of longstanding, garden-variety property doctrines, including the right of first possession, which awards title to unowned resources to the first person to take possession of them; the doctrine of relative title, which entitles occupants of property to exclude non-owners; and the doctrines of adverse possession (which applies to real property) and prescription (which applies to other forms of property and other rights), which take the logic of possession one step further by *removing* title from the owner when a nonowner takes physical possession and makes use of the property in stipulated ways for a sufficiently long duration of time. The same basic logic of possession informed the European doctrines of early international law, such as the "right of discovery" and the "right of conquest," which were used to determine which colonial power had the right to colonize a particular area by awarding property rights and the rights of territorial jurisdiction to whichever one succeeded in conquering a particular territory first. (This also served to "justify" the expropriation of land from its native inhabitants).[16]

Doctrines such as these are to be found in the property codes of most every developed legal system, including Islamic and Jewish law as well as Anglo-American law and the legal systems of continental Europe. This includes the Ottoman law codes (derived from Islamic law) that governed Palestine in the late nineteenth century when the modern Zionist movement to establish a Jewish homeland in Palestine first arose.[17] These Ottoman laws were largely preserved when Great Britain made Palestine its "mandate" following World War I. The land laws enforced by the British in mandatory Palestine were a combination of those inherited from the prior Ottoman regime (which the Ottoman authorities had already begun to modernize and reform in the years directly preceding the British mandate) and their own statutory innovations, such as the Land Transfer Ordinance of 1921, which restricted the ability of Jews to purchase Arab-owned land. When the Israeli state was established in 1948, and when it later assumed military control over the occupied territories in 1967, these British and Ottoman laws continued to be applied, albeit selectively (naturally, the British restrictions on land transfers to Jews were repealed) and, in the main, opportunistically, with new land laws passed by the Israeli parliament and new judicial doctrines developed that sometimes supplemented and sometimes supplanted the old

---

16. On the doctrines of discovery and conquest, see Joseph William Singer and Joseph P. Kalt, Myths and Realities of Tribal Sovereignty: The Law and Economics of Indian Self-Rule (2004).

17. *See* George E. Bisharat, *Land, Law, and Legitimacy in Israel and the Occupied Territories*, 43 Am. U. L. Rev. 467, 491–95 (1994); Alexandre (Sandy) Kedar, *The Legal Transformation of Ethnic Geography: Israeli Law and the Palestinian Landholder 1948–1967*, 33 N.Y.U. J. Int'l L. and Politics 923, 932–936, 949–966 (2001).

Ottoman and British land laws. In the 1950s, the laws of adverse possession were substantially modified with the aim of preventing Palestinians in Israel from establishing adverse possession claims.[18] But some version of the doctrines of adverse possession and legal prescription always remained in force, attesting to the utility and ongoing normative pull of the basic principle that *de facto* possession should, in certain prescribed circumstances, be recognized as constituting *de jure* rights to possession.

There are two major theories of adverse possession, each of which assigns a leading role to the psychological attachments formed by current possessors to their possessions. One of these, the utilitarian theory, also focuses on the practical problems of proof that arise when there is no reliable historical record, and the past is "lost in the mists of history." According to this utilitarian theory, the doctrine of adverse possession serves two basic functions. The first is to impose a statute of limitations on claims against trespassers because of the inevitable uncertainties that arise out of the vagaries of memory. On this account, adverse possession represents the (appropriate) triumph of "pragmatics" over "principle." In a perfect world, wrongs are "instantly uncovered" and the principles of corrective justice are vindicated.[19] But in the real world, problems of proof and the unreliability of memory and representations about the past mean that wrongs are frequently not uncovered for a long time, or not uncovered at all, and in any event, difficult to prove. "With time, memories fade and witnesses die: no one can recall who did what to whom," and even the "documentary evidence" may be "forged, lost, altered or destroyed."[20] In a world with such faulty means of reconstructing the historical record, it is better, on this view, for pragmatics to triumph over principle.

The second function attributed to adverse possession on the utilitarian account is to "quiet title." Eliminating lingering uncertainties about who owns what is thought to serve the positive utilitarian functions of enhancing the marketability of property and maximizing its productive use. By simply declaring the current possessor (who meets certain conditions) to be the legal owner, the uncertainty is dissolved. The utilitarian explanation for favoring the current possessor over other contenders is that "what comes last is more reliable and certain" than what came earlier for the simple reason that is more readily identifiable. Furthermore (and here is where a psychological attachment theory kicks in), to this is added the supposition that current occupants derive

---

18. On the changes implemented in adverse possession law, *see* Alexandre (Sandy) Kedar, *Legal Transformation*, at 952–966. For an overview of the various methods used to acquire Arab property and the legal regimes under which they were implemented, see generally Kedar, as well as Bisharat, *Land, Law, and Legitimacy*.

19. Richard Epstein, *Past and Future: The Temporal Dimension in the Law of Property*, 64 Wash. U. L. Q. 667, 675 (1986).

20. Epstein, *Past and Future*, 675.

a higher subjective utility from the property for no other reason than the fact that, because they currently occupy it, they have "developed expectations of continued control."[21]

As critics have observed, this is a somewhat dubious assumption, since the existence and strength of expectations are highly contingent matters, and, as the Palestinian refugee situation makes painfully clear, it is entirely possible for a nonpossessor to harbor expectations of coming into control of the resource, and to make continued emotional and economic investments in reliance on that expectation. (Conversely, an indifferent current occupant might have no expectations regarding the property at all.) In such situations, we can't rule out the possibility that the strongest degree of attachment and the highest level of emotional and economic investment are made by the party not in possession.

There could hardly be a better case in point than the Palestinian refugees—except, of course, for the Jews, who nurtured at least as strong an attachment to the same land over the course of two thousand years of exile. These mirror images of psychological attachment to a lost homeland more than suffice to demonstrate the falsity of the assumption that attachments to property necessarily wax with ongoing occupancy and wane with absence. But regardless of the correctness of its psychological suppositions, what is important is that conventional utilitarian reasoning about adverse possession makes psychological suppositions that grant importance to the psychological investments we make in land and the expectations we form when we do occupy land regarding its continued presence.

In American jurisprudence, this utilitarian theory of adverse possession is commonly associated with Oliver Wendell Holmes's famous saying that "man, like a tree in the cleft of a rock, gradually shapes his roots to his surroundings, and when the roots have grown to a certain size, can't be displaced without cutting at his life."[22] "Roots," according to the conventional utilitarian way of thinking, are understood to be a great personal benefit, both in and of themselves and as the source of innumerable further benefits, or gains in personal well-being. Conversely, being uprooted is understood to generate great personal, and social, costs.

A similar psychological assumption about the importance of "roots" and rootedness is given a different, less economic, and more psychoanalytic (or Hegelian) spin by the "personhood theory" of property, according to which a "bond develop[s] between adverse possessor and object over time"—not just an expectation of continued possession or an economic investment, but an emotional bond, in which a person's sense of self or "personhood" becomes

---

21. Margaret Jane Radin, *Time, Possession, and Alienation*, 64 Wash. U. L. Q. 739, 744 (1986).

22. *Quoted in* E. Allan Farnsworth, Changing Your Mind: The Law of Regretted Decisions 199 (2000).

bound up with the property.[23] On this theory (as on the utilitarian account), the converse assumption is also usually drawn, namely that, as the original title-holder is separated from the property, her "interest fades."[24] Why both theories make this assumption, belied by the all too common experience of exile, is worth pondering.

Despite the counterexample of exile, attachment is by its nature a present-oriented psychological mechanism, closely connected to the psychological mechanism of adaptation. Whereas collective memory is concerned with reconstructions of the past, attachments are what we form to the things that we *have*—to our present surroundings and holdings, to the people, places, and things that constitute our environment, to our experience and our reality in the here and now.

The fundamental psychological insight shared by personhood theory and the utilitarian/Holmesian conception of "man . . . gradually shap[ing] his roots to his surroundings" is that the psychological processes of attachment and adaptation are important features of our psyches. We all become attached to our present surroundings, and suffer a loss, sometimes a grievous loss, when we are forced to leave them.

It is hard to see what else could explain the otherwise shocking disregard for the past, and past injustices, displayed by the legal doctrine of adverse possession and the concept of facts on the ground. Perhaps the most shocking thing about the normative authority conferred on adverse possessors and other "creators" of "facts on the ground" is the flagrant disregard that it seems to display toward the canons of corrective justice. "Legalized theft" is perhaps the pithiest expression that commentators have offered to describe the paradox that seems to inhere in granting normative power to facts on the ground and thereby "turning facts into rights" and even wrongs into rights. The psychological and normative value accorded to "attachment," recognized by utilitarian and personhood theories of property, seems to play an important role in explaining this seeming disregard for the claims of corrective justice.

This psychological perspective may also help us to better understand what the presence of families adds to the case for subordinating the past-oriented claims of corrective justice to the present-day interests and needs of the current possessors. Obviously, the presence of children is not a necessary element for making out a successful adverse possession claim,[25] or for successfully establishing a "fact on the ground." But it is the case that the presence of children and family units greatly enhances their chances for success. That line in the PASSIA

---

23. *See* Margaret Jane Radin, *Property and Personhood*, 34 Stan. L. Rev. 957 (1982).

24. Radin, *Time, Possession, and Alienation*, 748–49.

25. To be clear, in drawing a connection between the concept of facts on the ground and the legal doctrine of adverse possession, I am *not* suggesting that the settlements in the territories satisfy the requirements of the legal doctrine.

report describing "the grandchildren living around the corner" is not a throw-away; it is doing a lot of powerful rhetorical work. Similarly, I would suggest that it is no accident that populating the settlements with families is a central component of the settlers' strategy of creating facts on the ground. (So, too, a large preponderance of successful garden-variety adverse possession cases feature family homes). Indeed, it could well be said that children are the ultimate "facts on the ground."

But what exactly does the presence of all those children signify, and what work are they doing that leads the mere fact of possession to acquire its evident normative power? It is not just that many of the families in the settlements are ultra-Orthodox Jews committed to a literal interpretation of the biblical injunction to be fruitful and multiply. The typical settlement in the territories exhibits a much higher birth rate than a place like French Hill, which, with its mix of secular and religious, mainly modern orthodox Jews, looks more like the secular and mixed Jewish neighborhoods of "Israel proper." The physical presence of each and every child contributes to the population count, and the siege mentality that sees the demographic "imbalance" as a threat to the Jewish character of the state might well conceive[26] of Jewish children as filling a security need in addition to fulfilling a biblical injunction. From the point of view that sees the "demographic threat" as a danger to the Jewish state as grave as any military attack, children are the ultimate physical facts on the ground, and procreation is the ultimate method of fact-creation.

But just as the fact of physically possessing land has more than a physical dimension, there is more to the presence of children on a settlement than their sheer physical, demographic presence. The presence of children also highlights the psychological features of attachment and adaptation that lead to the prioritization of needs of the present—and the needs of those who *are present*—over claims of right rooted in the past. The attachments that the children of the settlements have formed epitomize the attachments that hold all of the members of a settlement together. Furthermore, children are the ultimate innocents, singularly blameless for creating these attachments. We understand, as the psychological theory of attachment tells us, the need that children have for continuity, and the trauma that they will consequently experience if they are displaced—and we understand that the adults, too, have this need. A significant part of what makes the dismantlement of French Hill "inconceivable" is our reluctance to inflict this trauma, particularly on those who, like children, bear no responsibility for their being there or establishing the settlements in the first place.

In addition to attachment, children also highlight the psychological process of adaptation, which works together with the mechanisms of attachment and collective memory to make the present seem normal and dismantlement "inconceivable."

---

26. Pun intended.

To put it simply, children and families are markers of normalcy. Despite (and in considerable tension with) the conception of children as weapons in the demographic "war," children, and the domestic activities and enterprises that constellate around them, are the epitome of normal, civilian life—and the antithesis of the activities and social functions associated with the military needs or survivalist imperatives that characterize a military or pioneering "outpost." The more domestic life there is in a settlement, the more normal it looks, and the less it looks like a settlement.

Every settlement in the territories aims to achieve this sense of normalcy. But not every settlement has been as successful in achieving it as French Hill. In part this is a function of time—the more time passes, the more normalcy sets in. In part it is a function of proximity—the closer a community is to what is perceived to be Israel proper, the more normal it looks. (Being contained *within* the boundaries of a city widely viewed as an indivisible political entity was obviously a huge advantage). But success in producing a sense of normalcy is also, importantly, a function of the psychological perceptions we have about who we are and the kind of activities we are engaged in. Along with collective memory, which reshapes our sense of the origins of the community, and attachment, which bonds us to the community and makes it feel like "home," the psychological mechanism of adaptation plays a key role in producing this sense of normalcy.

But normalization is not an exclusively psychological phenomenon. To fully grasp the phenomenon, there are other facets of normalization that need to be understood, and for this we need to look beyond psychology to other theoretical frameworks. Three theories of normalization seem particularly well-suited to analyzing the phenomenon of facts of the ground, one being Foucault's conception of norms and normalization, another drawn from Carl Schmitt's theory of the state of emergency, and finally a third theory of normalization, the theory of "political normalization" developed by early Zionist thinkers as a response to European anti-Semitism and the perceived "abnormality" of being a stateless people. Each of these conceptions of normalization offers a different perspective on what transpires when facts on the ground undergo the transition from a state of apparent abnormality or social and legal "exceptionality" to a state of seeming normalcy and legal or quasi-legal acceptance.

Foucault uses the concept of normalization to describe the effects of "productive" as opposed to "juridical" power, juridical power being a top-down mode of governance, which dictates behavior through means of external coercion and violence, productive "biopower" being a mode of governance and reciprocal power relations that works through the formulation and internalization of norms.[27] Norms, as Foucault describes them, operate as a system of governance

---

27. I rely here on Francois Ewald's excellent explication of Foucault's concept of the norm. *See* Francois Ewald, *Norms, Discipline, and the Law, in* Law and the Order of Culture, 138–160 (Robert Post ed., 1991).

outside the juridical system of the law (although they have increasingly become the mode through which the law itself operates, the juridical being just one of the many forms that the law can take). Norms are a species of rules, but unlike more traditional juridical rules that emanate from the will of a sovereign on high, norms emanate from the population and its actual social practices. Norms are a standard of measurement based on the average, which itself is derived from the aggregate of actual events and its "observable regularities," which constitute the "constants of social life."[28] From this standpoint, "the important thing about events" is not what caused them to occur, but rather "*that* they occur, or rather that their occurrence is repetitive, multiple, and regular."[29]

As Francois Ewald notes in his excellent explication of Foucault's conception of norms and the normative, "[b]y the standards of an earlier world," the approach of the statistician "is most remarkable for his rigorous suspension of judgment. For him, events are facts with distinct boundaries in space and time—they are complete in themselves and have no cause, or past, or future," they "become purely accidental" and "for the purposes of statistics, they remain without victims and without a cause."[30] Here we see the rudiments of an explanation for why this empirical approach entails a rejection of corrective justice. Whereas "[L]egal judgments were traditionally based on an attempt to discover the cause of damages," motivated by the belief that "it was essential to find out whether damages were the result of an unpredictable natural event or whether they could be attributed to a particular person or institution who would be required to bear responsibility for the damages," in the system of judgment based on norms, "causality is superseded" and "a new rule of justice" is adopted, one that refers not to the past events and actions, "but rather to the existence of the group, a social rule of justice that the group is free to determine for itself, and on its own terms."[31]

Although Foucault nowhere, to my knowledge, analyzes the doctrines of adverse possession and prescription or the practice of establishing facts on the ground, this "new" normative paradigm that Foucault sees expressed in the practices and disciplines of the modern sciences and professions that shape modern society (e.g., medicine, psychology, insurance, etc.) is breathtakingly similar to the normative paradigm expressed in the legal and extralegal practices described as facts on the ground. As in the case of the actuarial sciences and other disciplines Foucault analyzes, the practices that grant normative force to facts on the ground rest on "an entirely different idea of justice"[32] from the one that animates the normal rules of property rights—an idea of justice that is derived from empirical behavioral norms rather than the principles of corrective justice, and that indeed

---

28. *Id.* at 144.
29. *Id.* (emphasis added).
30. *Id.* at 143.
31. *Id.* at 147.
32. *Id.*

contravenes the principles of corrective justice. It would be difficult to come up with a more apt description of these practices than the Foucauldian vision of the production of "biopower" and the translation of empirically observable norms into forces of normalization.

What this account of normalization leaves open is the question of why, or more precisely *when* the paradigm of corrective justice will be exchanged for this new "idea of justice." After all, the "old idea of justice," the juridical mode, based on the principles of corrective justice, persists alongside the norm-based conception described by Foucault, and it is not exactly clear when the norm-based conception will be favored over the traditional conception, or what causes this to occur. A theory that may help to shed light on this crucial issue is the theory of the state of emergency or "state of exception" developed by the controversial political theorist, Carl Schmitt.

Unlike Foucault, Schmitt does not explicitly address the concept of the norm, normalcy, or normalization. But his concept of the state of emergency as "the state of exception" points us toward an explanation of why and when the rules of corrective justice—and the rule of law more generally—will be suspended. And his idea of the permanent state of emergency offers an alternative understanding of the transition that abnormal situations, like facts on the ground, undergo as they come to seem normal and acquire normative force.[33]

As Schmitt helped us to see, a state of emergency (whether or not it is officially declared) is a "state of exception" in which the ordinary rules don't apply. In theory, the state of exception is triggered by the existence of an emergency, that is, an existential threat, which threatens our survival or our basic rights. In the state of emergency, our conduct is governed not by the rules of law that ordinarily apply to protect the rights of others, but rather, by the logic of necessity or exigency, which authorizes actions that violate the rights of others if undertaken to serve overriding needs, such as self-defense. An exception is built into the paradigm of corrective justice itself for such overriding needs, which in theory explains why and when such conduct will be justified. According to the conventional view of the state of emergency, emergency situations are by nature temporary, ending when the threat ends, and the necessity that justifies suspending the ordinary rules no longer obtains. Schmitt's innovation was to contend that the state of emergency is permanent, and that, in effect, we are always in a state

33. Schmitt expounded his theory in a number of books, including Carl Schmitt, Political Theology: Four Chapters on the Concept of Sovereignty (1922) and The Concept of the Political (George Schwab trans., 1976). His leading modern expositor is Giorgio Agamben. *See* Giorgio Agamben, State of Exception (2003). Another helpful expositor on whom I have relied is David Dyzenhaus. *See* David Dyzenhaus, *Schmitt v. Dicey:* Are States of Emergency Inside or Outside the Legal Order?, 27 Cardozo L. Rev. 5 (2006); and Legality and Legitimacy: Carl Schmitt, Hans Kelsen, and Hermann Heller in Weimar (1999).

of emergency, whether or not one is formally declared. Instead of ending after it is formally declared, the state of emergency is, according to Schmitt, perpetuated. And with the perpetuation of a state of emergency comes a perpetuation of the state of exception to the law—a perpetual suspension of the rule of law and all the "ordinary" rules that "ordinarily" subject our actions to the constraints that flow from the recognition of the rights of others. From the standpoint of empirical incidence, the state of legal exception and the state of legal normalcy have in effect traded places. What in theory is the rare, exceptional state of affairs—the suspension of "normal" law—has become "the new normal." And what in theory is the normal state of affairs—the state of affairs in which the normal rules of law apply—has become an illusion, as the exception swallows up the rule. In short, the state of emergency/the state of exception has been normalized.

Like Foucault's, this theory of normalization seems like a singularly apt description of the dynamics that propel the establishment of facts on the ground and their attainment of normalcy and normative force. The circumstances in which facts on the ground are created always entail some kind of emergency or exigent situation that justifies (or purports to justify) overriding the "usual" rules, be it a relatively minor emergency (such as the "cloud over title" that arises out of evidentiary ambiguities making it impossible to ascertain if a transfer was voluntary or forced and clouding the identity of the true owner), or be it a major emergency, such as a threat to personal or national security. There is always some exigency generating a need to override the rights that we "ordinarily" protect asserted in a facts on the ground situation.

It is telling in this regard how many transfers of Arab-owned or occupied land have occurred in Israel/Palestine under the mantle of some kind of emergency law, or military necessity, on *both* sides of the Green Line. The occupied territories are subject to military administration, and even though the international law that governs military occupations requires the military administration to enforce the preexisting civilian laws, it provides an *exception* to that requirement for situations when "military necessity" or security needs require overriding civilian law. Settlements have thus been founded under the exceptional "legal authority" of an exception to an exception to an exception, as, by law, civilian law is expected to give way to military rule, which in turn is expected to give way to the civilian laws of the prior rulers, which in turn is expected to give way to military necessity. On the other side of the Green Line, a formal declaration of a state of emergency has been in place since the 1948 war. Although not applied to most Jewish transactions, this state of emergency has never been repealed, and it has been selectively applied to Palestinian residents and citizens living within the boundaries of the Green Line to sanction property expropriations and transfers.[34]

---

34. Bisharat, *Land, Law, and Legitimacy*, 514–518.

The question is whether to accept this logic as a justification. It is always in the interest of those who are grabbing power or grabbing land to claim that they are justified in doing so, and the logic of necessity that defines the state of emergency is a justification that comes readily to hand. But if the justification is nothing more than a self-serving rationalization, then there is no reason for us to accept it, and therefore no reason to grant facts on the ground any normative force. We are back to nothing but brute facts and brute force, arbitrary power stripped of any normative claim to legitimacy or legality.

This was Schmitt's chief claim, that political power is essentially and necessarily arbitrary, and that the liberal aspiration to subject political power to the rule of law is an illusion. But one does not have to accept his diagnosis of the impossibility of establishing the rule of law in order to appreciate the challenge to the rule of law and the rules of corrective justice created by real and perceived emergencies. Even if the existence of an emergency is always a matter of subjective perception, the possibility that an emergency might arise is also reality that has to be reckoned with even by adherents to the rule of law. The real value of Schmitt's analysis is that, by pointing us away from the objective existence of an emergency, it points us toward an understanding of the other conditions that trigger the state of emergency. And, at the same time, it moves us toward an understanding of what perpetuates the state of emergency (and what perpetuating a state of emergency involves) that even those of us who remain committed to affirming the rule of law and applying the principles of corrective justice have to contend with.

What triggers the state of emergency after all is not anything as simple as the objective existence of an emergency or threat to personal or national security. On Schmitt's view, the assertion that such a threat exists is inherently subjective and subject to the inherently arbitrary authority of the sovereign, and he goes to great lengths to establish the lack of any necessary correspondence between what the sovereign declares and what an objective observer would agree is an emergency situation that justifies overriding rights and suspending the rule of law. And he is surely right to warn us against thinking that in every situation in which the logic of the state of emergency prevails, there is an objective threat. What *is* a constant feature of the situations in which the logic of the state of emergency is applied (above and beyond the ever-present element of arbitrary power) is a breakdown in the conditions that enable us to apply the ordinary rules of justice—not just a breakdown in the objective political conditions, but a breakdown in the *conceptual* distinctions on which the ordinary rules of justice depend.

Take the most basic conceptual preconditions for establishing the rules of corrective justice. In order to apply the rules of corrective justice that protect property rights and ensure just transfers, it must be possible to distinguish just from unjust transfers and to make clear assignments of moral responsibility for the commission of unjust acts (e.g., unjustified forced expropriations). It must be possible in other words to distinguish the victims and the perpetrators.

Facts on the ground confound these distinctions. They do not necessarily confound our ability to discern the victims of the situation, but they do make it extremely difficult to discern the perpetrators or to separate them from a broader, blameless or at least less blameworthy population, in which they are embedded. In short, they make it very difficult to make the requisite judgments about agency and moral responsibility. Facts on the ground confound our ability to assign moral responsibility to the present-day *de facto* occupants of the property by dispersing responsibility across multiple actors, by generating innocent parties (blameless children and good faith purchasers) and interspersing them amongst the present-day occupants, and by embodying a mixed set of motives that blurs the distinction between morally culpable actions and actions that are justified by "necessity" (even from the standpoint of corrective justice). Together, the diffusion of moral responsibility and the mixture of motives make it near to impossible to draw the clear-cut distinctions that the canons of corrective justice demand.

The diffusion of responsibility accomplished by facts on the ground is intimately related to the condition of "normalcy" toward which established settlements tend. A community in which people go about the ordinary business of civilian life, working, having a family, setting up businesses and homes, grabbing a slice of Domino's Pizza, and visiting their grandchildren around the corner is a state of affairs in which the presence of at least some people who are blameless seems undeniable, and in which a still greater number of people have only a tenuous connection to the original acts of wrongdoing that led to the founding of the community.

In the case of Israeli settlements and land development projects intended for Jews, there a diffusion of responsibility across multiple actors and a further diffusion of responsibility across time, as one generation gives rise to another and the original founders become outnumbered by new residents who were not directly involved in the actions that led to the founding, and may not even be aware of them. The diffusion of responsibility is exacerbated by the blurring of the distinction between public and private action that has been a significant feature of Zionist land settlement practices since the earliest efforts were undertaken to establish Jewish settlements in pre-state Palestine. The blurring of the boundary between public and private action has been a feature of virtually all of the Jewish property development projects undertaken before and after the establishment of the Israeli state and is by no means confined to the occupied territories, although it is a salient feature there as well.

The point is made with its greatest force when we look at the Zionist land acquisition practices that would seem to conform most closely to the prevailing norms of private, voluntary, market-based legal transfers, the land acquisition practices implemented by the budding Zionist organizations and their purchasing agents in the period prior to the establishment of the Jewish state. In its early phases, the three guiding objectives of the Zionist movement were "Jewish political autonomy," "Jewish labor," and "Jewish land," the understanding being that each was a prerequisite for the others. The pursuit of these three objectives was not necessarily linked to the maximalist of vision of a Greater Israel—that was a matter over which the Zionist movement was philosophically divided, and even those who supported an expansionist vision philosophically were led by pragmatic calculations to limit their territorial aspirations to only a part of Palestine and to concede the rest to the Arab population.[35] Likewise, the pursuit of the right of political self-determination wasn't necessarily linked to the idea of a Jewish *state*—that too was a matter of internal controversy, with some schools of Zionist thought favoring the establishment of a Jewish "homeland," a sub-state form of political autonomy within a larger multiethnic state, and only gradually succumbing to the emergence of the statist vision as the dominant school of Zionist thought. But the pursuit of even these limited territorial and political aspirations in a land that was populated by Arabs, ruled over by foreign powers (first the Ottomans, then the British), and hampered by laws that restricted the ability of Jews to purchase property, had to rely on the same basic technique of land acquisition that would later come to be identified with the policy of "creating facts" in the occupied territories. Notwithstanding the predominance of technically voluntary land sale transactions as the preferred mechanism for acquiring land, and notwithstanding the nominally private nature of these transactions, the political and legal constraints that the early Zionists faced forced them to adopt as a conscious strategy the establishment of *de facto* possession with the aim of gaining *de jure* recognition. This strategy was used to pursue a constellation of collectivist and nationalist goals, carried out by quasi-public, quasi-private, proto-state institutions with a mixture of market-oriented and socialist features.

Thus, in the first phase of Zionist settlement, which took place in the pre-state period from the late nineteenth century until the eve of the 1948 war, the favored mechanism for acquiring land was private purchase and sale agreements. Privately funded and owned corporations were established by Zionist organizations with the specific purpose of purchasing land. Their purchasing agents would enter into land sale agreements with the self-designated owners of "Arab land," local "notables," whose legal authority to sell the land was contested within the Arab community in light of the feudal arrangements that prevailed, but who simply disregarded concerns about the "proletarianization" of the Palestinian peasantry in pursuit of their own profit. Notwithstanding the passage of a British statute aimed at prohibiting these sales, willing buyers and willing sellers found ways to circumvent the legal restrictions on purchases by Jews,[36]

---

35. Gershon Shafir, LAND, LABOR, AND THE ORIGINS OF THE ISRAELI-PALESTINIAN CONFLICT (1996), xxiii.

36. On the British Land Transfer Ordinance of 1921, which restricted the sale of property to Jews, *see* Bisharat, *Land, Law, and Legitimacy*, at 494–97.

and most of the land acquired for Jewish settlement prior to the establishment of the Jewish state was acquired through this means.

In the same way that the conventional distinction between private (voluntary) and public (forced) transfers breaks down in the context of the early history of land settlement in Israel, this context also demonstrates a fusion of public and private *functions*, with private land acquisition serving as the basis for establishing political sovereignty—and communal institutions providing the means to acquire private property, which in turn was dedicated to collectivist labor and economic organizations. The early Zionists developed a variety of collectivist institutions and modes of economic organization, which subsumed private ownership to collective forms of governance, and the public distribution of resources and employment, and other public (e.g., nationalist) ends. Although, from a strictly legal point of view, these organizations were private—privately funded, privately owned and operated, staffed by private purchasing agents and other private officers—their internal organization was collectivist, and their aim was to lay the groundwork for a socialist Jewish nation and a socialist Jewish nation-state. Yet these socialist practices could no more be divided from the capitalist practices of a market economy that governed the larger economy than could the public, political dimension of these practices be divided from their private aspect. Ironically, the collective modes of property ownership developed by Zionist organizations served to give Jews the competitive edge they needed to prevail (or even just survive) in the market for labor and property in their competition with the local Arab population. Nonmarket methods and values determined relations within the Jewish population, but relations between Jews and Arabs took place primarily according to the norms of the market. One implication of this, as we have seen, is that many of the property transfers from Arabs to Jews occurred through the "normal" means of the market. Yet the mere fact that a land transfer occurred through the mechanisms does not dispose of the question of its initial—or later—validity.[37]

Many other distinctions that are usually subsumed under the basic public/private distinction can be seen to collapse as a result of the legally, politically, and morally ambiguous circumstances of the time. Such basic distinctions as intent versus effect, intentional harms versus accidents, fact versus value, past versus present, legality versus illegality, even the seemingly fundamental distinction of principle versus pragmatism breaks down. The supposed opposition between considerations of moral principle (i.e., corrective justice) and considerations of practical necessity and *realpolitik* itself collapses in light of the fact that *every* action undertaken in this volatile context is fueled by perceived, urgent needs. Even the fundamental distinction between religious and secular, spiritual and material domains, breaks down in the context of the "Holy Land," where both

---

37. *See* Shafir, LAND, LABOR, AND ORIGINS, 45–90.

Jews and Arabs ground their claims of ownership not only in the facts of occupancy and the urgency of present needs, but also in claims of historic and divine right.

This, then, is the chief distinguishing characteristic that marks almost every land acquisition project undertaken to advance the Zionist objectives of Jewish land settlement and sovereignty in Israel: not just the urgency of the needs that propelled the pursuit of these objectives, but the collapse of the most basic conceptual distinctions that together constitute the conceptual field of the normal (i.e., the material, the secular, the legal, the politically acceptable, the moral). The practice of creating facts on the ground both instantiates and responds to this condition of conceptual breakdown. Having broken down this conceptual field, and having licensed the violation of the ordinary rules that apply in normal conditions, the practice of establishing facts on the ground then operates to reconstitute the normal, "normalizing" the conditions that emerged out of the violation of the normal.

Regardless of the particular method employed by the public/private agents of Zionist policy—market transactions executed by nongovernmental or quasi-private actors, forced expropriations implemented by the state under the emergency laws or the laws of eminent domain—we see the same basic strategy of establishing *de facto* possession (whose legal or moral validity is susceptible to challenge) with the aim of having it turn into a kind of *de jure* possession, insulated by law, or if not by law, then by morality, or if not by morality, then by the prevailing winds of political opinion, from challenge. This is the basic "lesson that the Jews learnt" during the pre-state period of settlement, namely "that physical buildings had to be backed up by a demographic presence."[38] It is this lesson that led them to pursue the basic strategy of establishing as significant a *de facto* demographic presence as they could, through whatever means were most likely to gain *de jure* recognition. Where the established system of property law served their interests, the Zionists followed it. Where the established property regime thwarted their interests, they found ways to subvert it. But even when the law stood in the way, the basic logic of legal exceptions served to endow the circumvention of the law with its own kind of legality, allowing Zionists to claim either that their purchases were within the letter of the law, or alternatively, that (following the basic legal logic of prescription) holdings that were initially illegal had ripened into a *de jure* right to possession.

This was the strategy pursued within the constraints of British law, which sought to limit Jewish purchases of Arab property, in the period leading up to the establishment of the Jewish state. And this was the strategy pursued without constraint in the immediate aftermath of the war of 1948, when the newly founded Jewish state found itself, after successfully fending off Arab attacks, in

38. Facts on the Ground, 1.

possession of both sovereignty and land—including land that was privately owned and vacated by Arabs. As has been well documented, "a massive population transfer" had occurred by the war's end, with "Palestinians . . . forced to flee east and Jewish residents of the Old City . . . expelled west."[39] The mass exodus of Palestinians provided the newly established Jewish state with the opportunity to effect a large-scale transfer of ownership from Arabs to Jews, an opportunity that was quickly seized on and implemented through a variety of legal techniques. At the time, taking over the homes of Arab refuges satisfied pressing needs of the nascent state, needs of both nation-building and state-building, including housing the thousands of Jewish refugees who escaped from Europe during and after World War II, and the thousands more who took flight from Arab countries and other non-European countries where Jews were no longer welcome.[40]

These needs point not only to the blending of public and private objectives and merging of public and private agents, but also to the mixture of motives that, as much as the diffusion of responsibility, confounds our ability to draw the conceptual distinctions on which the ordinary law of just versus unjust transfers depend. The oft-heard condemnation of Zionism as a colonialist project, like most condemnations of colonialism, rests on easy distinctions between motives of "need" and motives of "greed."[41] But how is one to draw the distinction between need and greed (let alone settle the question of whether "Zionism is colonialism") in a context like that outlined above? If ever there were a situation governed by the emergency logic of necessity, one would think that housing refugees from the Holocaust (or providing refuge for the Jews of Europe *before* they were caught up in the maw of Holocaust) would be it. Yet it is also the case that expansionist dreams of a Greater Israel have fueled some of the settlement activity, and even the nonexpansionist policies of settlement have involved land grabs, i.e., forced, and in many cases, unjustified dispossession. Terms like colonialism, and sloganeering like "Zionism is colonialism," presuppose a facile distinction between motives of greed (e.g., land grabs, power grabs) and motives of need (e.g., survival and autonomy), which a nuanced grasp of the complex motives behind Israeli and Zionist settlement policy belies.

The needs for safe refuge and political self-determination highlighted by the Holocaust, which provide the indispensable backdrop to the history of Jewish land settlement in Israel/Palestine, bring us to the third theory of normalization that helps to shed light on the phenomenon of facts on the ground—the Zionist conception of restoring Jews to a condition of "political normalcy." It bears recalling

---

39. FACTS ON THE GROUND, 3.

40. *See* Bisharat, *Land, Law, and Legitimacy*, 505 (describing the "exigencies facing the new state of Israel" that "intensified the Zionist movement's impetus for land acquisitions.")

41. *See, e.g.*, Kedar, *Legal Transformation*, 996 ("I believe . . . that like in other settlers' societies, greed for land was the crucial motivating force.").

that the Zionist movement arose in late nineteenth-century Europe as a response to what seemed to be the otherwise insoluble predicament of Jewish life. Notwithstanding the existence for centuries of Jewish communities in their midst, European countries persistently discriminated against Jews, shutting them out of various professions, educational and social institutions, and denying them the right to own or farm agricultural land and other civil and political rights, such as the right to hold office. The increase in the incidence of violent anti-Semitic attacks in Eastern Europe, and the concomitant disillusion with the path of assimilation in Western Europe convinced the early Zionists that the only cure for the "abnormal" status of the Jews was "political normalcy." "To become a people like all other people" was the basic prescription of all Jewish political ideologies at the time that sought to find a cure to the problem of anti-Semitism.

For Zionists, that meant that Jews must "become a nation like all other nations."[42] As the historian Yuri Slezkine put it, Zionism "argued that the proper way to overcome Jewish vulnerability was not for everyone else to become like Jews but for the Jews to become like everyone else."[43] And to become like everyone else, in the context of nineteenth-century Europe, was to become a political nation, possessed of its own nation-state, within which Jews would be allowed to exercise all of the economic and social rights denied them by gentile states. The recent rise in anti-Semitism was seen as proof that even when host states extended legal rights and privileges to Jews, they could not be relied on to continue to afford Jews tolerance or equal treatment. And the Dreyfus Affair was seen as proof that even when gentile society professed to accept Jews (so long as they shed their offensive "tribal" ways), and even when Jews accepted this invitation to assimilate (through conversion or other forms of cultural "self-betterment"), anti-Semitism was bound to resurface and express itself in ugly forms of persecution. The long and the short of it was that there was no solution to "the Jewish question" other than overcoming the "abnormal" condition of being a religious minority, a stateless nation, a landless people, dwelling in another nation-state. And to overcome that abnormal condition was precisely to attain the status of "political normalcy," which, according to the Zionist diagnosis and prescription for the Jewish problem, entailed *Jewish political sovereignty* over land, *Jewish ownership* of land, and *Jewish labor* on the land.[44] *What* land was initially up for grabs, as early Zionists considered the possibilities that were dangled for creating a homeland for the Jews in other parts of the world, such as Uganda. But the cult of the land and the basic idea that a nation-state with territorial sovereignty—"a nation like all other nations"—was necessary to

---

42. *See* Anita Shapira, *Herzl, Ahad Ha-'Am, and Berdichevsky: Comments on their Nationalist Concepts*, 4 JEWISH HIST. 59 (1990).

43. Yuri Slezkine, THE JEWISH CENTURY 2 (2004).

44. *See generally* SHAFIR, LAND, LABOR, AND ORIGINS.

solve the "pathology" of the Jewish condition in the Diaspora were central tenets of the Zionist movement.

It has often been noted that the Zionist diagnosis of "the Jewish question" mirrored the diagnosis of the Jewish problem of the European anti-Semite. The problem for (or with) Jews from both perspectives was that they were "pariahs," "unproductive," "parasites" who, failing to perform the productive work of tilling the land, were forced into the role of "usurers" in the budding capitalist economy. Jews, on this analysis, had produced both an overly large capitalist class and a landless proletariat, which explained their overrepresentation among both capitalists and communists.[45] What they sorely lacked was a core of landed cultivators and a self-sufficient economy based on the "dignity of labor."

Just as the Zionist diagnosis of Jewish "abnormality" mirrored the stereotypes of the anti-Semite, so too their proposed cure of political normality mirrored the contemporary visions of political and economic independence that abounded in the larger European culture. To find in nationalism the cure for political and economic dependence and physical vulnerability was nothing more than to subscribe to the reigning political ideology of the day. That said, relatively few people subscribed to the Zionist vision of establishing a Jewish nation-state until the close of World War II.[46] As David Myers and Gershon Shafir have observed, the period in which Zionism arose was a period of enormous intellectual and political ferment in which most Jews absorbed with solving "the Jewish question" gravitated toward other political ideologies, including various forms of socialism, internationalism, and nonstatist (or even antistatist) forms of Jewish cultural autonomy or religious rebirth.[47] Only a narrow segment of the Jewish population endorsed Zionism. Non-Jewish support was even weaker, though Zionists did succeed in obtaining some backing for their political project of establishing a Jewish homeland in Palestine, most crucially from the British, who sometimes thwarted but at other times supported the Zionist goal of creating a Jewish homeland in mandatory Palestine. However, it was not until the full horror of the Holocaust had been revealed that the majority of Jews, and the world community at large, endorsed the creation of a Jewish state and, with that, the Zionist aspiration for "political normalcy." As Gershon Shafir observes, "territorial nationalism—so different from and alien to the [traditional] ethnic Jewish way of life—was, as it were, imposed on Jews as a last resort, in response to Nazi persecutions and genocide, and forced migration from Eastern Europe,

---

45. On the stereotyping of Jews as pariahs, parasites, and usurers, *see* THE JEWISH WRITINGS: HANNAH ARENDT (Jerome Kohn and Ron H. Feldman eds., 2007), in particular, "Antisemitism," *id.* at 52.

46. *See* Shafir, LAND, LABOR, AND ORIGINS, 7; *see also* David N. Myers, "Beyond 'Statism': A Call to Rethink Jewish Collectivity," unpublished manuscript on file with the author.

47. *See id.*

North Africa, and the Middle East."[48] The support for the creation of the State of Israel following World War II, like much of the support for Israel today, rested on the perception that "in this century, the potentially tragic consequences of the severance of Jews from a territory of their own were only too clearly revealed, justifying a desire for *political normalcy* by standards of the modern world order."[49]

Only with a fuller picture of the practical and conceptual conditions of normalcy can we understand what precisely is involved in the normalization of "the abnormal," whether the reference is to the abnormal condition of "a people without a land," or to exigent conditions that lead to the suspension of the rules that ordinarily govern land transactions, as in a state of emergency. Insights drawn from Foucault and Schmitt's conceptions of normality/abnormality provide us with that understanding. The fascinating thing about the case of Israel/Palestine is that from a Zionist perspective all these different conceptions of abnormality converge: the abnormal political condition of the Jews *is* the exigency that, from a Zionist perspective, serves to justify the Jewish acquisition of privately owned "Arab land." On this view, Jewish life is a perpetual emergency, which justifies the creation of facts on the ground, which in turn generate a new condition of normality.

The siege mentality of the emergency theory of rights and power encoded in Zionism is not, of course, unique to Zionism. The Zionist case is but an example of a much broader phenomenon, the use of emergency powers to establish a new regime, and the subsequent normalization of that state of emergency. The phenomenon that Schmitt examined and that formed the disturbing core of his theory of politics, the normalization of the state of exception, is a subject of increasing concern, as more and more countries around the world invoke states of emergency and institute emergency law without any foreseeable end. The practice of creating facts on the ground is fueled by the same basic logic as emergency law, which holds that exigent circumstances justify overriding the laws that "ordinarily" protect civil rights. Normalizing the state of emergency and legitimating the changes in the distribution of rights and power that result in emergency conditions is the ultimate function of the policy of creating facts on the ground.

This understanding can help us see more clearly the range of practices to which the concept of facts on the ground applies, and to get a better grasp of the normative implications of the practice in light of that conceptual range. What I hope this analysis shows is that the concept of creating facts on the ground applies to a much broader range of practices than is commonly understood. The distinguishing features that my analysis has tried to reveal are not limited to the

48. Shafir, LAND, LABOR, AND ORIGINS, 8.
49. *Id.* at xxii (emphasis added.)

case of settlements in the occupied territories; they are present in the land settlement practices implemented on the other side of the Green Line in Israel Proper—and innumerable other land acquisition and development projects around the world. Indeed, the main conceptual implication of this analysis is that it is very difficult to draw a clear line between land settlement projects that partake of the logic of creating facts on the ground and those that do not. On my analysis of the meaning of the term, it should be understood as applying not only to clearly illegal occupations of property of the sort that we see in the occupied territories but also to acquisitions of property of merely questionable validity and perhaps even to some acquisitions that comport with the rules defining legally valid transfers but are nonetheless of dubious, or ambiguous, moral validity. So understood, the term applies to a broader range of practices in the Israeli case, not limited to the occupied territories, and also to a wide variety of phenomena outside the Israeli case. Besides the obvious examples of states engaged in classic projects of colonialism, there are innumerable examples of states, sub-state groups, and other actors (e.g., squatter movements) engaging in the creation of facts on the ground, amassing private property through whatever available means, circumventing legal obstacles, and transforming private property into political sovereignty or sub-state forms of political autonomy.

Widening our understanding of the practices appropriately described as creating facts on the ground should help to correct a disturbing tendency toward exceptionalism that dogs the discourse about Israeli policy, and that indeed has dogged Jewish ventures throughout Jewish history, even when the venture is to try to escape the condition of exceptionality for a condition of "normalcy." The exceptionalism of the pro-Israel camp is a "positive exceptionalism" that insists on the moral superiority of the Jewish state as supposedly evidenced in such doctrines as the Israeli military doctrine of purity of arms, according to which Israeli soldiers are supposed to answer the highest moral standards even on the battlefield. Alongside (and in considerable tension with) the more pragmatic Zionist vision of becoming a "nation like all other nations," this more lofty moral vision of Israel as "a light unto other nations" has led many supporters of Israel to *disbelieve* the claims of Israel's critics, according to which its land settlement practices in the territories (and elsewhere) are unjust and unjustifiable, and have to be reversed.

On the other side of the debate, anti-Zionist discourse presents a perfect mirror image of the Zionist claim of Israeli moral exceptionalism, only here the exceptionalism is of a negative sort, singling Israel out for criticism, ignoring comparable or still more egregious actions undertaken by other political actors around the world, and subjecting Israel to a double standard. This practice of selectively subjecting Israel to a higher moral standard than other nations and actors, which is blind to the ubiquity and the occasional benignity of the practices dubbed "creating facts on the ground," is another disturbing variant of Israeli exceptionalism.

Both of these forms of exceptionalism need to be rejected. In my own view, the Israeli case is not exceptional but rather exemplary. It is exemplary because Jews epitomize the features that lead groups in general to seek to form colonies and that lead them, further, to adopt the strategy of creating facts on the ground in order to overcome the obstacles to achieving that end. As seen in the analysis above of "the Jewish problem," the "problem" with Jews in the Diaspora has always been their "refugee status," their status as "pariahs," "parasites," a landless nation within another nation, the quintessential Malthusian "surplus population." Other European colonialist movements also were motivated by the desire to solve the problem of their own "surplus populations." They obviously had other motives as well, but the motives of greed are not easily separated from the motives of need, in particular the need to satisfy the basic needs of economic and physical survival of these "surplus populations."

Inasmuch as other groups have assumed the status of refugees, diasporic populations, surplus populations whose basic needs can't, or won't, be met by the "home country," all these groups are now (the social equivalent of) Jews. That is, they occupy the same place as the Jews occupied in the Jewish question—which is to say, they occupy no place that they can call their own. What the Jew in the Jewish question attests to is the stubborn physicality, the sheer materiality, of human existence. The problem with a population deemed to be "pariah" or "surplus" is that it has to go somewhere. Ruling out "the perennial suggestion for solving the Jewish question by slaying all the Jews,"[50] it has to *be* somewhere, and that means that there has to be a *place* for them to be. This alone may explain why the logic of property—inherently exclusionary, innately absolutist, fixated on such base, materialist concerns as land and other physical and economic resources—is difficult, if not impossible to transcend. Even the most integrationist, "anti-groupist" social philosophy must come to terms with people's basic need for a physical place to be—a place in which to live and work and satisfy one's basic physical and economic needs. And that means coming to terms with the competition for scarce resources, and the complex group dynamics that competition sets in motion.

Of course, the need for *a* place to be does not by itself dictate the choice of *where* to be, and it is always possible to fantasize another place devoid of the "demographic problem" that necessitates the exclusionary tactics of facts on the ground—and to castigate the group that has engaged in those tactics for failing to find that mythical other place. It is possible, in other words, to fault the Zionists not for seeking to fulfill their basic aims—sovereignty over land, property rights in land, labor on the land—but for seeking to fulfill them in Palestine where another population already had established the moral (if not the legal) rights to territorial sovereignty and ownership. But where, then, should the Zionists have

---

50. Arendt, Jewish Writings, 47.

sought to fulfill their aims? Here again we confront the stubborn materiality, the sheer physicality, of human existence. Follow every counterfactual (e.g., the Uganda option) to its bitter end and you will find there—a bitter end. Because the bitter fact is that there is no place on earth where the basic aims of Zionism could have been pursued with any realistic chance of success without displacing another population.

The equally bitter irony—and tragedy—is that in implementing their aims, the Zionists recreated the Jewish question as the Palestinian question. It has been said that the Palestinians have become the Jews' Jews and the Arabs' Arabs—as sure a testimony to the troubling persistence of "the Jewish question" as one could find. Whoever occupies the status of the refugee, the displaced person, the dispossessed, is destined to become the pariah, the parasite, the "surplus" population so long as the logic of property (and economic competition between groups) persists. That logic will inevitably motivate attempts on the part of the pariah population to establish facts on the ground in a desperate attempt to try to get back "home." This may not constitute a justification for a policy that inflicts the same harm on others that those who engage in it are trying to heal. But it helps us to understand what motivates the policy, and what that policy entails, both conceptually and practically. And with that understanding in place, we can move toward a less simplistic assessment of the policy's moral and political validity.

From the earliest days of modern Zionism, private land acquisition and the establishment of political sovereignty have gone hand in hand in Israel, bearing out the old legal realist dictum that property and sovereignty, private ownership and the exercise of political power, are not two distinct things, but rather, two inseparable aspects of a single phenomenon.[51] The legal realists made this point about established nation-states whose exercise of sovereignty was a given. But the point is equally applicable to nationalist movements involved in the *creation* of sovereign states. Indeed, the fusion of property and sovereignty is more readily apparent in the processes of state creation and nation building than it is in the context of established states, which can more easily conceal the dependency of private rights on the exercise of power by political entities. In quite visible ways, nationalist movements, colonialist movements and the proto-state organizations that they spawn fuse the public functions of establishing and exercising political sovereignty over territory with the functions of private land acquisition, allocation, and ownership. They do so in pursuit of objectives that cannot always be neatly separated into morally justificatory ("need") and morally blameworthy ("greed") categories. And they do so through agents and via methods that cannot be cleanly separated out into morally blameworthy as opposed to blameless actors and actions. It is in recognition of these ineliminable political, moral, legal, and factual ambiguities that we have coined the concept of creating facts on the ground.

51. *See* Morris Cohen, *Property and Sovereignty*, 13 CORNELL L. Q. 11 (1927).

6. COMMONS AND LEGALITY

AVITAL MARGALIT

I. INTRODUCTION

In recent years, scholars of various disciplines have examined commons governance in highly detailed and nuanced analyses.[1] This scholarship is characterized by an attempt to situate the commons in their economic, political, legal, ecological, social, and cultural environments. Instead of a reductive one-dimensional analysis focusing either on the internal arrangements of the commons or on state regulation, we now have multidimensional dynamic analyses that describe the interactions between the commons and its different environments.

Despite enriching our understanding of the interplay among the physical, social, and political dimensions of the commons, most of this literature adheres to rational-actor theories of social life, neglecting the cultural life of the commons. The absence of cultural analysis is most evident in their treatment of law. While the current literature calls for the utilization of a variety of conceptual frames and theories derived from the social sciences in order to provide sophisticated analyses of the environments in which the commons operate, upon encountering the legal realm they adopt, almost invariably, the concept of law as an external set of rules and sanctions. Law is habitually viewed as an externally imposed constraint, and even, on occasion, as a threat to the efficient management of the common resource.[2] While at times, the law does indeed amount to such a matrix of rules and sanctions, the place, role, and meaning of law in the life of the commons is much more complex and should also be studied from a cultural perspective. Seen from such a perspective, legality, constituted by the rules of

1. A bibliography prepared in 1989 contained about 5000 studies of common property cases and hundreds more studies have been published since. Important collections of such studies can be found in The Question of the Commons: The Culture and Ecology of Communal Resources (Bonnie J. McCay and James A. Acheson, eds., 1987), Common property Resources: Ecology and Community-Based Sustainable Development (Fikret Berkes ed., 1989), Rights to Nature: Ecological, economic, and Political Principles of Institutions for the Environment (Susan Hanna, Carl Folke, and Karl-Goran Maler eds., 1996), The Drama of the Commons (Elinor Ostrom, Thomas Dietz, Nives Dolšak, Paul C. Stern, Susan Stonich, and Elke U. Weber eds., 2002), and The Commons in the New Millennium: Challenges and Adaptation (Nives Dolšak and Elinor Ostrom, eds., 2003).

2. *See* Arun Agrawal, *Common Resources, and Institutional Sustainability*, *in* The Drama of the Commons, *supra* note 1, at 41, 58.

state law and the internal law of the commons, operating through both formal and informal sanctions and embedded in the everyday life of the commons, is accorded its place as endogenous to the commons phenomena.

Analyzing the current trend in the theory of the commons with regard to the contextualization of the commons, and perceiving the commons as organizations having internal structure and culture and interacting with their environments, this chapter suggests a more dynamic, multidimensional frame of analysis, one that will examine the interaction between internal variables of the commons and environmental variables, and do so along a time axis. Moreover, exposing the assumptions underlying current theory regarding the role of law in relation to the commons, this chapter offers a cultural approach with which to analyze the relationship between the commons and legality. The efficacy of this socio-legal framework will be tested through the case of the *kibbutz* and its legal environment.

II. CONTEXTUALIZING THE COMMONS

The vast literature on the commons includes general theories or models of the commons as well as more case-specific analyses. Both approaches are necessary components of our discourse on the commons, but in this part I shall briefly demonstrate and evaluate the turn to contextuality in commons analysis.

A. The Turn Towards Contextualization in Commons' Analysis

1. The Economically-Oriented Perspective The classical, economic-oriented analysis of the commons[3] begins with the work of Garrett Hardin and Harold Demsetz, although it is by now well established that both were referring to an "open access" regime and not to a commons or communal property, where a resource is owned or used by a group according to specific rules and regulations.[4]

---

3. For an analysis of the economic-oriented formulation of the commons problem as an artifact of the economic professional community, *see* the argument of Riles in Ravi Kanbur and Annelise Riles, *And Never the Twain Shall Meet? An Exchange on the Strengths and Weaknesses of Anthropology and Economics in Analyzing the Commons, in* The Contested Commons: Conversations Between Economists and Anthropologists 266 (Pranab Bardham and Isha Ray, eds., 2008).

4. *See* Robert C. Ellickson, *Property in Land,* 102 Yale L.J. 1315, 1322–1323 (1993); A. P. Lino Grima and Fikret Berkes, *Natural Resources: Access, Right-to-Use and Management,* in Common Property Resources, *supra* note, 1 at 32, 38–39; and Henry A. Regier, Richard V. Mason, and Fikert Berkes, *Reforming the Use of Natural Resources, id.* at 110, 114–118. On the typology of property regimes, *see generally* Margaret A. McKean, *Success on the Commons—A Comparative Examination of Institutions for Common Property Resource Management,* 4 J. Theoretical Politics 247, 250–253 (1992).

Hardin's famous prediction of "the tragedy of the commons"[5] was based on a parable, and began with a call for the readers to "picture a pasture open to all." Under this analysis, the rational actions of self-interested persons in a commons tend to lead to undesirable consequences both for the individual and the community as a whole. As Hardin concluded, "[F]reedom in a commons brings ruin to all." Hardin's solution to the commons problem is "mutual coercion that is mutually agreed upon by the majority of the people affected."

Hardin's analysis of the commons was one-dimensional. It looked at the interaction among his hypothetical self-interested individuals living in a world without any historical, social, or cultural context. The political context appeared only if we understand Hardin as suggesting state regulation as a solution, but even in this regard, Hardin gave no account of the nature of such state and its other relationships with those subject to its power.

Demsetz's[6] contribution to the literature on the commons was a cost-benefit analysis that attempted not only to explain the transition from common property to private property rights, but also to substantiate the ascendancy of the latter. According to Demsetz, the primary function of property rights was to create incentives to internalize externalities (external costs and benefits) that arise when the gains of internalization become greater than its costs. Thus, the emergence of property rights is connected to the emergence of new externalities. In a commons, no one person bears all of the costs that that person's exercise of his communal right generates. Others bear most of these costs. Hence, there is an incentive to overexploit the resource.[7] Private property rights constitute a solution because each person shares both the costs and the benefits from his own activities. This internalization guarantees that each owner will fully take into account the effects of his own activities on his neighbors and on subsequent generations.

To illustrate his arguments, Demsetz described the transition from a commons into a private property land regime among Indians of the Labrador Peninsula.[8] The relevant externality in this case is the overhunting of game triggered by the introduction of a fur trade that increased the value of furs. Demsetz's efficiency theory of property regimes, though telling an evolutionary story, was mainly one-dimensional and, other than acknowledging certain changes in external circumstances as the source for new kinds of externalities, focused exclusively on the manifestation of an individually-oriented perspective and

---

5. Garrett Hardin, *The Tragedy of the Commons*, 162 Science 1243 (1968).

6. Harold Demsetz, *Toward a Theory of Property Rights*, 57 Am. Econ. Rev. 347 (1967).

7. *Id.* at 354.

8. Demsetz was criticized for his selective reliance on anthropological information provided by Eleanor Leacock in her research on the Montagne Indians. *See* Eric T. Freyfogle, *Land Use and the Study of Early American History*, 94 Yale L.J. 717, 740 (1985).

maximization of individual well-being.[9] Demsetz also disregarded other cultural, social, and political aspects of the community whose history he analyzed, as well as the ramifications of the encounter between this community and the outside world as evidenced in the practices and norms of fur trading and in the colonial political power supporting this trade. [10]

Subsequent scholars have refined Demsetz's cost-benefit analysis by examining the efficiency of the commons in a somewhat more contextualized manner.[11] A good example is Robert Ellickson's contention, based on the histories of American pioneer settlements, that commonses are more efficient in what he termed "large events," where there are increasing returns to scale and the desirability of spreading risks.[12] Ellickson concluded that, where rules and practices among members are already established, the response of a group is more efficient than the response of individuals. Ellickson's analysis was more attentive to the context in which the commons operated than preceding studies. He mentioned both external variables stemming from the unique economic environment of the American frontier and internal variables such as the rules and practices of the group. However, Ellickson utilized the history of the pioneer settlements merely to illustrate a prestated theory, and his description of the context was brief and insufficient, neglecting to consider other important variables of the political and social environment.

2. The Institutional-Economic Approach Notwithstanding Hardin's and Demsetz's assertions, advanced game theory has persuasively proved the possibility of voluntary cooperation, allowing a view of the commons, not as tragically doomed, but as a viable option.[13] Empirical data has demonstrated that people in

---

9. For a critique on Hardin's and Demsetz's ontological and cultural assumptions, *see* Carol M. Rose, *Property as Storytelling: Perspectives from Game Theory, Narrative Theory, Feminist Theory*, 2 YALE J. L. & HUMANITIES 37, 40–48 (1990); James E. Krier, *The Tragedy of the Commons, Part Two*, 15 HARV. J. L. & PUB. POL'Y 325, 336–338 (1992).

10. For some elaborated theories on the transitions between property regimes that take context seriously, *see* Stuart Banner, *Transitions between Property Regimes*, 31 J. LEGAL STUD. 359 (2002); Henry E. Smith, *Exclusion Versus Governance: Two Strategies for Delineating Property Rights*, 31 J. LEGAL STUD. 453 (2002); Katrina Miriam Wyman, *From Fur to Fish: Reconsidering the Evolution of Private Property*, 80 N.Y.U. L. REV. 117 (2005); and Daniel Fitzpatrick, *Evolution and Chaos in Property Rights Systems: The Third World Tragedy of Contested Access*, 115 YALE L.J. 996 (2006).

11. Stevenson's comprehensive economic-mathematical analysis, which compared the efficiency of private and common property regimes in Swiss Alps grazing areas, can also serve as an example for a contextualized efficiency-theory of commons. Stevenson examined and compared among three different common property regimes: shared alps, community alps, and *korporation* alps, each with its unique history and governing rules. *See* Glenn G. Stevenson, COMMON PROPERTY ECONOMICS (1991).

12. Ellickson, *supra* note 4, at 1322–1344.

13. *See* ROBERT AXELROD, THE EVOLUTION OF COOPERATION (1984); MICHAEL TAYLOR, THE POSSIBILITY OF COOPERATION (1987); Elinor Ostrom, Roy Gardner, and James

various cultures have successfully developed norms and institutions that result in the efficient management of common property.[14] A dominant line of research, operating within the boundaries of rational choice theory, aims at delineating the contours of successful institutional arrangements of commons' management.

Scholars who work within this institutional perspective typically offer a list of "design principles for institutions" based on inferences made by reflecting on a substantive number of case studies of the commons.[15] While there are differences in method and emphasis among these studies, the structure of their suggestions is similar.[16] Their lists of design principles refer to the resource system, characteristics of the users' group, the institutional arrangements, and the external environment.

Elinor Ostrom's search for design principles illustrates the nature of contextualization through institutional analysis.[17] From the empirical data, Ostrom generalized several design principles, those essential elements or conditions that help account for the success of the institutions. Among these are the setting of clearly defined boundaries that differentiate common pool resources (CPRs) from cases of open access, that is, principles that constitute the institutional arrangements, such as congruency between appropriation and provision rules, and local conditions stemming from the environment in which the CPR operates, collective choice arrangements that ensure users' participation in decision-making, gradual sanctioning in cases of disobedience of the rules, and the availability of low-cost mechanisms for conflict resolution. According to Ostrom, the users' group in successful CPRs is characterized by relative stability, geographical proximity, homogeneity, and an intricate web of connections among participants who share a past and expect to share a future.

In addition to these internal design principles, Ostrom paid attention to the external environment.[18] Key is her assertion that, in order to assure the success of a CPR, there should be minimal recognition by the state of the right to organize.

Walker, Rules, Games and Common-Pool Resources (1994); and Armin Falk, Ernst Fehr, and Urs Fischbacher, *Appropriating the Commons: A Theoretical Explanation, in* The Drama of the Commons, *supra* note, 1 at 157.

14. For a concise summery of these studies and the history of the institutional analysis of the commons, see Thomas Dietz, Nives Dolšak, Elinor Ostrom, and Paul C. Stern, *The Drama of the Commons, in* The Drama of the Commons, *supra* note 1, at 3, 11–26.

15. *See* Robert Wade, *The Management of Common Property Resources: Collective Action as an Alternative to Privatization or State Regulation,* 11 Cambridge J. Eco. 95 (1987); Robert Wade, Village Republics: Economic Conditions for Collective Action in South India (1988) [1994]; and McKean, *supra* note, 4, at 257–276.

16. *See* Agrawal, *supra* note 2, at 46–54, 61–63.

17. Elinor Ostrom, Governing the Commons: The Evolution of Institutions for Collective Action (1990).

18. Another external variable mentioned by Ostrom is relevant to more complex situations of "nested" CPRs, those which are part of larger systems. *Id.* at 101–102.

Accordingly, the autonomy of the CPR should not be challenged by external government authorities.

On its face, the "design principles" are multivariant and multidimensional, referring to the many variables both internal and external to the commons. In comparison with the more traditional economic analysis, the institutional approach takes a leap forward toward the contextualization of our understanding of commons. However, as will be elaborated in the next section, the institutional analysis is limited in its effort of contextualization, and significantly more is needed in order to achieve a more sensitive contextualized analysis of the commons.

B. A Dynamic Contextualized Analysis of Commons

The institutional-economic analysis of the commons does advance our understanding of which factors enhance the probability that an efficient, self-managed commons will survive and which risks should be avoided. As many analysts have noted, while rich in insights, this approach nevertheless has several limitations that prevent it from providing an adequately complex understanding of the forces affecting the commons.[19]

First, scholars of the institutional-economic approach are apt to pay relatively little attention to the relationships between commons and their ecological, technological, economic, social, political, cultural, and institutional environments. They tend to treat commons almost as if they are isolated, neglecting to connect their findings on internal variables to external ones.[20] In more recent literature, theoretically-based criticism of such neglect may be discerned. For example, Victoria Edwards and Nathalie Steins advocated perceiving "the entire resource system, and the wider social, cultural, ecological and economic environment in which it is embedded" as the "correct subject for research."[21] In such a research

---

19. The lists of design principles should not be deemed exhaustive. Instead, they may be supplemented. A study of the commons may be enhanced by examining additional variables. For example, it may be fruitful to compare cases where the common resource is a product of existing social relations with cases where people "came to the resource" and a community evolved out of the need to manage the resource; cases where the prevailing surrounding culture stresses norms of trust and cooperation with cases of a culture of competitiveness and suspiciousness; cases where cooperation is only instrumental to solving collective action problems with cases where cooperation itself is part of the ideological tenets of the group; or cases where the surrounding political and social environment has remained relatively stable with cases where revolutions, colonialism, and other destabilizing events have occurred.

20. *See* Agrawal, *supra* note 2, at 58–59; David Mosse, *The Symbolic Making of a Common Property Resource: History, Ecology, and Locality in a Tank-irrigated Landscape in South India*, 28 DEVELOPMENT & CHANGE 467, 470 (1997).

21. *See* Victoria M. Edwards and Nathalie A. Steins, *Special Issue Introduction: The Importance of Context in Common Pool Resource Research*, 1 J. ENVIRON. POLICY PLAN. 195,

project the commons becomes embedded.[22] The outcome of expanding the scope of investigation to include the environments results in a more realistic understanding of the commons, but it comes at a price: the ability to translate reality and present its complexity in a relatively clear and simple model is lost.

Second, current studies of the institutional-economic thesis belabor the compilation of lists of design principles. The perception of design principles as lists should be replaced by the conceptualization of the principles as a set of interconnected variables, thus transferring attention to the study of causal relations.[23]

Third, the underlying assumptions of the institutional-economic analysis regarding human nature and the nature of a community further limit the scope of the investigation into the dynamic of the commons. The institutional-economic approach perceives the participants in the commons through the lenses of the rational self-interested individual, bringing into the common predetermined preferences or shaping them according to the payoff system of the institutional arrangements of the commons. The commons as a social entity or community is analyzed as a cost- minimizing mechanism. The community is conceptualized as an instrument whose goal is to promote the well-being of its members. As Annelise Riles correctly stated, such a rational actor approach fails to explain the complexity of the social world of the commons with its different patterns of norms, rules, sanctions, and behaviors.[24]

Incorporating the frames of thought suggested by the institutional-economic approach with those offered in more recent writings, which look at the commons from a cultural perspective, this section of the paper offers a structure for a dynamic contextualized analysis of the commons. This structure examines four dimensions of the commons as follows.

1. **Inside the common.** When studying a commons, the researcher looks at variables such as the physical characteristics of the resource and their symbolic meanings;[25] the mechanisms of resource management; the

---

196 (1999). For a suggestion of an analytical framework for the analysis of contextual factors in multiple-use commons, *see* Victoria M. Edwards and Nathalie A. Steins, *A Framework for Analysing Contextual Factors in Common Pool Resource Research*, 1 J. ENVIRON. POLICY PLAN. 205 (1999).

22. *See* Rob van Ginkel, *Contextualizing Marine Resource Use: A Case from the Netherlands*, 1 J. ENVIRON. POLICY PLAN. 223, 224 (1999).

23. *See* Agrawal, *supra* note 2, at 45–46, 53 ("lists of factors can be only a starting point in the search for a compelling theorizing of how these factors are related to each other and to outcomes. Instead of focusing on lists of factors that apply to all commons institutions, it is likely more fruitful to focus on configurations that contribute to sustainability").

24. *See* Riles, *supra* note 3.

25. On the symbolic meaning of common resources, see Mosse, *supra* note 20, at 472. On the symbolic meaning of resources, *see generally* Arjun Appadurai, *Introduction:*

content of the norms and rules governing the commons; the life-cycle stage of the organization;[26] the level of obedience to the rules and legitimization accorded to decision-making institutions, an in-depth study of the social and demographic characteristics of the users' group and the nature of social dynamics among the group's members (including social stratification, power relations, and conflict management), as well as the symbolic cultural life of the commons.

2. **Outside the commons**. The researcher also studies the ecological, economic, social, and political environments in which the commons is situated. Key is the study of the institutional arrangements and modes of operation of the state and state agencies. It may also be the case that the commons is part of an organizational field that mediates between it and the state.[27] Where relevant, it may be beneficial to examine the characteristics of such an organizational field, its cultural life, and power structure, as it may have a significant effect on the culture and practices of the commons.
3. **Studying interactions**. Since internal and external variables interact with each other in a multiplicity of forms and directions, generating diverse effects on the commons, it may be useful for the researcher to pay attention to the patterns of such interactions.
4. **Studying changes**. A study of the commons conducted along a time axis may enrich our understanding of the mode of operation and effects of internal and external variables, the interactions between them at any

---

Commodities and the Politics of Value, *in* THE SOCIAL LIFE OF THINGS 3 (Arjun Appadurai ed., 1986); Helga Ditmar, THE SOCIAL PSYCHOLOGY OF MATERIAL POSSESSIONS: TO HAVE IS TO BE (1992); HISTORY FROM THINGS: ESSAYS ON MATERIAL CULTURE (Steven Luban and W. Davia Kingery, eds., 1993).

26. Similar to other organizations, the life of a self-managed commons entails different stages of development and transition. Ostrom suggested that the same theory and analysis may be applied to study the processes of institutional provision and institutional change. *See* Ostrom, *supra* note 17, at 140–141. It is, however, questionable whether the interplay among the various internal and external design principles would have the same patterns of interaction, independent of the life-cycle stage that the commons is experiencing at the time of the investigation.

27. According to Scott, organizational fields are defined in terms of shared cognition or normative frameworks, or a common regulative system. *See* W. Richard Scott, INSTITUTIONS AND ORGANIZATIONS 56 (1995). According to this conceptualization, organizations that do not "belong" to one industry may form an organizational field provided they share "an area of institutional life." *See* Stephen J. Mezias, *Using Institutional Theory to Understand For-Profit Sectors: The Case of Financial Reporting Standards*, *in* THE INSTITUTIONAL CONSTRUCTION OF ORGANIZATIONS: INTERNATIONAL AND LONGITUDINAL STUDIES 164 (W. Richard Scott and Soren Christensen eds., 1995) (referring to the 200 largest firms in the U.S. as an organizational field because they compare themselves to one another and takes the others' patterns into their considerations).

given time, and the dynamic of changes within the commons, and in its relationships with the environment.[28]

The proposed framework for conducting an analysis of the commons is structural in nature, allowing a great degree of flexibility in constructing explanations and importing insights from various schools of thought on the nature of social action into the analysis. It is neither reductive, nor exhaustive, but rather is open ended, leaving ample room for case-specific sensitivity. This framework may be useful for conducting a case study of a certain commons or when looking for ways to "heal" a failing commons, as well as when formulating a policy regarding the appropriate patterns for construction and management of a commons. The contention here is not that the study of a commons invariably necessitates the examination of all internal and external variables and their interaction in the past and present. In some cases such a comprehensive examination may not be needed, while in others it may only be necessary with regard to certain variables and interactions. Usually, it will be difficult, if not impossible, to predetermine the desired extent and scope of the research. However, the framework may be useful in such cases by suggesting dimensions of inquiry and directing the conduct of an initial study aimed at determining which variables and dimensions should be explored in a more thorough and detailed manner.

III. COMMONS AND LEGALITY

A. Legality and the Theory of Commons

The scholarship on commons has become more and more sensitive to the broader context of the environment in which commons operate, or at a minimum, has become conscious of the need to develop more responsive and nuanced theories and methods of inquiry regarding the relationship between the commons and the environment. With respect to the legal sphere, such sensitivity is sorely lacking.

Law is usually perceived in commons' scholarship as part of the state's devices. On occasion, the analysis does not relate directly to the law, but merely provides a general treatment of the interaction between the commons and state authorities. Analysts perceive the law as external to the commons and occasionally even perceive it as a threat to efficient self-management of the resource. The dominant theory simply asserts the "design principle," under which the state should accord the commons a minimal recognition of rights to organize and establish its own rules.[29] They argue that the state should allow the commons to

28. On the importance of the time axis, *see* van Ginkel, *supra* note 22, at 230, and Mosses, *supra* note 20, at 470.

29. *See* Ostrom, *supra* note 17, at 101: "[I]f external governmental officials presume that only they have the authority to set the rules, then it will be very difficult for local

develop its institutional framework without being threatened by state intervention in its internal affairs and that state legislation should be limited to enabling statutes. Normatively, this argument promotes recognition of the commons' right to conduct its affairs autonomously. The assertion of commons' autonomy stems from a policy emphasis on community management, based on efficiency theories, an extreme ideology of communitarianism, or on the view that the revival of local communities is the answer to the plight of an indigenous commons.[30]

Such a treatment of the law is flawed both normatively and descriptively. Law is not merely an external factor; it is also endogenous to the commons constituting an integral part of its cultural environment. Law contributes to providing and sustaining the commons in more than one respect, though its practices may be indirect and not easily revealed or measured. Normatively, it is questionable whether the commons should be accorded autonomy with regard to all its internal arrangements and operations.

1. Imposition of Law Scholars of the commons strongly tend to perceive the state's regulation of the commons as an imposition of law that threatens the desired ability of the commons to self-regulate its internal affairs. From a normative point of view, this perception is problematic. Moreover, the observation is not empirically substantiated.

Many of the examples used to support this claim discuss colonized commons, where the intervention of colonial authorities, carried out through the imposition of legal and market institutions, has led to the weakening or even the destruction of communal or tribal common ownership.[31] Indeed, a dominant strand in the literature on law and colonialism focuses on the cultural differences between the colonized people and the law imposed on them by the colonizers, evidenced by the exercise of power through the imposition of the colonizer's law.[32] This literature views the law as external to the social actors and

---

appropriators to sustain a rule-governed CPR over the long run." *See also* Wade, *supra* note 15, at 105. Carol Rose observed that Ostrom's analysis of CPRs as prior to politics is a modern version of Locke's social contract theory. *See* Carol Rose, *Property as the Keystone Right?*, 71 NOTRE DAME L. REV. 329, 333–334 (1996). In part, this argument does not do justice to Ostrom, especially if we note the importance she ascribed to the role of state agencies in the process of providing institutions. It is fair to say that Ostrom viewed the state as a threat when it intervenes in a successful CPR situation or prevents the creation of one, but not otherwise.

30. *See* Mosse, *supra* note 20, at 468, 471.

31. *See, e.g.*, Thomas R. Berger, VILLAGE JOURNEY: THE REPORT OF THE ALASKA NATIVE REVIEW COMMISSION (1985); Stuart Banner, *Conquest by Contract: Wealth Transfer and Land Market Structure in Colonial New Zealand,* 34 LAW & SOC'Y REV. 47(2000); and Fitzpatrick, *supra* note 10, at 1011–1016.

32. *See, e.g.*, Frederick Cooper, *Contracts, Crime, and Agrarian Conflict: From Slave to Wage Labor on the East African Coast, in* LABOUR, LAW, AND CRIME 228 (Francis Snyder and Douglas Hay, eds., 1987).

examines the impact of law on society, finding that the law usually destroyed existing traditional authorities and relationships, norms and cultural values, and economic self-sufficiency.[33]

In more recent "law and colonialism" literature, analyses of the relationships between colonizers and colonized has become more complex than previously portrayed. This literature teaches that there are various dialectical and mutually constitutive relationships between state law and unofficial forms of order. The emphasis is both on the ways in which state law penetrates the other normative order and exercises its constitutive power, as well as on the diverse reactions of variously affected social fields. Unofficial normative orders are depicted as resisting state law, manipulating it to their needs and even exercising constitutive power on state law.[34] At times, the penetration of the colonial legal system was not always complete,[35] resulting in a gap between the declarations of the colonial administration and its actual success in transforming the colonized society.[36] In some cases, different classes of the colonized society differed in their ability to resist or manipulate the situation of the plurality of normative orders.[37] What emerges clearly from this literature is the wide range of reactions of the colonized, and their ability, albeit limited, to negate the effects of the "imposition." Nonetheless, looking solely at colonial experience in order to generate a general assertion about the inherent danger to the commons as a result of the application of an imposition, may be unnecessarily restrictive.

---

33. *See* Robert L. Kidder, *Toward an Integrated Theory of Imposed Law, in* THE IMPOSITION OF LAW, 289, 292 (Sandra B. Burman and Barbara E. Harrell-Bonds, eds., 1979).

34. *Id.* at 291–303. *See also* June Starr and Jane F. Collier, *Introduction, in* HISTORY AND POWER IN THE STUDY OF LAW 1, 9 (June Starr and Jane F. Collier, eds., 1989); Sally Engle Merry, *Law and Colonialism,* 25 LAW & SOC'Y REV. 889 (1991).

35. In some cases, the legal system did not penetrate the whole territory of the colonized people. *See, e.g.,* June Prill-Brett, *Ancestral Land Rights and Legal Pluralism: Another Land Reform in the Highlands of Northern Philippines,* 9 LAW & ANTHROPOLOGY 43 (1997). Moreover, it is clear that in some cases, the indigenous people continued with their former ways as much as they could, and yielded to colonial power only when they had no other alternative. *See, e.g.,* Sally Falk Moore, *Treating Law as Knowledge: Telling Colonial Officers What to Say to Africans about Running "Their Own" Native Courts,* 26 LAW & SOC'Y REV. 11, at 12 and 42 (1992).

36. *See* Nicholas B. Dirks, *From Little King to Landlord: Colonial Discourse and Colonial Rule, in* COLONIALISM AND CULTURE 175 (Nicholas B. Dirks ed., 1992) (examining the gap between colonial legal discourse regarding imposition of new legal categories and the actual minor differences it created in everyday life of land relations in south India).

37. *See, e.g.,* Jacqueline Vel, *Umbu Hapi Versus Umbu Vincent: Legal Pluralism as an Arsenal in Village Combats, in* LAW AS A RESOURCE IN AGRARIAN STRUGGLES 23, 25 (Franz von Benda-Beckmann and M. van den Velde, eds., 1992). On the lack of attention to the role of the elite in the law and colonialism literature, *see* Nathan J. Brown, *Law and Imperialism: Egypt in Comparative Perspective,* 29 LAW & SOC'Y REV. 103, 105 (1995).

In a federal system a common may avoid the imposition of law by moving to another jurisdiction whose policies toward the common are more favorable. However, exercising the exit option is not always possible, or it might be too costly, as, for example, where the common resource is a natural geographically situated resource.

Moreover, while law was, and still is, a mechanism of domination, at times it can also be benign, even beneficial. The literature on commons includes many examples where state intervention or involvement was instrumental to the sustainability of commons and the rejuvenation of its community. There are new and innovative ways through which the state comanages resources with communities or is involved, directly or indirectly, in supporting the revitalization of self-management of common resources by local-level communities.[38] Against a background of the conflicting historical evidence, it seems that, although a healthy suspicion of state authority may not be unfounded, it must also be contextualized and translated into an assertion of a need for a strong autonomy only where justified.

2. The Autonomy of the Commons In its direct treatment of law, or through reference to the state generally, a dominant argument in the literature on commons calls for the recognition of the right of the commons to be left alone. The normative issues that this argument implicates deserve detailed discussion that is beyond the scope of this chapter. What follows is merely a statement of some initial thoughts on the subject.

The question of the commons' autonomy is similar to the question of group rights. As the modern Western state has expanded the use of its regulatory powers, the question of the relationship between the state, representing society at large, and subgroups, minorities, and other private associations has became more significant. In recent decades, scholars from a variety of disciplines have advanced arguments regarding how the modern liberal state ought to treat such communities. The suggestions have ranged from total assimilation to multiculturalism, from state intervention to state tolerance.[39]

Promoting the idea of the right to culture, some have argued, similarly to the arguments made in commons' scholarship, that the state should respect the

---

38. *See* Filkret Berkes, *Cross-Scale Institutional Linkages: Perspectives from the Bottom Up*, *in* THE DRAMA OF THE COMMONS, *supra* note 1, at 293, 298–299, 301–310.

39. *See, e.g.*, WILL Kymlicka, LIBERALISM, COMMUNITY, AND CULTURE (1989); Charles Taylor, *The Politics of Recognition*, in MULTICULTURALISM: EXAMINING THE POLITICS OF RECOGNITION 25 (Amy Gutmann ed., 1994); THE RIGHTS OF MINORITY CULTURES (Will Kymlicka ed., 1995); Deborah Rhode, *Association and Assimilation*, 81 NW. U. L. REV. 1061 (1986); Robert Post, *Cultural Heterogeneity and Law: Pornography, Blasphemy, and the First Amendment*, 76 CALIF. L. REV. 297 (1988); Aviam Soifer, *Freedom of Association; Indian Tribes, Workers, and Communal Ghosts*, 48 MD. L. REV. 350 (1989); and Mark D. Rosen, *The Outer Limits of Community Self-Governance in Residential Associations, Municipalities, and Indian Country: A Liberal Theory*, 84 VA. L. REV. 1053, 1061 (1998).

distinct cultural norms and the laws of subgroups, and accordingly, should leave the governance of internal affairs to the subgroups, imposing only minimal constraints. However, respect for group autonomy may entail a price tag where the fundamental rights of group members as citizens of the state or the rights of outsiders are compromised.[40] Where a commons denies a member her share in the enjoyment of the common resource on which her subsistence depends, where a member is denied her right to participate in collective decision-making, where the commons arbitrarily sanctions a member or puts unjustified limitations on members' right to exit, or when the commons is involved in discriminatory practices of exclusion[41]—should the state refrain from intervening?

Moreover, in dealing with natural resources, the internal rules of the commons and its degree of success in sustaining such resources may have negative externalities on the surrounding environment. When confronted with a failing commons, would an intervention whose aim is to prevent such externalities be unjustified because it infringes on the autonomy of the commons?

These are core questions, and require treading a fine line between group rights and member rights, based on our normative stand. However, one may argue that the specific implementation of the preferred policy should be context-sensitive.

3. Commons and Legal Environments The treatment of law in commons' scholarship can be classified as a rational-materialistic perspective that conceptualizes organizations as rational wealth maximizers, perceiving law to be a system of incentives and penalties. Because of its emphasis on organization-level rational action, this perspective tends to assume that organizational identities, interests, and capacities exist independently of the law.[42]

Looking at the relationship between the commons and legality from a cultural perspective leads to a more complex and enriched understanding. The cultural perspective sees organizations as cultural rule-followers that use law as a system of moral principles, scripted roles, and symbols. Organizations look to law for normative guidance as they seek their place in a socially-constructed cultural reality.[43]

The sociological new-institutionalism literature on law and organizations emphasizes both the constitutive functions of law and the complex, mutual

---

40. *See generally*, Is Multiculturalism Good for Women (Susan Moller Okin with respondents, Joshua Cohen ed., 1999).

41. On a normative model of commons that preserves exit while promoting cooperation, *see* Hanoch Dagan and Michael A. Heller, *The Liberal Commons*, 110 Yale L.J. 549, 566–602 (2001). On the right to entry, *see id.* at 570–571.

42. *See* Lauren B. Edelman and Mark C. Suchman, *The Legal Environment of Organization*, 23 Ann. Rev. Sociology. 479, 484–485 (1997).

43. *Id.* at 482, 495.

constitutive relationship between organizations, and their legal environment.[44] While law provides the categories and definitions through which organizations construct an understanding of themselves and their environment, the organizations themselves take part in the process of constructing these categories and definitions,[45] thus constituting the endogeneity of the law.[46] The same holds true with regard to commons. For example, Kenneth Ruddle[47] described how customary informal law governing Japanese fishery for centuries was enacted, with some amendments, as state law. This is a case where the "bottom up" and the "top down" were successfully linked as a constitution of historical continuity.

The cultural perspective on the position and role of law in the life of organizations, and the evidence emerging from case studies on commons, demonstrate that law may both be imposed on the commons, as well as be constructed by the commons. Law affects the commons and, in turn, is affected thereby. There is no room for an *a priori* assertion regarding the incidence of one direction of influence over the other.

B. The Dynamic Analysis of Legality and Commons

Legality is part of the commons, and should, therefore, be incorporated into the dynamic, contextualized analysis of the commons. Where appropriate, the formal internal laws of the commons, its prevailing social norms and the interaction between the two, should be investigated. Various social and cultural components may be examined in this regard, including acquiring knowledge of the system of order, its legitimacy, practices of use, avoidance or resistance of law, and the modes of thought through which the participants in the commons conceptualize and assign meaning to their actions in the legal realm. The dimension of the environment can also be part of the study, namely, the formal and informal legal practices of the state and its agencies, and, where relevant, the legal realm of the organizational field with which the common is affiliated. It may be useful to

---

44. *Id.* at 492–506 (1997). *See also* Mark C. Suchman and Lauren B. Edelman, *Legal Rational Myths: The New Institutionalism and the Law and Society Tradition,* 21 LAW & SOCIAL INQUIRY 903, 909–928 (1996).

45. On the mutually constitutive approach to law, *see generally* Austin Sarat and Thomas R. Kearns, *Beyond the Great Divide: Forms of Legal Scholarship and Everyday Life, in* LAW IN EVERY DAY LIFE 21, 22 (Ausin Sarat and Thomas R. Kearns, eds., 1993); Kitty Calavita, *Blue Jeans, Rape, and the "De-Constitutive" Power of Law,* 35 LAW & SOC'Y REV. 89, 100–103 (2001).

46. On the endogeneity of law, *see* Lauren B. Edelman, *The Legal Lives of Private Organizations, in* THE BLACKWELL COMPANION TO LAW AND SOCIETY 231, 238–245 (Austin Sarat ed., 2004).

47. Kenneth Ruddle, *Solving the Common-Property Dilemma: Village Fisheries Rights in Japan Coastal Waters, in* COMMON PROPERTY RESOURCES, *supra* note 1, at 168. *See also* James M. Acheson, *Where Have All the Exploiters Gone? Co-Management of the Maine Lobster Industry, id.* at 199.

study these two dimensions together, since internal law and state law (and the law of the organizational field) interact with one another, generating different social outcomes. In certain cases, the time-axis may be helpful in understanding the levels of legal orders and their interaction.

A contextualized analysis may be achieved by utilizing numerous theoretical concepts. Of course, no one theoretical framework is able to capture the full scope and variety of legalities. To illustrate the merits of a contextual analysis three concepts are suggested here as a possible starting point for the study of the legal life of the commons.

First, looking at the interaction between different levels of legality in the commons—the internal and the external, and studying such interaction along a time axis—it is worthwhile to use the insights of the "legal pluralism" literature.[48] By offering the insight that the legal field contains a plurality of normative orders, the perspective of legal pluralism enables an examination of the multifaceted relations between state law and other legal forms of ordering within a society, the commons being one of them. This perspective questions when and why state law shapes the other systems of law and vice versa. The examination of the internal processes, forces and cultural components of semiautonomous fields may help explain why the interaction between them adopts one character or another. Moreover, since legal pluralism views the mutually-constitutive relations between the levels of legality as a process, where appropriate, the analysis may also be sensitive to the time-axis and examine the dynamic interaction in both its stable and/or changing facets. However, the literature of legal pluralism does not provide the tools for such an examination and should, therefore, be supplemented by other perspectives on legal phenomena.

Second, the concept of legal consciousness, meaning the cognitive schema of thought found among the participants of a social group regarding the legal realm,[49] may provide a way to study the mutual-constitutive relations between the levels of legality.[50] According to Patricia Ewick and Susan Silbey, this is the study of "how legality is experienced and understood by ordinary people as they engage, avoid and resist the law and legal meaning" within structural

48. *See* Sally Falk Moore, LAW AS PROCESS: AN ANTHROPOLOGICAL APPROACH 55–6 (1978); Marc Galanter, *Justice In Many Rooms: Courts, Private Ordering, and Indigenous Law*, 19 J. LEGAL PLURALISM 1 (1981); Peter Fitzpatrick, *Law and Societies*, 22 OSGOODE HALL L.J. 115 (1984); John Griffiths, *What Is Legal Pluralism?*, 24 J. LEGAL PLURALISM 1, 38 (1986); and Sally Engle Merry, *Legal Pluralism*, 22 LAW & SOCIETY REV. 869 (1988).

49. On schemas of thought, *see* William H. Sewell, Jr., *A Theory of Structure: Duality, Agency, and Transformation*, 98 AMERICAN J. SOCIOLOGY 1 (1992).

50. On the uses of the concept "legal consciousness," *see* David M. Engel, *How Does Law Matter in the Constitution of Legal Consciousness?*, *in* HOW DOES LAW MATTER? 109 (Austin Sarat and Garth Bryant, eds., 1998); Austin Sarat, "*. . . the Law is All Over": Power, Resistance, and the Legal consciousness of the Welfare Poor*, 2 YALE J. L. & HUMANITIES 344 n.1 (1990).

constraints.[51] It is collectively, not individually, constructed, and thus, is historically situated and shaped.[52] The legal consciousness of the commons mediates the understanding of the participants both with regard to official and unofficial law within the commons and with regard to state legality. The participants experience and understand the interaction between the commons and state law through the terms, perceptions, and schemas of their culture. Where the commons is affiliated with an organizational field, this wider field should also be looked at as an arena for the production and reproduction of legal consciousness.

Finally, insights based on new-institutionalism scholarship can assist in understanding those processes within the commons and its environment that constitute legal consciousness.[53] The sociological new-institutionalism theory of organizations focuses on the effects that cultural beliefs produce on organizations by operating in their environments.[54] Thus, the theory is able to generate important insights regarding the commons as organizations and their cultural worlds, including the legal sphere and legal consciousness as an institution.[55] The neo-institutionalism literature is helpful in understanding the source of institutionalized, or taken-for-granted,[56] schemas and how they become institutionalized. For example, using the term isomorphism, Paul DiMaggio and Walter Powell described the attempts of organizations to resemble in their structures and activities the dominant established patterns within their environment. They point to three types of isomorphic processes: coercive isomorphism (resulting from "formal and informal pressures exerted on organizations by other organizations upon which they are dependent"), mimetic isomorphism

---

51. *See* Patricia Ewick and Susan B. Silbey, The Common Place of Law: Stories from Everyday Life 35 (1998).

52. *Id.* at 46. *See also* Laura Beth Nielsen, *Situating Legal Consciousness: Experiences and Attitudes of Ordinary Citizens about Law and Street Harassment*, 34 Law & Soc'y Rev. 1055, 1060 (2000).

53. On the merits of combining insights from the literatures on legal consciousness with neo-institutional approaches, *see generally* Eric W. Larson, *Institutionalizing Legal Consciousness: Regulation and the Embedding of Market Participants in the Securities Industry in Ghana and Fiji*, 38 Law & Soc'y Rev. 737, 738–740 (2004).

54. *See* Scott, *supra* note 27, at 31, 92–132.

55. *See id.* at 64–89. The term "institution" was defined by Scott in the broadest terms: "Institutions consist of cognitive, normative and regulative structures and activities that provide stability and meaning to social behavior . . . Although constructed and maintained by individual actors, institutions assume the guise of an impersonal and objective reality." *Id.* at 33–34. On the maintenance and persistence of institutions, *see* Lynne G. Zucker, *The Role of Institutionalization in Cultural Persistence*, *in* The New Institutionalism in Organizational Analysis 83 (Walter W. Powell and Paul J. DiMaggio, eds., 1991). More recent writing focuses mainly on explaining institutional change. *See generally* Elisabeth S. Clemems and James M. Cook, *Politics and Institutionalism: Explaining Durability and Change*, 25 Annual Rev. Sociology 441 (1999).

56. *See* Zucker, *supra* note at 85.

(imitation arising out of uncertainty), and normative pressures (stemming primarily from professionalization).[57] Others have pointed at variances among organizations in their vulnerability to the pressures of the environment and have noted diverse modes of reactions toward such pressures.[58] In more recent writings, scholars of new-institutionalism have introduced into their analyses the notions of interests, agency, and power, especially in regard to institutionalization and deinstitutionalization processes.[59] In line with this literature, an analysis of legality in the commons may trace the processes of the institutionalization of schema of legal consciousness throughout the different levels of legality, exhibiting sensitivity both to environmental pressures and to struggles among members of the commons over power, control, and legitimization.

Combining the legal pluralism perspective, the concept of legal consciousness and the study of the emergence and institutionalization of cultural schemas as part of the organizational processes and their interrelationship with their environment, provide a framework for a dynamic multidimensional contextualized analysis of legality in the commons. Such framework is not the only model that may be generated to examine the commons and legality from a cultural constitutive approach; in some contexts it may be useful in framing the questions to be asked, while in others it might be irrelevant. A framework for analysis should also be contextualized.

IV. LEGALITY IN THE *KIBBUTZ*

The Israeli *kibbutz* is an intriguing site for testing competing theories regarding the relationship between the commons and legality, and more generally, for reflecting on the importance of multidimensional dynamic analyses of the relationship between the commons and their environments.

The *kibbutz* is—or at least used to be—a commune, a community of people holding and managing all property together and distributing its benefits equally

57. *See* Paul J. DiMaggio and Walter W. Powell, *The Iron Cage Revisited: Institutional Isomorphism and Collective Rationality in Organizational Fields, in* The New Institutionalism, *supra* note 55, at 63, 64–5, 67–70.

58. *See* Christine Oliver, *Strategic Responses to Institutional Processes,* 16 Academy of Management Review 145 (1991). For an analysis of organizational responses to pressures from the legal environment, *see* Lauren B. Edelman, *Legal Environments and Organizational Governance: The Expansion of Due Process in the American Workplace,* 95 American J. Sociology 1401 (1990); Jeb Barnes and Thomas F. Burke, *The Diffusion of Rights: From Law on the Books to Organizational Rights Practice,* 40 Law & Soc'y Rev. 493 (2006).

59. *See* Paul DiMaggio, *Interest and Agency in Institutional Theory, in* Institutional Patterns and Organizations 3, 12–16 (Lynne G. Zucker ed., 1998); Paul J. DiMaggio, *Constructing an Organizational Field as a Professional Project: U.S. Art Museums, 1920–1940, in* New Institutionalism, *supra* note 55, at 267.

with no direct link between work or other contribution to commune life and any form of monetary remuneration for it.[60] At the same time, the *kibbutz* provides for all the needs of its members (such as food, housing, education, and health) through collective consumption, constituting what has become known as the general guarantee for all members. In this way, the *kibbutz* adheres to the maxim of "from each according to her ability, to each according to her needs." As an intentional community, the *kibbutz* is an exemplary and equitable way of communal living for people who believe in the ideals of equality, brotherhood, and mutual assistance. Communal ownership of property is a means to achieve these goals.

In what follows, this chapter provides a short demonstration of the use of a multidimensional dynamic analysis in the study of legality in both the past and the present of the *kibbutz*.

A. Looking at the Past

The question of legality in the *kibbutz* has attracted scholarly attention, with two main arguments offered. Both refer to the internal dimension of the *kibbutz* life as an organization.

One line of reasoning was raised by Richard Swartz in his by now classic study on social control and social structure.[61] Studying the *kibbutz* in the late 1940s, Swartz argued that social control in the *kibbutz* was exercised through nonlegal sanctions as applied by the community as a whole or its general assembly. Because the *kibbutz* lacked any specialized agency for social control, Swartz concluded that there was no formal legal control within the *kibbutz*. Swartz based his explanation on the special features of the *kibbutz* and its social and economic structures. Because the *kibbutz* is a primary group with face-to-face interaction based on its collectivist economy, the exercise of nonlegal sanctions is efficient, with no need for the formal exercise of law. Swartz's argument resonates with more recent writings on law and social norms, with its contention that the efficient exercise of social control in small, close-knit, and nonhierarchical communities explains the lack of application of state law and even ignorance of law among such communities.[62] When looking at legality solely from the internal

---

60. The first *kibbutz* was established in 1910, and today there are over 270 *kibbutzim* spread throughout Israel. Interestingly, while the Israeli *kibbutz* is renowned around the globe, and over the years, almost every one of its facets has attracted the attention of various academic disciplines, though the past and present of the *kibbutz* generate fascinating questions for those interested in the phenomena of the commons, an analysis of the kibbutz as a community holding common property is rare. A notable exception is the inclusion of the kibbutz in Ellickson's analysis of communes. *See* Robert C. Ellickson, *supra* note 4, at 1315, 1344–1348 (1993).

61. *See* Richard D. Swartz, *Social Factors in the Development of Legal Control: A Case Study of Two Israeli Settlements*, 63 YALE L.J. 471 (1954).

62. *See, e.g.*, Robert C. Ellickson, ORDER WITHOUT LAW: HOW NEIGHBORS SETTLE DISPUTES (1994).

dimension and from an economic-oriented perspective, Swartz's argument is plausible. However, the question arises as to whether such an analysis is sufficient in order to fully grasp an understanding of the role that legality plays on the *kibbutz* commons. As will be demonstrated below, the answer is no.[63]

Another argument with regard to legality and the *kibbutz* is Allan Shapiro's suggestion that, initially, the *kibbutz* was ideologically against the law, and this ideology acted against bringing legal control into the kibbutz.[64] Shapiro argued that, initially, the *kibbutz* regarded law as "alien to the familial intimacy of the *kibbutz*," The social relationships among *kibbutz* members living in a small, close-knit group were based, at least in their eyes, on intimate face-to-face interactions. There was no place for legal control, with its impersonal character, in the daily life of the *kibbutz*. Shapiro looked at only one cultural component—an antilaw norm, and, again, only at the internal dimension of the social life of the *kibbutz*.

In fact, a closer historical study reveals the limitations of both of these arguments. During the 1920s, the corporate structure of the *kibbutzim* went through a process of formalization and was legalized under state law as a cooperative society. Neither Swartz nor Shapiro paid attention to the fact that the *kibbutz* was governed by rules, enacted under state law,[65] and that it was state law that conferred authority on the *kibbutz* general assembly to formulate regulations and reach decisions in particular cases. The question of the relationship between the *kibbutz* and the Cooperative Societies Ordinance, 1933, or the state agency of the Registrar of Cooperative Societies is not raised in their exchange.[66] Also, during the same period, the *kibbutzim*, as part of belonging to the organizational field of the labor-movement in Palestine, formulated their constitutions as entities affiliated with such movement.

The study of the legal consciousness of the *kibbutz* found that while the *kibbutz* was in compliance with the dictates of state law, the fact that the *kibbutz* was a legal entity under state law with binding rules of association did not

---

63. For further criticism on Swartz, *see* John Griffiths, *The Division of Labor in Social Control, in* 1 TOWARD A GENERAL THEORY OF SOCIAL CONTROL 37, 40–7 (Donald Black ed., 1984).

64. *See* Allan E. Shapiro, *Law in the Kibbutz: A Reappraisal*, 10 LAW & SOC'Y REV. 415 (1976). Shapiro also argued that although the social conditions on the kibbutz changed, the *kibbutz* did not develop legal control in Swartz's sense of the term.

65. "Rules" is the legal term used in the Cooperative Societies Ordinance, 1933, for the bylaws of a society defined thereunder, denoting its articles of association.

66. Similar neglect is found in other ethnographic works on the *kibbutz* that examined the ways in which the *kibbutz* settled disputes. *See* Terence M. S. Evens, *Stigma, Ostracism, and Expulsion in an Israeli Kibbutz, in* SYMBOL AND POLITICS IN COMMUNAL IDEOLOGY 166 (Sally Falk Moore and Barbara G. Myerhoff, eds., 1975); Michael Saltman, *Legality and Ideology in the Kibbutz Movement, reprinted in* THE SOCIOLOGY OF THE KIBBUTZ 125 (Ernest Krausz and David Glanz, eds., 1983).

become common knowledge among *kibbutz* members, and those who were aware of the rules did not imagine them as having a role in the regulation of the everyday life of the *kibbutz*. Such estrangement from the rules was a taken-for-granted, institutionalized component of the *kibbutzim*'s culture.[67]

The estrangement from state law should be understood against the background of the process of the structuring of the organizational field to which the *kibbutzim* belonged, namely, the organizational field of the labor movement in Palestine and its major organization, the General Federation of the Jewish Workers in Palestine (the Histadrut).[68] It was in this formative period that the *kibbutzim* and other organizations in the field were established and incorporated under state law. The cultural components of the field and of the different organizations comprising it emerged at that time. It was a process embedded in ideological controversies and, even more, in a power struggle over domination of the field.

An exacting historical study reveals that estrangement was an instilled and manipulated legal consciousness that became institutionalized.[69] The estrangement of the *kibbutzim* from state law served the interests of the Histadrut leadership through the creation of a dependence thereon in the *kibbutzim*'s relations with the state. Thus, it was not the legal nature of the rules as law generally or as state law particularly that distanced the *kibbutzim* from them, since law was a major arena for the *kibbutzim*'s ideological debates and struggles over power. The alienation was due to the operation of mechanisms of legal domination by the political leaders.

Estrangement from state law became an institutionalized legal consciousness of indifference. Several variables contributed to the institutionalization of this legal consciousness, mainly the routine nature of the practices of estrangement.[70] In the case of the *kibbutzim*, the practices that became routine both created and maintained the institution of the legal consciousness of indifference.

The state authorities' nonintervention in the internal affairs of the *kibbutzim*—though formally they had the power to do so—contributed to the persistence of estrangement. Political considerations accounted for this policy by the state. During the Mandate period, the British emphasized the development of cooperatives among the Arab population and generally considered the Jewish cooperative

---

67. *See* Avital Margalit, *The Kibbutz and State Law: The Construction of Legal Estrangement*, Haifa L. Rev. (forthcoming)(in Hebrew).

68. *See* Avital Margalit, *Law, Organization, and Corporate Structure in the Workers' Society*, 26 Tel Aviv U. L. Rev. 451 (2002)(in Hebrew).

69. *See* Margalit, *supra* note 67.

70. Routines are repetitive patterns of activity or organizational performances that can operate as carriers of institutions. *See* Sidney G. Winter, *Survival, Selection, and Inheritance in Evolutionary Theories of Organization*, *in* Organizational Evolution: New Direction 269, 274–7 (Jitendra V. Singh ed., 1990).

sector as capable of taking care of its own affairs. This policy of nonintervention persisted long after the establishment of the State of Israel, mainly because of the relatively formidable political power of the *kibbutzim*. State supervision of compliance with law was limited to the formal requirements of the Cooperative Societies Ordinance.[71] The lack of state supervision contributed to the self-perception of the *kibbutzim* as being autonomous from the state and enhanced the sense of belonging to the organizational field.

To conclude, contrary to the arguments based on one-dimensional analysis according to which the absence of law in *kibbutz* daily life was an outcome of the efficiency of nonlegal sanctions or an antilaw cultural norm, the dynamic multidimensional analysis proves that the *kibbutzim* were not by nature strangers to state law, but were actively manipulated into becoming estranged from it.

B. Looking at the Present

In the mid-1980s, most *kibbutzim* experienced a grave economic crisis that can only partially be attributed to causes inherent in the commune system.[72] The sudden and unexpected slump in the *kibbutz* economies dealt a serious blow to the pride and self-image of *kibbutz* members, as well as to the standing of the *kibbutz* in the eyes of the Israeli public. The crisis was followed by waves of departures by members from *kibbutzim*. The sense of security stemming from the promise of the general guarantee was shattered and calls for the need to change the *kibbutz* became common. While about third of the *kibbutzim* still adhere to the fundamental ideological values adopted by the early *kibbutzim*, the majority of the *kibbutzim* have, to various degrees, modified the communal aspects of their life, limiting the scope of the general guarantee and demanding personal responsibility in its stead and constituting a direct connection between members' work and their monetary remuneration, thus introducing precepts of a market economy into the *kibbutz*. New mechanisms of management and collective decision-making were introduced, all with the same aim—decreasing the level of participation and cooperation, thereby lessening the power of the community. These modifications are an outcome of long and hard-fought struggles among rival sectors within the *kibbutz* movement. Such struggles

---

71. On the preference of state agencies to adopt culturally constructed, easily observable symbols of compliance, *see* Lauren B. Edelman, *Legal Ambiguity and Symbolic Structures: Organizational Mediation of Civil Rights Law*, 97 American J. Sociology 1531, 1568 (1992).

72. On the current crisis in the kibbutzim, *see generally*, Crisis in The Israeli Kibbutz (Uriel Leviatan et al., eds., 1998), 22 J. Rural Cooperation (nos. 1–2) (special issue: *The Kibbutz in the Mid 1990s: Crisis and Changes*) (1994); Eliezer Ben-Rafael, Crisis and Transformation: the Kibbutz at Century's End (1997); Eli Avrahami, The Changing Kibbutz: An Examination of Values and Structure (2000); Daniel Gavron, The Kibbutz: Awakening from Utopia (2000).

exposed the internal hierarchies that stratified the supposedly egalitarian *kibbutz*. The modifications benefited mostly the relatively young professionals among *kibbutz* members resulting in the emergence of new legal facets of *kibbutz*. The *kibbutzim* rediscovered and adopted state law and the rules as part of their patterns of discourse and action.[73] *Kibbutz* officials as well as members became aware of the *kibbutz* as a legal entity with legal obligations and rights under state law. Seeking legal advice became common, and there were numerous cases where *kibbutz* members filed grievances with the Registrar of Cooperative Societies or state courts.

Initially, when the legal aspects of the *kibbutz* first became exposed to its members, state agencies were generally reluctant to intervene and did so only as a last resort. Only close to a decade after the *kibbutz* crisis first emerged did the state finally exercise its regulatory powers with regard to them. Currently, newly enacted regulations pursuant to the Cooperative Societies Ordinance, under which all *kibbutzim* are incorporated,[74] and decisions by the governing body of the Israel Lands Administration from which the *kibbutzim* lease most of their lands, allow the *kibbutzim* to privatize their property in part both by conferring on their members' private holdings in housing and also, to some extent, in its productive assets. This introduces private property rights in that which was previously held communally.

How may we explain these changes in the *kibbutzim*? Is the transformation toward the emergence of private property rights an outcome of new externalities? Is it an outcome of the failure of the *kibbutzim* to follow desirable design-principles of successful commons? What part did the changing preferences and ideological tenets of the members play in the impetus toward privatization? What role did the decline in the status of the *kibbutz* play in the larger Israeli society? Why do some *kibbutzim* continue to adhere to their traditional commons model while others are happy to remold their property regime? In light of the contentions presented in this chapter, there is no single, simple answer.

This complexity can be illustrated by considering the dissociation of the housing arrangements from the other assets of the *kibbutz*, resulting in the registration of each house as the private property of members.

It seems that there was no negative externality directly or exclusively linked to communal housing that may account for the introduction of private property. Generally, the internal rules regarding the allocation of housing units in the *kibbutz* were undisputable. One could argue, however, that because home is the most important cultural symbol of identity, relationships, and belonging, having private property rights in their homes, played a role in restoring and enhancing the

73. *See* Uri Zeligman (Registrar of Cooperative Societies), *The Changing Kibbutz and its Legal Status*, 28 Me'befnim 52 (1999) (Hebrew).

74. On the new regulations, see Amnon Lehavi, *Mixing Property*, 38 Seton Hall L. Rev. 137, 168–172 (2008).

members' sense of security. However, the privatization of housing was possible only because the state, as the land owner, allowed this legal transformation long before the *kibbutzim* contemplated such dramatic change in their way of life.

Such possible explanation, however, does not give an answer to the question why the scheme of privatization was not adopted by all *kibbutzim*, or at least by those who are in grave economic difficulties. As this example illustrates, the search for an explanation for the changing face of the *kibbutz* necessitates utilizing a dynamic multidimensional framework that would take into account both internal and external factors and would look for an integrated explanation.

The same premise holds true with regard to the question of legality that relates to the emergence of an awareness of the legal realm in the life of the *kibbutz* and its members, changes in the internal mechanisms of social control and their effectiveness, changes in the legal environment, in Israel generally and the *kibbutz* particularly, and the interaction and mutually intertwined influences of the various levels of legality. Only such dynamic multidimensional analysis would be able to provide us with sufficient answers to the intriguing question of the role law played in the transformation of the *kibbutz*.

V. CONCLUSIONS

This chapter advocated the merits of using a dynamic multidimensional framework of analysis of the commons, one that directs our attention toward the interactions between the internal arrangements and culture of the commons and its ecological, political, social, and economic environments. This proposal emphasized the desirability of a similar contextualized analysis regarding the place, role, and power of the legal realm in the life of the commons and proposes a framework for such an analysis. Taking the existence of a plurality of legal-normative orders as its underlying assumption, this chapter suggested viewing the commons as an organization situated within a legal environment and interacting with such an environment on a multitude of levels and forms. This proposition also presented the concept of the cultural schema of legal consciousness as mediating between the commons as an organization and its legal environment. Delving deeper into the question of legality in one commons—the *kibbutz*—this chapter demonstrated how rich and nuanced our understanding of legality in the commons becomes when considering the commons not merely as an economic enterprise, but also as a social and cultural field of human interaction. Understanding the place, function, and power of legality in a commons, necessitates, therefore, empirical observations, directed by a framework based on a dynamic multidimensional analysis to assist in contextualizing the relationship between the commons and legality.

7. PROPERTY IN A QUEUE

KEVIN GRAY

I. INTRODUCTION

Queuing behavior is an extraordinary and—so far as legal scholars are concerned—little analyzed social practice. Queues are interesting not least because "they manifest much of the complexity of real life in a limited, concentrated experience."[1] I want to focus here on the simplest example of the queue—the physical line-up for service such as might be found at one's local post office, bank, supermarket, cinema, or airport check-in.[2] On a larger scale, the object of scrutiny includes the mass queue of persons waiting for tickets for some sporting spectacle or seeking admission to some exhibition or entertainment.[3] It is the task of this chapter to explore the moral and social geography of the queue in an attempt to determine whether the queue embodies a regulatory structure that replicates or mimics any of the more readily recognized features of municipal legal phenomena. In particular, we shall be concerned to examine the proprietary implications or connotations of the social protocol of lining up. With the queue we suddenly come close to the moment of formation of a certain kind of order—the creation of a normative regime that governs a significant aspect of social

---

1. F. Neil Brady, *Lining Up for Star-Wars Tickets: Some Ruminations on Ethics and Economics Based on An Internet Study of Behavior in Queues*, 38 J. Business Ethics 157, 158 (2002).

2. I propose to leave aside the more complex issues that surround, say, the allocation of replacement body parts or the provision of public housing units or even the traffic of digital information. I shall likewise pass over other nonphysical queuing mechanisms such as remote telephonic queuing, which so intensifies the frustration of commercial transactions for the modern consumer (*see* Deborah K. Unzicker, *The Psychology of Being Put on Hold: An Exploratory Study of Service Quality*, 16 Psychology and Marketing 327 (1999)).

3. It matters not for the purpose of this paper whether the resource that is made available to queuers at the point of service is or is not exhaustive by nature. In other words, it is irrelevant whether the desired resource for which the queuers stand in line is available in sufficient supply to satisfy the needs of all within the queue. The possibility in some cases that the resource may run out does not alter the fundamental dynamic of the queue, but merely enhances for the queuer the significance of his or her place within the line. Exhaustion of supply simply entails that the unsuccessful queuer's investment of time has been wholly lost. The focus of this paper is not, therefore, the question whether the queuer will ultimately get anything by waiting in line, but rather an enquiry as to what precisely the queuer can be said to own or hold *while waiting*.

activity and interaction. Several fascinating questions arise. How, if at all, does this creative moment connect with the origins of property? Does the institution of the queue help to explain the deep foundations of property? Does the queue contain a distant echo of some primeval proprietary "big bang" so that the beginnings of property are still perceptible in the way we behave in the various waiting lines we encounter in our everyday lives? Do our experiences of the queue tell us anything about the software of the mind (and, especially, about the way in which we conceptualize proprietary rights and relationships)? What follows is ultimately an examination of the nature of proprietary experience. How, exactly, do we *think* property?

Underlying the present chapter is the hypothesis that, in the daily business of lining up for service, we engage in a range of very elementary proprietary perceptions. But what, precisely, is there to feel proprietary about in a queue? The queue is, of course, a direct response to a mismatch of supply and demand—in this case a mismatch between the number of clients seeking a particular service and the ability of the service-provider instantly to satisfy that need. The service-provider externalizes part of the cost of delivery by imposing on the client the disbenefit of waiting for service. In the process the client forfeits the opportunity cost of the time spent waiting in the queue. The proprietary dimension of the line-up could simply be about the control of physical space within the line—and to a degree it certainly is. However, the conclusion reached in this chapter is that, in the behavioral protocol of the queue, we also experience a deeply personal sense of ownership of *time* and of the derogation from self-respect and self-propriety occasioned by any violation of the spatio-temporal ownership represented by each place in the waiting line.

II. THE QUEUE AS A MEDIUM OF POWER AND CONTROL

The phenomenon of the queue is intimately associated with the social organization of time and, as Barry Schwartz so aptly reminded us, "the distribution of waiting time coincides with the distribution of power."[4] Power, said Schwartz, entails "the capacity to provide scarce services which people must wait to receive" and to be kept waiting is "to be the subject of an assertion that one's own time (and, therefore, one's social worth) is less valuable than the time and worth of the one who imposes the wait."[5] The institution of the queue is therefore more than

4. Barry Schwartz, Queuing and Waiting: Studies in the Social Organization of Access and Delay 5, 44 (1975).

5. Barry Schwartz, *Waiting, Exchange, and Power: The Distribution of Time in Social Systems*, 79 American Journal of Sociology 841, 856–857 (1974).

a matter of abstract ordering—it is a "social occasion,"[6] with all the relativities of ascendancy and suppliance that such an occasion connotes. Waiting is all about the asymmetrical allocation of power between superordinates and subordinates. But although asymmetries of power may explain why waiting occurs, the inner dynamic of the queue is itself the product of an extraordinary exercise in psychological control.[7] The queue is, effectively, a mechanism of social regulation in which a randomly assembled group of strangers is caused to act, quite counterintuitively, in a particular way. Previously unrelated persons are somehow persuaded to subscribe collectively to a normative code that they then police themselves. At its core the queue incorporates a fundamental, and deeply democratic, principle of "ordinality"[8]—a rule of "first come, first served" (FCFS)[9] or, as it is alternatively known, "first in, first out" (FIFO).[10] Although this principle presents an obvious impediment to immediate goal satisfaction, the distribution of service according to order of arrival is widely viewed as an important restraint upon an otherwise anarchic struggle for personal advantage. In this sense the queue already carries an echo of a proprietary function. Like the institution of property, the queue exists only because there are limits (real or imagined) on the availability of certain desired resources. The pattern of structured waiting overseen by the queue is an almost unique species of spontaneous self-discipline in which the potentially anomic force of the crowd is converted by tacit agreement into a deferment of individual gratification in the interests of some higher social order or objective.

The enduring mystery of the queue relates to the origins of this convergence of behavioral forms. Queuing practice is more than merely an instance of externally observable custom or predictable regularity. As H. L. A. Hart would have said, the queue evinces, in however fragile a fashion, an "internal aspect" in which the members of the waiting line exhibit a "critical reflective attitude to certain patterns of behaviour as a common standard." This attitude reveals itself in "criticism . . . demands for conformity, and in acknowledgements that such criticism and demands are justified, all of which find their characteristic expression in the normative terminology of 'ought,' 'must,' and 'should,' 'right' and 'wrong.'" Violation of the norms of the queue "is not merely a basis for

---

6. Stanley Milgram, Hilary James Liberty, Raymond Toledo, and Joyce Wackenhut, *Response to Intrusion into Waiting Lines*, 51 J. Personality and Social Psychology 683 (1986).

7. The queue is "a psychological as well as a social structure" (Barry Schwartz, *Queues, Priorities, and Social Process*, 41 Social Psychology 3, 9 (1978)).

8. Edward T. Hall, The Silent Language 201 (1959).

9. *See* Randolph W. Hall, Queueing Methods For Services and Manufacturing 417 (1991).

10. *See* Alec M. Lee, Applied Queueing Theory 18 (1966).

a prediction that a hostile reaction will follow but a *reason* for hostility."[11] In the view of Neil MacCormick, the queue "belongs to a form of normative order that exists because there is an overlapping, largely shared, common understanding of the right way to behave."[12] It is the internalized order of the queue—the self-realization of its normative structure—that provides the focus of the remainder of this chapter.

III. THE NORMATIVE MERITS OF THE QUEUE

The waiting line may well reflect unattractive disparities of power in human relations, but for all its demerits the phenomenon of the queue can rightly be said to promote certain valuable social ends. The FCFS rule has the enormous virtue of "ethical simplicity."[13] The principle of ordinality gives transparent force to some elementary concept of social or procedural justice.[14] It also displays a profoundly equalitarian character: waiting in line is one of the great levelers of humankind.[15] The queue is no respecter of persons.[16] In the citizenship of the queue no rank is relevant other than the rank order of one's position as determined by the coldly neutral datum of sequential arrival in the line.[17] There is also some reason to believe that the FCFS rule is an expression of a more general value structure historically associated with certain segments of Western society.[18] Above all, the

---

11. H. L. A. Hart, The Concept of Law 56, 88 (1961).

12. Neil MacCormick, *Norms, Institutions, and Institutional Facts*, 17 Law and Philosophy 301, at 308–309 (1998).

13. Brady, *Lining Up for Star-Wars Tickets*, *supra* note 1, at 161.

14. *See* Richard C. Larson, *Perspectives on Queues: Social Justice and the Psychology of Queueing*, 35 Operations Research 895 (1987); M. Groth and S.W. Gilliland, *The Role of Procedural Justice in the Delivery of Services: A Study of Customers' Reactions to Waiting*, 6 J. Quality Management 77 (2001); Anat Rafaeli, Greg Barron and Keren Haber, *The Effects of Queue Structure on Attitudes*, 5 J. Service Research 125, 128 (2002).

15. The transformative role of the queue should not be underestimated. For instance, there is evidence that the shared wartime experience of queuing for rationed supplies helped to break down prewar patterns of deference to one's superior within a socially stratified system (*see* Joe Moran, *Queuing up in Post-War Britain*, 16 Twentieth Century British History 283, 286–289 (2005)).

16. There is a certain social equity in the idea that queuers are bound together in a situation of shared disadvantage (*see* Charles H. Cooley, Human Nature and the Social Order 281–282 (1983) (1902)).

17. *See* Edward T. Hall, The Silent Language 201 (1959).

18. *See* Schwartz, Queuing and Waiting, *supra* note 4, at 108. It has been suggested that respect for the impersonal ordinality of the queue may correlate with a modern diminution of kinship bonds, a social process that has allowed individuals to be "recognised as persons of potentially equal worth, with equal rights that need to be respected by all other persons, regardless of their social connections" (*see* Stuart Corbridge, *Waiting in Line, or*

key benefit conferred by queuing protocol is that of perceived "fairness" or "fair play" in the provision of service as between rival and highly appetitive claimants.[19] The FCFS rule ensures "a direct correspondence between inputs (time spent waiting) and outcomes (preferential service),"[20] a result that "resonates affinity" with a capitalist (if not Marxian) criterion of distributive justice.[21] In many contexts the queue thus replicates the allocative mechanism that would likely have been agreed by all relevant parties behind a Rawlsian "veil of ignorance."[22] Moreover, by eliminating preemptive strikes for selfishly desired objectives, the FCFS rule effectively inhibits conflict and, in the eyes of some observers, "offers a peculiarly public performance of governmentality, or what Foucault called the ethical government of the self."[23] Thus, for Stanley Milgram and his collaborators, the queue could indeed be described as "a classic illustration of how individuals create social order, on the basis of a rudimentary principle of equity, in a situation that could otherwise degenerate into chaos."[24]

IV. THE BASIC PRINCIPLES OF THE QUEUE

So far we have described the queue as being anchored in a fundamental principle of ordinality: prior arrival confers superiority in the rank order of the queue. However, priority of arrival is only a necessary, and not in itself sufficient, precondition of access to the service that the queue seeks. Deeply embedded in the phenomenology of the queue is the notion that the priority gained on arrival must be sustained by the active maintenance of one's "place" within the line. To abandon one's position in the queue—to "renege" (in the technical jargon of the queue-watcher)—is to forfeit the priority secured by first arrival. It is this combination of ideas—physical entry into the queue coupled with the continuance of a self-validating presence within the queue—that offers further clues to

---

the Moral and Material Geographies of Queue-Jumping, in GEOGRAPHIES AND MORALITIES: INTERNATIONAL PERSPECTIVES ON DEVELOPMENT, JUSTICE AND PLACE 187 (Roger Lee and David M. Smith eds., 2004)).

19. "[P]eople sense a kind of fairness about queues that they don't see in exclusively economic solutions . . . Lines may not be efficient, but they are reasonably fair" (Brady, *Lining Up for Star-Wars Tickets, supra* note 1, at 164). *See similarly* Thierry Meyer, *Subjective Importance of Goal and Reactions to Waiting in Line,* 134 JOURNAL OF SOCIAL PSYCHOLOGY 819, 820 (1994)(a "fair attempt to control inequity in the distribution of a scarce resource").

20. Leon Mann, *Queue Culture: The Waiting Line as a Social System,* 75 AMERICAN J. SOCIOLOGY 340, 346 (1969).

21. Schwartz, QUEUING AND WAITING, *supra* note 4, at 199.

22. *See* JOHN RAWLS, A THEORY OF JUSTICE 136–142 (1973).

23. Stuart Corbridge, *Waiting in Line, supra* note 18, at 192.

24. Milgram et al., *Response to Intrusion into Waiting Lines, supra* note 6, at 683.

the social and philosophical dynamic of waiting in line. We shall have to subject both of these component elements to further examination, but the feature that unites them is, of course, the dimension of *time*. Time not only is significant in determining the sequence of arrivals, but has a further relevance in measuring commitment to the discipline of the queue and, in consequence, the socially adjudged appropriateness of each queuer's claim to preferential service.

V. TIME AND THE NORMATIVE CODE OF THE QUEUE

The process of queuing involves a more complex network of relationships than might at first be envisaged. Relevant participants include, of course, the server who performs the frontline task of supplying a desired service for the person at the head of the queue (selling a ticket, answering an enquiry, handing out a food parcel, etc). There is, obviously, the individual queuer. Then again there is the collectivity of persons who constitute the remainder of the queue. Other *dramatis personae* include the queuer's friends, family, or associates (who may want to come and join him) and also complete strangers (who may become nonconsensual intruders in the line). For all of these people time has a value, since time is "a generalized resource whose distribution affects life chances with regard to the attainment of other, more specific kinds of rewards."[25] Time provides an essential gateway to ever more highly desired forms of preference satisfaction. But time is valuable not merely because it is the *sine qua non* of access to productive achievement and personal fulfillment. Unlike many other resources it is finite and nonfungible; its progress is irreversible. "For many, time is not just a scarce resource; it is *the* scarce resource."[26] In an increasingly frenetic society, we have become "time-poor" and therefore more time-conscious.[27] And the phobia associated with a loss or deprivation of time is reinforced by some residual folk memory of a religious era—perhaps most closely linked with the Protestant tradition—which emphasized the "moral preciousness of time."[28] The Protestant work ethic and the belief that each must ultimately account to God for the use of time combined to generate an enduring detestation of idleness. On this view time belonged to God alone,[29] with the consequence that only productive uses of

---

25. Schwartz, *Waiting, Exchange, and Power, supra* note 5, at 868.

26. France Leclerc, Bernd H Schmitt, and Laurette Dubé, *Waiting Time and Decision Making: Is Time Like Money?*, 22 Journal of Consumer Research 110 (1995).

27. Moran, *Queuing up in Post-War Britain, supra* note 15, at 304.

28. Schwartz, Queuing and Waiting, *supra* note 4, at 154–155.

29. *See* R. H. Tawney, Religion and the Rise of Capitalism 55 (1980).

time were worthy in His eyes. In Max Weber's illuminating account, waste of time became "the first and in principle the deadliest of sins."[30]

Thus it is that, in the context of the queue, a number of people have potentially conflicting interests in the intangible and inelastic commodity of time. And, in regulating access to productive time, the queue is fundamentally a mechanism for allocating the disadvantages of delay between the various players involved. As every queue-watcher confirms, the process of waiting is painful.[31] It is almost always a thoroughly negative experience.[32] Waiting time is dead time[33]—a perception richly corroborated in the literature on queuing.[34] In many contexts the queue has become a potent symbol of unhappiness and social unrest.[35] The process of waiting imposes, in short, a demoralization cost of some significance. Waiting accentuates an implicit inferiority and "subserves the distribution of power that it presupposes."[36] The compulsory immobility of the queuer induces exaggerated, but no less palpable, feelings of powerlessness, *ennui*, anxious

---

30. Max Weber, The Protestant Ethic and the Spirit of Capitalism 157 (1958) (1930).

31. Schwartz, Queuing and Waiting, *supra* note 4, at 167.

32. *See* Larson, *Perspectives on Queues, supra* note 14, at 897. As William James famously observed, unoccupied or idle time weighs much more heavily than fruitfully employed time (William James, The Principles of Psychology 410 (1952) (1891)).

33. We spend a nontrivial portion of our lives waiting in a linear physical formation for the delivery of certain goods and services. All of us "throw away the small-change time—five minutes here, a quarter hour there—that accumulates in any ordinary day" (quote contained in Schwartz, *Waiting, Exchange, and Power, supra* note 5, at 842). Various estimates have been made of the time spent queuing. One much quoted statistic was produced during the 1980s by a consulting firm, Priority Management Pittsburgh, to the effect that average Americans spend five years of their lives waiting in lines (compared, incidentally, with four years doing housework) (*see* Jeff Berner, The Joy of Working from Home: Making a Life while Making a Living 46 (1994)). Even if the time spent in queues has been more heavily curtailed in recent years by the prevalence of online retail transactions, the statistic retains a certain force.

34. *See* David H. Maister, *The Psychology of Waiting Lines, in* The Service Encounter 113 (John Czepiel, M.R. Solomon, and D.F. Surprenant eds., 1985); J. Watt, *Effect of Boredom on Time Perception,* 69 Psychological Reports 323 (1991); Michael K. Hui and David K. Tse, *What to Tell Customers in Waits of Different Lengths: An Integrative Model of Service Evaluation,* 60 Journal of Marketing 81, 82 (1996).

35. One of the most iconic political images of the modern British era comprised, under the striking headline "LABOUR ISN'T WORKING," a photograph of a long line of people stretching away into the distance, all supposedly queuing to reach the unemployment office (Moran, *Queuing up in Post-War Britain, supra* note 15, at 292–293). It was this message that so powerfully struck a chord with the British electorate in May 1979 and swept the Conservative Party under Margaret Thatcher into almost twelve years of unrivalled power.

36. Schwartz, *Waiting, Exchange, and Power, supra* note 5, at 856–857.

watchfulness, stress, frustration, and even, on occasion, uncontrolled rage.[37] To wait in line is to endure "an interval of non-being, the black space between events and the outcome of desires."[38] The personal cost of being caught in this limbo is intensified both by the sense of degradation inherent in waiting[39] and by an enhanced awareness that "time, a fraction of one's life, is being stolen away, irrecoverably lost."[40] For some, the imposition of delay even comprises a ritual insult[41]—a process of deprivation rendered all the more offensive because the queue becomes, yet more insidiously, a location of entrapment where participants are lured into escalating commitment. The greater the sunk cost of invested time, the more difficult it is to abandon the line.[42]

VI. PROPRIETARY CONNOTATIONS OF THE QUEUE

There seems to be widespread agreement amongst queue-watchers that a waiting line, although comprising only a random and temporary collocation of strangers, constitutes a "miniature social system" or an "embryonic social system with a set of norms for controlling conflict."[43] On closer analysis the device of the queue also discloses certain distinctly proprietary connotations or characteristics.

---

37. *See* Edgar Elías Osuna, *The Psychological Cost of Waiting*, 29 J. Mathematical Psychology 82, 82–83 (1985); Thierry Meyer, *Subjective Importance of Goal and Reactions to Waiting in Line, supra* note 19, at 820. The sunk cost of time generates a "striking increase in the degree of negative reciprocity" experienced by those who wait (Robert J. Oxoby and Diane Bischak, *Passing the Time: Other-Regarding Behavior and the Sunk Cost of Time, in* University of Calgary Department of Economics Discussion Paper 2005–03 at 22 (⟨http://econ.ucalgary.ca/fac-files/rjo/disc05-03.pdf⟩ (accessed 3 February 2009).

38. L. Morrow, *Waiting as a Way of Life*, Time, July 23, 1984, at 65. The queuer often lapses into a state of mindlessness or automaticity (*see* John A. Bargh and Tanya L. Chartrand, *The Unbearable Automaticity of Being*, 54 American Psychologist 462 (1999)).

39. *See* Schwartz, Queuing and Waiting, *supra* note 4, at 173.

40. Morrow, *Waiting as a Way of Life, supra* note 38, at 65.

41. *See* Schwartz, Queuing and Waiting, *supra* note 4, at 171 ("to render oneself motionless for the sake of another has always been one of the most humiliatingly radical forms of subordination").

42. *See* Hal R. Arkes and Catherine Blumer, *The Psychology of Sunk Cost*, 35 Organizational Behavior and Human Decision Processes 124, 137–138 (1985).

43. Mann, *Queue Culture, supra* note 20, at 349; Mann, *The Social Psychology of Waiting Lines*, 58 American Scientist 390 (1970). As a form of collective behavior, the queue can be said to embody a coordinated pattern of relationships governed by a shared set of beliefs (*see* Clark McPhail and Ronald T. Wohlstein, *Collective Locomotion as Collective Behavior*, 51 American Sociological Rev. 447 (1986); Milgram et al., *Response to Intrusion into Waiting Lines, supra* note 6, at 688).

A. Priority of Arrival

In attaching consequence to the order of arrival, the underlying norm of queuing behavior draws upon one of the most primitive canons of property jurisprudence—the idea that "first in time is first in right."[44] This ancient mantra has long served as a beacon illuminating the path toward a resolution of human conflicts. In the words of Lawrence Berger, people "follow it as an unwritten law in their social interaction,"[45] a proposition that can be verified, even at an early stage in human development, in any children's playground or school yard and, somewhat later, in any supermarket car park. Moreover, the rationale of first occupancy as the origin of preferential claims taps into some of the classic justificatory theories of property.[46] Temporal priority as a ground of right has a venerable philosophical provenance and may well draw additional strength from labor-based theories that found proprietary entitlement on the investment of personal effort (here the effort of the queuer in taking trouble to initiate or enter or remain in the queue).

The attribution of advantage on the footing of first arrival or first possession is at least as old as Roman law[47] and plays upon primal impulses and perceptions that lie deeply buried in the subconscious reaches of the human psyche.[48] In the view of many commentators, the rule of first possession remains "the dominant method of initially establishing property rights."[49] In contexts that are otherwise morally neutral, the factor of time (i.e., the publicly observable fact of

---

44. Richard A. Epstein, *Past and Future: The Temporal Dimension in the Law of Property*, 64 WASH. U. L. Q. 667, 669 (1986).

45. Lawrence Berger, *An Analysis of the Doctrine that "First in Time is First in Right,"* 64 NEB. L. REV. 349, 350 (1985).

46. *See* Richard A. Epstein, *Possession as the Root of Title*, 13 GA. L. REV. 1221, 1222 (1978–79); Carol M. Rose, *Possession as the Origin of Property*, 52 U. CHI. L. REV. 73 (1985–86).

47. *See* W. W. Buckland, A TEXTBOOK OF ROMAN LAW 205–208 (3rd ed. rev'd by P.G. Stein, 1963); J. Roland Pennock, *Thoughts on the Right to Private Property*, *in* NOMOS XII: PROPERTY 176 (J. R. Pennock and J. W. Chapman eds., 1980). "[A]s between mere possessors prior possession is a better right" (*Mabo v. Queensland (No 2)* (1992) 175 CLR 1, 210 per Toohey J.).

48. Anthropological research indicates that a principle of first possession was recognized by many primitive peoples (*see* W. SCHMIDT, DAS EIGENTUM AUF DEN ÄLTESTEN STUFEN DER MENSCHHEIT, BAND I, DAS EIGENTUM IN DEN URKULTUREN 192 (1937); W. NIPPOLD, DIE ANFÄNGE DES EIGENTUMS BEI DEN NATURVÖLKERN UND DIE ENTSTEHUNG DES PRIVATEIGENTUMS 83 (1954)).

49. *See* Dean Lueck, *The Rule of First Possession and the Design of the Law*, 8 J. LAW & ECON. 393 (1995). Even today sophisticated legal systems resort to relatively crude rules of thumb in the desperate attempt to provide a superficially principled scheme for the allocation of valued assets. Thus the lawyer brought up in the Anglo-American tradition still intones that "where the equities are equal, the first in time prevails."

first arrival) is commonly regarded, *faute de mieux*, as having a specially significant role in dictating distributional outcomes. In such cases the fragile discriminant of chronology offers a plausibly objective ground of distinction between competing (and otherwise inseparable) claims and, in the case of the queue for service, has the further advantage that sequence of arrival is a highly visible phenomenon. The immediate dividend is the avoidance of anomie and—precisely for this reason—temporal order begins, more subtly, to generate its own moral merit and to become an acceptable tool of social and economic governance.

B. Persistence of Presence

Mere prior arrival is not, of course, enough to determine the relative strength of claims within a queue. The normative code of the queue requires that each member should continue to stand in line for such period of time as is needed to reach the service point at the head of the queue. Central to the practice of queuing is the idea that the claim to service is forgone unless the queuer maintains a physical or territorial presence within the line. To validate the priority obtained through early arrival, the queuer must spend time in the queue "not only to demonstrate to latecomers that he occupies a given position, but also to demonstrate that his right to priority is confirmed by an unquestionable willingness to undergo further suffering to get the commodity."[50] In this way the subculture of the queue derives one of its most important elements from a Western perception of time, where "great emphasis is placed on priority by time serving."[51] The investment of time and suffering tends to generate enormous respect for claims of priority within a society that endorses the correlation of effort and reward and in which the equilibration of personal discomfort and personal gain is widely regarded as a foundational principle of distributive justice.[52] In a context where few objective factors separate the claims of competitors for a desired good, the normative order of the queue thus falls back on a primitive criterion of voluntarily

50. Mann, *Queue Culture, supra* note 20, at 344. It is, of course, true that certain service-providers nowadays issue sequentially numbered queue tickets, thereby releasing the queuer from the necessity of maintaining an active presence in the line-up and leaving current priority to be indicated by an overhead display (*see* Moran, *Queuing up in Post-War Britain, supra* note 15, at 297).

51. Mann, *The Social Psychology of Waiting Lines, supra* note 43, at 390. It is not without interest that, in certain non-Western societies where time is less highly valued and less closely regulated, the queue functions much less effectively or—in some cases—not at all (*see* Edward T. Hall, The Silent Language 23–41 (1959); R.L. Lee, *Malaysian Queue Culture: An Ethnography of Urban Public Behavior*, 12 Southeast Asian Journal of Social Science 36, 39 (1984)).

52. *See* George C. Homans, Social Behaviour: Its Elementary Forms 75 (1961); Schwartz, Queuing and Waiting, *supra* note 4, at 93–94.

undertaken exposure to the pain or disamenity of standing in line.[53] The willingness to suffer otherwise purposeless hardship is viewed as a potent surrogate for a Lockean investment of labor.

C. The Property of the Queuer

It is of the essence of the waiting line that each queuer controls a crudely defined three-dimensional zone that symbolizes his or her rank within the line, the precise locus of that control gradually shifting as the queue shuffles its way forward toward its destination. The queuer holds, in effect, a kind of mobile property in land, a portable space that is uniquely and recognizably his or hers and is defensible against all comers.[54] But the proprietary quality of the claim rests on rather more than the assertion of rights over a physical territory. Queuing behavior is all about the ownership, management, and conservation of the commodity of *time*. Time constitutes a latent, but all-important, fourth dimension in the parceling up of rights in a queue. None of this should surprise any land lawyer brought up in the common law tradition. Time has always been an essential component of the common law explanation of real ownership: the various "estates" in land were (and still are) defined by a coefficient of time.[55] For centuries the venerable doctrine of estates has encapsulated the idea that one can have property in time.[56]

---

53. One of the virtues that the queue rewards is patience—a term whose semantic roots are precisely those of passion or suffering (*see* SCHWARTZ, QUEUING AND WAITING, *supra* note 4, at 183).

54. *See* Robert Sommer, *Studies in Personal Space*, 22 SOCIOMETRY 247, 247–248 (1959), and compare W. H. Auden's classic calculation of the extent of personal space: "Some thirty inches from my nose, The frontier of my Person goes . . ." ("Thanksgiving for a Habitat" (I. Prologue: The Birth of Architecture (Postscript)) in W. H. AUDEN: COLLECTED POEMS 519 (Edward Mendelson ed., 1976)). Auden's estimate of preferred interpersonal distance is borne out, at least in Anglo-American culture, by various studies. For example, in his discussion of "proxemic zones," Edward Hall defined the "far phase" of "personal distance" (as distinct from intimate, social or public distance) as comprising a span of two and a half to four feet (THE HIDDEN DIMENSION: MAN'S USE OF SPACE IN PUBLIC AND PRIVATE 113–114 (1966)).

55. KEVIN GRAY and SUSAN FRANCIS GRAY, ELEMENTS OF LAND LAW para 1.3.5 (5th ed., 2009). *See Walsingham's Case* (1573) 2 Plowd 547, 555, 75 ER 805 at 816–817.

56. Nor, incidentally, was the common law any stranger to the queue. The flexibility afforded by the rich taxonomy of time-related estates allowed interests in land to be ordered sequentially. For centuries the process of family endowment among the members of a social élite was heavily dependent on the construction and maintenance of complex chains of successive entitlement to dynastic wealth (*see* LLOYD BONFIELD, MARRIAGE SETTLEMENTS 1601–1740: THE ADOPTION OF THE STRICT SETTLEMENT (1983); Alain Pottage, *Proprietary Strategies: The Legal Fabric of Aristocratic Settlements*, 61 MOD. L. REV. 162, 172–174 (1998)).

The modern phenomenon of the physical line-up for service is likewise directed toward a power-related ordering of property in time. By making the client wait for a desired service, the service-provider converts the queuer's time to its (i.e., the service-provider's) use. But, as against all persons *other* than those ahead in the line, the queuer can assert a different kind of property in time. Whereas most of the common law estates in land were diminished by the passage of time, the entitlement that the queuer values and defends—let us, for the moment, simply call it the queuer's "mobile estate" in land—is far from a wasting asset. It draws its primary strength precisely from the *effluxion* of time. The service-provider may have assumed immediate possession of the queuer's time, but the queuer holds, as it were, a reversionary estate that gathers significance with every passing moment. Although the queuer plainly suffers a loss of productive time by having to wait, the queuer can claim, in turn, that his or her place in the line symbolizes a property in *spent* time—an investment that has escalating value as the queuers progress toward the service point. Indeed, the steadily increasing likelihood of eventual access to service represents the only compensation that the queuer will ever receive for the imposed disbenefit of having to queue. While the service-provider has plainly made a preemptive raid upon the commodity of time, the queuer—in the cascade-effect of this pyramidal ordering of time—has acquired a time-related and time-generated "estate" that can be asserted against the rest of the world except those ahead in the queue.[57] Not by accident does recent queue scholarship confirm that a significant component of the queuer's experience of standing in line involves the making of "downward comparisons" with persons behind in the queue.[58]

VII. SEMANTIC AND CULTURAL CONNOTATIONS OF THE QUEUE

It is also worth observing, at this point, that the social practice of queuing is bound up in an ancient nexus of interpenetrating semantic links. It may be recalled that the radical meaning of the term "estate" is drawn from the Latin *stare* (to stand). Embedded in the etymology of "estate" is the very notion of "standing"—the physical process of bipedal nonmobile self-support. In one archaic use of the term, the word "estate" connoted a relative standing or "status"—the condition or position in which one stood relative to others within

57. This analysis sits quite comfortably with leading perceptions of property as consisting primarily in *control over access* to valued goods and desired benefits (*see Yanner v. Eaton* (1999) 201 CLR 351 at [18] per Gleeson C.J., Gaudron, Kirby and Hayne JJ. (High Court of Australia); Kevin Gray, *Property in Thin Air*, 50 CAMBRIDGE L.J. 252 at 299 (1991)).

58. *See* Rongrong Zhou and Dilip Soman, *Looking Back: Exploring the Psychology of Queuing and the Effect of the Number of People Behind*, 29 JOURNAL OF CONSUMER RESEARCH 517, 518–519 (2003)).

a socially stratified community. References to one's "estate" reverberated with an inbuilt sense of ranking or ordering.[59] So, as the queuers stand in line, maintaining their respective places, each is asserting a species of "estate"—a relative status—that is inherently linked with, and is calibrated by, the commodity of time. Each queuer's *status* or *estate* constitutes a bundle of entitlement in an amalgam of time and place—an entitlement that is opposable not only against those further back in the queue, but also against all others who have not yet joined the line. It is, indeed, this profoundly proprietary perception of the queuer's claim that accounts for, and gives color to, the behavioral patterns that comprise the empirically observable emanations of queuing conduct. Although the social cohesion of the queue may be a product of collective rationality—quite possibly a prudential or learned response to a particular mismatch of supply and demand—it is the instinctive, even if seldom articulated, proprietary characterization of the queuer's rights that triggers a range of reactions to the classic problems of the queue.[60]

At this juncture it can also be queried whether there is more than a mere semantic link between "estate" ownership and the practice of standing in line. There is, in fact, some tentative evidence of a cultural or socio-legal affinity between the Anglo-Saxon conceptualism of estate ownership and the interpersonal discipline of the queue. The practice of queuing tends to be most strongly prevalent in jurisdictions that have always been familiar with the legal apparatus of "estates" in land, that is, with the sequential arrangement of various grades of time-bounded ownership. It has been wickedly observed that "[a]n Englishman, even if he is alone, forms an orderly queue of one."[61] Writing in 1944, George Orwell likewise noted the willingness of the English to stand in line,[62] a process of social self-regulation that has been traced through into more recent times by professional scholars of the queue.[63] Although there is also now a suggestion

---

59. We have only to revisit the well-known, if somewhat dated, lines of the hymn composed by Mrs. Cecil Frances Alexander (1818–1895): "The rich man in his castle, the poor man at his gate, God made them, high and lowly, and ordered their estate."

60. Some of these classic problems are highlighted in *Legislative Drafting* 55 CLARITY (May) 4 (2006). Here Clarity, the international association promoting plain legal language, used the practice of queuing as a focus for a special master class devoted to drafting a "Queues Bill" for the "governance of queues in public places." I am grateful to Professor Peter Butt, a past President of Clarity, for drawing this exercise to my attention.

61. GEORGE MIKES, HOW TO BE AN ALIEN: A HANDBOOK FOR BEGINNERS AND MORE ADVANCED PUPILS 44 (1946) ("Queueing is the national passion of an otherwise dispassionate race. The English are very shy about it, and deny that they adore it").

62. George Orwell, *The English People, in* THE COLLECTED ESSAYS, JOURNALISM AND LETTERS OF GEORGE ORWELL, VOL. 3: AS I PLEASE 1943–1945 2 (Sonia Orwell and Ian Angus eds., 1968).

63. *See* Thomas L. Saaty, *Ordering Disorderly Queues, in* QUEUING THEORY: RECENT DEVELOPMENTS AND APPLICATIONS 209 (R. Cruon ed., 1967); Moran, *Queuing up in Post-War Britain, supra* note 15.

that the social code of the queue is beginning to break down amidst the incivility of an increasingly yobbish subculture in Britain,[64] there remains some ground for hypothesizing that the characteristically English discipline of the queue may owe something to a subliminal absorption of "estate" methodology within a wider popular consciousness.[65] It may just be that, over many centuries, the orderly sequencing of entitlement inherent in the doctrine of estates percolated more generally into a public mindset that responds positively to a norm of queue formation. In some deep sense each citizen knew his or her place in the grand scheme of things.

The possibility of such a cultural association is supported by the negative correlation that seems to exist between queue discipline and those non-common-law-based legal systems which have no knowledge of any doctrine of estates. It has long been recognized, for example, that respect for the queue is an Anglo-Saxon[66] rather than a Latin phenomenon.[67] In recent years student visitors to England from continental Europe have been targeted with lessons in the art of queuing.[68] One intriguing study of queuing in Hong Kong's Disneyland has also pointed to the strong resistance to queuing culture exhibited by mainland Chinese visitors to the park as compared with the greater degree of queue conformity evident among the colonially influenced Hong Kong Chinese.[69] Nor is it without significance that, in preparation for the 2008 Olympic Games, the 15 million inhabitants of Beijing were reportedly indoctrinated, through the medium of

---

64. David Stewart-David, *The Stressful Queue*, 4 LOGISTICS AND TRANSPORT FOCUS 50 (2002).

65. The process may have been reinforced by the literary manipulation of successive land entitlements in works such as Jane Austen's PRIDE AND PREJUDICE and SENSE AND SENSIBILITY. *See, e.g.*, Günther H. Treitel, *Jane Austen and the Law*, 100 LAW QUARTERLY REV. 549, 557–567 (1984); Luanne Bethke Redmond, *Land, Law and Love*, 11 PERSUASIONS, THE JANE AUSTEN JOURNAL 46 (1989); Gavin Little, *Literature and Legal History: Analysing Methodology*, 3 ENTERTAINMENT AND SPORTS L.J. (2006).

66. *See* EDWARD T. HALL, THE SILENT LANGUAGE 157, 201–202 (1959); ALEC M. LEE, APPLIED QUEUEING THEORY 19, 115 (1966); SCHWARTZ, QUEUING AND WAITING, *supra* note 4, at 108; Milgram et al., *Response to Intrusion into Waiting Lines, supra* note 6, at 688; Corbridge, *Waiting in Line, supra* note 18, at 183–184.

67. It has been suggested that countries whose linguistic roots are within the Romance family (e.g., France, Italy, and Spain) score much higher on a "power distance" scale than countries whose linguistic roots are Germanic (e.g., England). Larger "power distance" connotes a cultural acceptance of inequality, privilege, patronage, and the idea that "might prevails over right" (GEERT HOFSTEDE, CULTURES AND ORGANIZATIONS: SOFTWARE OF THE MIND 42 (1997)).

68. *Foreign Students Given 'Queuing' Lessons*, BBC NEWS, 5 August 2002, http://news.bbc.co.uk/1/hi/england/2169460.stm) (accessed February 3, 2009).

69. Henry Fountain, *The Real Line Dividing Cultures*, INTERNATIONAL HERALD TRIBUNE ASIA-PACIFIC, 18 September 2005) (http://www.iht.com/articles/2005/09/18/news/lines.php) (accessed February 3, 2009).

mobile phone text messages, in the practice of queuing. The Chinese Communist Party designated the eleventh day of each month as "Queuing Day" and, under the banner "To queue is civilized, to be polite is glorious," volunteer wardens attended at bus stops in a concerted attempt to instigate a general acceptance of queuing protocol.[70] In Calcutta, as Cornell economics professor Kaushik Basu has noted, the drive toward instilling a similar queue discipline began some years earlier, once again taking the form of volunteers with loudspeakers "urging anarchic gatherings of men and women at bus stops to stand in line."[71]

VIII. PROPRIETARY BEHAVIOR WITHIN THE QUEUE

The subliminal understanding that the queuer has some kind of elementary or symbolic "estate" reflects a mindset that taps deep into our biosocial drives and motivations. The imperative to conserve and protect assets in our possession may simply be rooted in our evolutionary biology. Some have even spoken of a "property recognition gene" as playing an important role in the natural selection of our species.[72] Moreover, the queuer's perception of, and willingness to defend, his own stake within the artificial order of the waiting line provides another vivid demonstration of the "endowment effect."[73] According to this widely accepted analysis of human behavior,[74] the sheer fact of possession confers on one's holdings an additional, subjective, and economically irrational value. A thing, once acquired, seems to its possessor more precious than was thought immediately prior to its acquisition. This "endowment effect," when coupled with the closely allied theory of loss aversion,[75] emphasizes the heightened salience of apprehended deprivation. Thus it is that those who stand in line resort, perhaps instinctively, to well-known proprietary strategies in their

70. *Wait for It: Queueing Joins the Olympics*, TIMES, 12 February 2007, at 33; *Form a Line, Please!* (http://english.cri.cn/3100/2007/02/11/1261@195043.htm) (accessed February 3, 2009).

71. Kaushik Basu, *Queues and Capitalism* (2004), http://news.bbc.co.uk/1/hi/world/south_asia/3579988.stm (accessed February 3, 2009).

72. Jeffrey E. Stake, *The Uneasy Case for Adverse Possession*, 89 GEO. L.J. 2419 at 2425 (2001). *See also* Owen D. Jones and Sarah F. Brosnan, *Law, Biology, and Property: A New Theory of the Endowment Effect*, 49 WM. & MARY L. REV. 1935 (2008).

73. *See* Richard H. Thaler, *Toward a Positive Theory of Consumer Choice*, 1 JOURNAL OF ECONOMIC BEHAVIOR AND ORGANIZATION 39 (1980); Daniel Kahneman, Jack L. Knetsch, and Richard H. Thaler, *The Endowment Effect, Loss Aversion, and Status Quo Bias*, 5 J. ECONOMIC PERSPECTIVES 193 (1991).

74. *See* Brian Knutson, G. Elliott Wimmer, Scott Rick, Nick G. Hollon, Drazen Prelec, and George Loewenstein, *Neural Antecedents of the Endowment Effect*, 58 NEURON 814 (2008).

75. According to the theory of loss aversion, losses have a greater subjective impact than objectively commensurate gains (*see* Jeffrey E. Stake, *The Uneasy Case for Adverse Possession*, *supra* note 72, at 2459).

manipulations of, and responses to, the queue-form. Whether consciously or not, they put into practice many of the perceptions and devices associated with proprietary advantage or entitlement.[76] As we shall see, queuers assert and enjoy a "property" in the waiting line that is considered to be alienable but not generally shareable, which is defensible but not ultimately survivable.

A. Reserving Places

Persistence of physical presence is an important component of the discipline of the queue. In the orthodox theory of the queue the person who abandons his or her place in the line prima facie forfeits any claim to priority.[77] The man who steps out of the tiresomely lengthy queue at the post office is taken irreversibly to have reneged or renounced his ranking in the ordinality of entitlement. Such "property" as he previously held in relation to the queue has now simply evaporated. Even if a couple of minutes later he regrets his act of abandonment, he will be expected, under the normal convention, to rejoin the queue at its rearmost point. One's position in the queue is, uniquely, a *worked* space; and to fail to work the space is to forgo the benefits associated with that space.

Yet it is notorious among queue-watchers that the queue, particularly in its larger-scale or marathon manifestations, is an evolutive social mechanism. The waiting line is a social system that breeds collaborative or mutually supportive subsystems based on acts of local cooperation or "local conspiracy."[78] Such strategic developments serve to ease the discomfort of waiting, thereby reducing the overall stress of queue discipline. One such renegotiation or modification of queuing norms is the practice of allowing "time-outs" or relaxations of the requirement of constant physical presence within the line. These collectively endorsed variations can take several forms, most involving some kind of vicarious or token representation in the queue. Over limited periods the participants in a line-up frequently recognize the validity of a substitutionary presence (whether established by a human associate or by some inanimate object) as part of a locally intuited or implicitly bargained compromise of the conventional rules of the queue.[79] Yet, by allowing such strategies of symbolic retention, modern

---

76. In what follows there is inevitably some resonance of the "law ways" uncovered in primitive social systems by Llewellyn and Adamson Hoebel (*see* Karl N. Llewellyn and E. Adamson Hoebel, The Cheyenne Way: Conflict and Case Law in Primitive Jurisprudence (1941)).

77. Brady, *Lining Up for Star-Wars Tickets*, *supra* note 1, at 161.

78. *Id.* at 162.

79. Leon Mann's classic study of crowds waiting in line for several days for tickets to the 1967 AFL World Series in Melbourne observed that groups of queuers commonly organized a "shift" system in which one or two members of the group physically guarded the group's position until relieved by someone else as custodian of the group's place in the line. Other queuers who had come to the line alone preserved rank order during temporary absences by the placing of some token item of personal property as a position marker.

queuing behavior merely replicates—in some subliminal mimicry—a timeless normative device for the preservation of territorial advantage. The age-old Roman formula of *corpus* and *animus* presumed a man's possession of land to persist even in the absence of personal physical presence, so long as the claimant could point to an underlying *animus possidendi* (or intention to possess) coupled with a *corpus possessionis* (such as might be constituted by the proxy presence of a slave or son or hirer who happened to be in practical control of the land in question).[80] In this way classical Roman law oversaw the displacement of crudely physical identifications of human territorial presence by a vastly more subtle and sensitive understanding of the control relationships that may emerge between people and defined geographical spaces.[81] In endorsing a similarly sophisticated protocol of valid time-outs, modern queuing behavior merely plays out the ancient drama of *corpus* and *animus* as its instinctive response to the problem of delay and the need to minimize the vexation of the waiting line. This translation of antique legal liturgy into modern social practice becomes a recurrent feature of our analysis of the phenomenon of the queue.

B. Trading Places

A different range of standard proprietary ploys comes to the fore with the question whether (and if so, to what extent) a queuer's position in a physical waiting line can be made the subject of a dealing or disposition to others. As noted earlier, the queue for service generates an accretion of value in spent time and the commodity of spent time may have widely divergent values for different people. The queue therefore affords an opportunity for various kinds of transaction with the place or position that symbolizes each queuer's accrued entitlement. In so far as facility for commerce (i.e., the potential for alienation) is commonly viewed as an essential indicium of a property right, these manipulations of the valuable asset

---

At some points in the wait, two thirds of the places in the line were held by objects rather than people (Mann, *Queue Culture, supra* note 20, at 345–346; *The Social Psychology of Waiting Lines, supra* note 43, at 392).

80. W. W. Buckland, A Textbook of Roman Law 202 (3rd ed. rev'd by P.G. Stein, 1963); J. A. C. Thomas, Textbook of Roman Law 143–146 (1976).

81. Many modern legal systems have built explicitly upon these Roman foundations in predicating the circumstances in which a personal presence can be deemed to continue notwithstanding actual physical absence. See, for instance, much of the residential tenancy legislation found throughout the common law world, where requirements of continued occupancy by a tenant have been held satisfied, not by physical presence on the part of the tenant, but merely by "some visible state of affairs in which the animus possidendi finds expression" (*Brown v. Brash and Ambrose* [1948] 2 KB 247 at 254–255). Similar solutions have emerged in the context of continuity of occupation for the purpose of "overriding interest" protection pursuant to England's Land Registration Acts of 1925 and 2002. *See generally* Gray and Gray, Elements of Land Law paras 4.7.8, 8.2.83 (5th ed., 2009).

encapsulated within the queuer's ordinal ranking inevitably have a proprietary resonance.

The most straightforward proprietary dealing in which the queuer may engage is the transaction of gift. The normative code of the queue views as entirely legitimate the simple act of voluntary transfer of one's place to another (i.e., to a donee). Provided that the transaction accords the donee, in the strictest terms, no privileges (actual or potential) beyond those already enjoyed by the donor, the singular act of gift operates by way of direct substitution and involves no negative externalities for other members of the queue. The donor releases his or her place to the donee and immediately abandons the queue and any personal claim to priority. Much more problematic is the possibility that an existing queuer may attempt to use his or her place in the queue as an object of largesse to be divided among or shared with a number of friends or associates. This distributive version of the act of gift clearly entails negative consequences for members of the queue behind, the introduction of newcomers into the line inevitably detracting from the priority already earned by those who have invested time standing in line. Such a maneuver resembles the long discontinued historic process of "subinfeudation" or, in more modern terms, a declaration of trust of one's "property" in the queue in favor of another or others. Curiously there appears to be some support, within the normative code of the queue, for the idea that under certain heavily controlled conditions existing queuers may "keep a place" for, and eventually import, another person into the line to stand alongside them.[82] Although this custom of place keeping is commonly a cause of friction—precisely because it *does* involve negative externalities—the privilege is sometimes tolerated, especially where it is invoked in favor of a spouse or a particularly close associate of the queuer.[83]

Another form of dealing with the "property" held by the queuer involves the sale of his or her place within the waiting line. Since the ranking of individuals in the queue cannot normally reflect the differential opportunity cost of their time, there is every incentive for Pareto-improving trades.[84] Even though it marks the ultimate commodification of time, profitable commerce in the asset of queue position is a phenomenon experienced right around the globe. Many people are

82. Mann, *Queue Culture*, *supra* note 20, at 349; Bernd H. Schmitt, Laurette Dubé, and France Leclerc, *Intrusions into Waiting Lines: Does the Queue Constitute a Social System?*, 63 Journal of Personality and Social Psychology 806, 807, 814 (1992); Brady, *Lining Up for Star-Wars Tickets*, *supra* note 1, at 159. *See also Legislative Drafting*, 55 Clarity (May) 7 (2006).

83. Kaushik Basu, *Queues and capitalism*, 2004, http://news.bbc.co.uk/1/hi/world/south_asia/3579988.stm (accessed February 2, 2009).

84. Felix Oberholzer-Gee, *A Market for Time: Fairness and Efficiency in Waiting Lines*, 59(3) Kyklos 427, 428 (2006). As a former Chief Justice of Ireland once observed, there is nothing unlawful in the sale of one's position in a waiting line (*Maher v. Minister for Agriculture and Rural Development* [2001] 2 IR 139 at 186 per Keane C.J.).

prepared to pay in order to reduce or eliminate waiting times. Such deals can occur indirectly, as, for example, where Hong Kong property speculators reportedly pay a daily queuing fee in the region of HK $1,000 to individuals who, on their behalf, wait in line for the chance to purchase apartments in a new development.[85] Likewise Leon Mann's study of Melbourne's mass queues of football fans in the 1960s revealed a substantial proportion of professional queuers (or freelance "scalpers") who waited in line for tickets that were destined for immediate onward transfer.[86] Direct "on the spot" sale of the queuer's physical position within the line is rarer, but certainly not unknown: Leon Mann reported the practice of trading places within line-ups for smash hits on Broadway during the 1950s.[87] By contrast, the conventional discipline of the queue is much more aggressively opposed to any attempt by an existing queuer to charge a fee for allowing a complete stranger to "cut into" the queue immediately ahead of him. Such market transactions, since they inflict the clearest prejudice upon the interests of those waiting behind in the line, are undertaken—if at all—only with some sense of embarrassment, shame, or guilt on the part of the profiteer.[88] To sell priority within the queue in this way is, effectively, to facilitate the antisocial practice of queue-jumping.

C. Taking Places

Proprietary perceptions of queuing behavior acquire a further dimension when attention is focused on the response of queue members to any attempted bypass of that most elementary precept of collectively endorsed queue discipline, the basal principle of "first come, first served" (the FCFS rule). Such violations of the normative code of the waiting line connote the clearest threat to both private and public conceptions of justice. The shadow of John Rawls hangs heavily, of course, over any discussion of justice—that "first virtue of social institutions"—and for Rawls it was an intrinsic requirement of an individual's humanity that he or she

---

85. *See Choi Man Wai v. HKSAR* [2001] 4 HKCU 1; *HKSAR v. Lam Chin Cheung, Raymond* [2001] 666 HKCU 1.

86. Mann, *Queue Culture, supra* note 20, at 343; Mann, *The Social Psychology of Waiting Lines, supra* note 43, at 390.

87. There is evidence that "placeholders" are routinely employed on Washington's Capitol Hill, on a remarkably profitable basis, to remain in line for hours (or sometimes days) for general-public seats at scheduled committee hearings, only to be replaced at the last moment by those client-lobbyists who wish to influence legislative initiatives (*see* Brian Montopoli, *The Queue Crew: Waiting in Line for a Living, in* Legal Affairs, January/February 2004).

88. Quite frequently, as reported in one study, the individual who allows an interloper to cut into the queue in return for an offer of money reward subsequently turns down the fee (*see* Oberholzer-Gee, *A Market for Time: Fairness and Efficiency in Waiting Lines, supra* note 84, at 432–437).

should be treated in a manner that fosters positive self-regard.[89] But concerns for individual dignity are merely a personalized emanation of a more public, more general quest for the achievement of a just society. Public and private interact continuously. Respect for personhood is a vital component of moral community—and no less so where that moral community is, in microcosmic form, the physical queue for service. It follows that notions of justice and fairness have been extensively canvassed in the literature of queue scholarship.[90] It should cause no surprise that these twin concerns should fasten, in large part, upon "impolite arrivals" in the line,[91] i.e., illicit attempts to disrupt the conventional order of the queue.[92] In all those social contexts where the discipline of the queue has taken root, nonconsensual physical entry within the waiting line (i.e., "queue-jumping") is commonly viewed as meriting social disapproval except in extraordinary circumstances of need or emergency. The mischief of queue-jumping is twofold, these two aspects relating respectively to the *private* and *public* impacts of the conduct in question.

First, the act of queue-jumping imposes an immediate cost or disbenefit upon all individuals in a queue who stand behind the point of intrusion. Their waiting time is inevitably (albeit sometimes only marginally) increased. In terms of a more clearly proprietary analysis, the victims of the intrusion have suffered a taking of their *property*—property in the form of spent time. The value of their investment—the sunk cost of time—has been diluted by the invasion of the interloper. An ancillary feature of this deprivation is the diminution of self-respect occasioned by the intrusion. By his obvious indifference to the stored value of the queuers' investment of time, the interloper has imposed an additional demoralization cost—a uniquely personal deficit—upon those who suffer the impact of his arrival in the line.[93] This disregard for personal dignity—even if involving no actual physical contact—is precisely the kind of wrong encapsulated

89. John Rawls, A Theory of Justice 3, 178–179 (1973).

90. The issue of fairness in the queue is very important to people in the waiting line—"perhaps even more important than the duration of the wait" (David Raz, Hanoch Levy, and Benjamin Avi-Itzhak, *A Resource-Allocation Queueing Fairness Measure*, 32 ACM SIGMETRICS Performance Evaluation Review 130 (2004). In Richard Larson's words, "fear of social injustice can often dominate queue waiting times" (*Perspectives on Queues*, *supra* note 14, at 896).

91. Jingwen Li, *From FIFO to LIFO: A Functional Ordering of Service Delay via Arrival Discipline*, 33 J. Applied Probability 507, 508 (1996).

92. Some violations are, of course, indirect. For example, a queuer who enters a supermarket express check-out queue with more than the permitted number of items is engaging in an act of queue-jumping just as surely as the person who buts his way into a more general queue.

93. For a classic discussion of demoralization costs, *see* Frank I. Michelman, *Property, Utility, and Fairness: Comments on the Ethical Foundations of "Just Compensation" Law*, 80 Harv. L. Rev. 1165, 1214 (1966–67).

within the common law notion of assault.[94] The act of encroachment is, moreover, an act of forcible dispossession—an offence against a peculiarly individualized sense of territoriality[95] or personal space. Some commentators refer to this bundle of essentially private consequences in terms of an "individual costs" analysis of queue-jumping.[96]

Second, the nonconsensual infiltration of the queue-jumper inflicts a rather different, and much more public, form of injury upon the social microcosm of the queue. The interloper's invasion is stigmatized not only because of its negative impact on individual queuers, but also because it connotes contempt for the entire normative order of the queue.[97] The indignation aroused by the encroachment derives, in part, from "the perceived disrespect the intruder has shown the system of social rules under which all members of the moral community are expected to live."[98] A significant disruption of a particular social order has occurred.[99] Waiting lines "are a public matter and therefore demand ethical behavior."[100] The act of invasion betokens a moment of systemic rejection and renunciation—a purely self-interested betrayal of the collective cultural values embodied in the institution of the waiting line. The social distaste generated by the interloper's disregard for these values has been described by some commentators in terms of "moral outrage"[101]; and the inevitable response to this disrespect (and the "unjust" consequences with which it is associated) is an emotion of moralistic anger directed against the wrongdoer.[102]

Queue-watchers have suggested that on entering the miniature social system of the waiting line, queuers "assume roles that may entail obligations if the system is under threat" and are therefore "motivated by concerns that transcend

---

94. From a very early stage the common law afforded extensive protection to sophisticated human sensitivities. The solicitude for the psyche that is demonstrated in the recognition of the wrong of assault remains "the only instance in English jurisprudence of a mere offensive sensation unaccompanied by any untoward psychosomatic symptoms, let alone external trauma, giving a cause of action for damages" (JOHN G. FLEMING, AN INTRODUCTION TO THE LAW OF TORTS 3 (1967)).

95. *See* Stanford M. Lyman and Marvin B. Scott, *Territoriality: A Neglected Sociological Dimension,* 15 SOCIAL PROBLEMS 236 (1967).

96. *See* Schmitt et al., *Intrusions into Waiting Lines, supra* note 82, at 806.

97. SCHWARTZ, QUEUING AND WAITING, *supra* note 4, at 94; Milgram et al., *Response to Intrusion into Waiting Lines, supra* note 6, at 684, 686–687.

98. Dale T. Miller, *Disrespect and the Experience of Injustice,* 52 ANNUAL REVIEW OF PSYCHOLOGY 527, 535 (2001).

99. For a vivid description of the naïve queuer's reaction to the interloper, *see* CHARLES H. COOLEY, HUMAN NATURE AND THE SOCIAL ORDER 282 (1983) (1902) ("Then he will certainly be angry").

100. Thomas L. Saaty, *Ordering Disorderly Queues, in* QUEUING THEORY: RECENT DEVELOPMENTS AND APPLICATIONS 210 (R. Cruon ed., 1967).

101. Schmitt et al., *Intrusions into Waiting Lines, supra* note 82, at 806.

102. *See* Miller, *Disrespect and the Experience of Injustice, supra* note 98, at 535.

individual cost considerations."[103] The collective response to queue violation by forced entry is, then, plainly one of general social disapproval. The expression of this disapproval ranges all the way from polite reminders of the existence of the queue, through hostile stares and gestures to vociferous jeering and outright acts of physical violence aimed at ejecting the trespasser from the line.[104] It is "[f]orce [which] underlies all allocative systems . . . all private ownership rights are ultimately founded on the ability to forcefully exclude potential competitors."[105] Yet one of the more fascinating findings of queuing research is the relative infrequency of direct physical action directed toward the expulsion of an interloper from the line.[106] There often appears to be a deep ambiguity in the response to acts of trespass within the line and, in this context, two aspects of the queue's reaction to violators have a particular significance for the property lawyer.

First, the classic studies of queuing behavior indicate that the primary responsibility for responding to an act of intrusion is seen as resting with those in the close vicinity of the trespass and, in particular, with the person standing right behind the point of forced entry.[107] Under the social code of the queue, this individual is regarded as owing a kind of fiduciary duty to the remainder of the waiting line to defend the integrity of the queuing system.[108] Placing the burden of resistance on the shoulders of the immediate victim is frequently rationalized on the surmise that this person, "either through his passive looks or careless surveillance . . . must have given some encouragement to the queue jumper"[109] or has been "careless in guarding his territory"[110]—a judgment that is strongly reminiscent of one of the standard rationales of adverse possession in the law of realty.[111] As always, the queuer's position in the waiting line is a worked space and failure to *work* the space, not least by defending it against all comers, may

---

103. Schmitt et al., *Intrusions into Waiting Lines, supra* note 82, at 814.

104. Where the stakes are highest (as, for example, in a queue for a limited supply of petrol or Cup Final tickets), the sanction will tend toward the more severe end of the scale. In his study of Melbourne football fans, Leon Mann recounted that five individuals were hospitalized after four different brawls broke out over queue-jumping in the ticket lines (*see* Mann, *Queue Culture, supra* note 20, at 347; Mann, *The Social Psychology of Waiting Lines, supra* note 43, at 392). *See also* Milgram et al., *Response to Intrusion into Waiting Lines, supra* note 6, at 684–685.

105. John Umbeck, *Might Makes Rights: A Theory of the Formation and Initial Distribution of Property Rights*, 19 ECONOMIC INQUIRY 38, 39, 57 (1981).

106. *See* Mann, *Queue Culture, supra* note 20, at 347.

107. Mann, *Queue Culture, supra* note 20, at 348.

108. *See* Schmitt et al., *Intrusions into Waiting Lines, supra* note 82, at 814. "[T]hose closest to the disruptive event are felt to have a special obligation to deal with it. There may be reluctance on the part of people further back in the line to do someone else's duty" (Milgram et al., *Response to Intrusion into Waiting Lines, supra* note 6, at 688).

109. Mann, *Queue Culture, supra* note 20, at 348.

110. Mann, *The Social Psychology of Waiting Lines, supra* note 43, at 392.

111. *See* GRAY and GRAY, ELEMENTS OF LAND LAW paras 9.1.7, 9.1.11 (5th ed., 2009).

lead to disadvantageous consequences that mimic the traditional legal response to displacements of a more general proprietary order.

The attention of property lawyers is also drawn instinctively to a *second* feature of the queue's ambivalent reaction to violators of the FCFS principle. There is evidence that the queue is a powerfully adaptive social institution, equipped with a significant capacity to absorb disturbances of the normative order of the waiting line. For this reason the queue often forbears to react aggressively against wrongful intrusion, preferring instead to co-opt within the line the very trespasser whose actions pose a danger to its survival. As Stanley Milgram and his research team concluded, "[o]nce an intruder is part of the line, she or he has an investment in its continued existence."[112] Others have emphasized that the greatest threat to the order of the queue is the appearance of *disorder*. Prolonged or violent confrontations with isolated trespassers detract from the perception that the queue has a stable and orderly structure, engendering instead an apprehension that the queue is fragile and noncohesive. At this point there is a "danger of complete disintegration" of the waiting line.[113] Over-ready resort to violent ejection of an interloper "seems to represent a kind of public acknowledgment that the queue is no longer organized and under control," an implicit concession that may well encourage an epidemic of queue-jumping.[114] The waiting line therefore exhibits, quite commonly, a preparedness to "ignore, adjust to, and tolerate" disturbances rather than risk the "escalation of a localized incident into a general fracas."[115] As Barry Schwartz once wrote, "the chaotic dissolution of the queue can be forestalled not only by the default of deviance but also by its contingent toleration." [116]

The prudential, self-serving logic that underlies the preservation of the integrity of the queue mirrors exactly the systematic deception practiced by the more general notion of property. The trappings of property as an institution are fiercely defended lest anyone perceive that the *imperium* of property has no clothes. On a daily basis we all participate in a mutual conspiracy of property talk, allowing ourselves to believe the shared pretence that proprietary analysis betokens a stable, ordered structure of entitlements to the goods of life.[117] We tolerate the mumbo-jumbo of property not least because the crude linguistic shorthand of our proprietary allusions promotes a certain low-level communicative efficiency. Rarely does anyone break rank in this exercise of juristic solidarity, although the High Court of Australia came close some years ago in suggesting that "it may be . . . that 'the ultimate fact about property is that it does not really exist: it is

112. Milgram et al., *Response to Intrusion into Waiting Lines, supra* note 6, at 689.
113. Mann, *The Social Psychology of Waiting Lines, supra* note 43, at 392.
114. *See* Mann, *Queue Culture, supra* note 20, at 349.
115. Milgram et al., *Response to Intrusion into Waiting Lines, supra* note 6, at 688.
116. SCHWARTZ, QUEUING AND WAITING, *supra* note 4, at 96.
117. *See* Gray, *Property in Thin Air, supra* note 57, at 252, 305.

mere illusion.'"[118] For the most part, however, we rally together to preserve the systemic integrity of property as a normative order and, historically, one of the principal ways in which this order has been maintained lies in the conscious condonation of certain isolated misappropriations of entitlement. Thus for example seisin, even when based on wrongful possession, was always accorded a certain protection by the common law "in the interests of peace."[119] From the earliest days of the common law there was a large social interest in "the quieting of possession."[120] Although—perhaps *because*—it allows the maturing of wrongs into rights, the law of adverse possession has served to promote the overall stability and integrity of the regime of property.[121]

In a variety of contexts—whether the arena of international law or a modern municipal legal order or even the humble microcosm of the queue—property is an organic phenomenon. It has a certain self-defining quality. It comprises, is founded upon, and is ultimately no more than, socially or politically constituted fact.[122] It is for this reason that statutes of limitation regularize what are usually relatively minor deviations from existing property allocations. By incorporating a principle of efficient trespass, the law ensures that land titles conform to lived boundaries. In so doing, the law marks a controlled trade-off between moral right and social reality—an absorption of wrongdoing within the mainstream of proprietary entitlement—which, in the long perspective of legal history, has reinforced rather than weakened the institution of property. It seems that the social mores of the queue involve a degree of elasticity that serves essentially similar purposes.

IX. CONCLUSIONS

The practice of queuing for service provides an intriguing subject for the property theorist. Here, in a context clearly distanced from any formal application of proprietary language or doctrine, we have a rare opportunity to witness the genesis of a legal institution. Modern astronomers are able to gaze across space and observe in real time the birth of a star many eons ago. In much the same way, by analyzing the conventions of queuing behavior, today's property theorists can catch a fleeting glimpse of the creation of proprietary order. Out there in the parallel universe of everyday sociality we find a behavioral form

---

118. *Yanner v. Eaton* (1999) 201 CLR 351 at [17] per Gleeson C.J., Gaudron, Kirby and Hayne JJ.

119. *Minister of State for the Army v. Dalziel* (1944) 68 CLR 261 at 276 per Latham C.J.

120. *See A'Court v. Cross* (1825) 3 Bing 329 at 332–333, 130 ER 540 at 541 per Best C.J.

121. *See* Gray and Gray, Elements of Land Law paras 9.1.6–9.1.12 (5th ed., 2009).

122. Kevin Gray and Susan Francis Gray, *The Idea of Property in Land, in* Land Law: Themes and Perspectives 18–27 (S. Bright and J. K. Dewar eds., 1998).

that mirrors back to us some of the mechanisms by which human beings have striven to reduce or control the potential anomie of competitive existence.

As Neil Brady has said, the queue discloses "the quintessential ethical conflict in economics and society: the pursuit of self-interest in a context of general fairness."[123] Central to the management of this fundamental tension between self-advancement and common civility is some deep, largely inarticulate, awareness of property, or, more accurately, an awareness of "propriety."[124] If our investigation of the phenomenon of the queue has highlighted one thing, it is that queuing behavior bears the imprint of elementary property forms. Embedded in the mores of the queue are rudimentary perceptions of ownership, self-ownership, and personhood. In the queue are found the coded traces of proprietary order and, perhaps more importantly, some clue as to the origins of that order. It is true that the substantive content of the property notion has always proved tantalizingly elusive. But it may just be, as evidenced in the queue, that the element of "boundary" that is implicit in the conceptualism of ownership performs a minimal, but still meaningful, role in curtailing the human impulse toward purely predatory behavior.[125]

In the context of the queue, the idea of "boundary" has both a *public* and a *private* dimension. At the public level, the queue sets in place a moral geography that demarcates the waiting line as the exclusive channel of access to a desired service. Those outside the queue are clearly beyond the bounds of the distributional system comprised in the queue and, in the normative order of the waiting line, have no preemptive right to accelerated service. To a greater or lesser degree, the collectivity of the queue mediates relationships between the personnel waiting in line and upholds the immunity of the group from destructive invasion by strangers. At the private level, the queue recognizes the spatio-temporal ownership represented by each place in the line and operates a normative convention that there may be no nonconsensual advancement of position within the queue. Under this convention each queuer is entitled to defend against opportunistic attack the personal space that was assumed on arrival and which symbolizes both the queuer's ordinal ranking and the stored value of his or her commitment to the queue.

But why should the "silent language"[126] of the queue endorse these essentially proprietary responses? The answer seems to lie in an implicit compromise of self-interest—a social compact aimed at maximizing personal advantage while limiting interpersonal conflict and averting general anomie. As has often been

---

123. Brady, *Lining Up for Star-Wars Tickets, supra* note 1, at 157.

124. *See* Gregory S. Alexander, Commodity and Propriety: Competing Visions of Property in American Legal Thought (1997).

125. *See* Kevin Gray, *There's No Place Like Home!*, 11 J. South Pacific Law 73, 87 (2007) (http://www.paclii.org/journals/fJSPL/vol11no1/pdf/Gray.pdf).

126. Edward T. Hall, The Silent Language 15 (1959).

said, property is socially constructed. Thus, for John Wiseman, the queue rests on a "perceived congruence between individual and collective rationality." In Wiseman's analysis, the queue has "an undeniable collective rationality (when compared with the alternative chaos)" in circumstances where a sufficient number of persons see the queue "as being a rational alternative for themselves as individuals."[127] In effect, the queue socializes the acquisitive impulse for the sake of an ulterior benefit conferred on all who are prepared to play by house rules. The queue comprises, in this way, a self-governance mechanism calculated to promote and secure an average reciprocity of advantage.

The trigger for queue formation requires, of course, a critical mass of persons who are prepared to commit themselves to its distinctive normative order. Some four decades ago Leon Mann described the relative drawing power of "stimulus queues" at bus stops and library issue desks, noting the critical number of queuers required in different contexts to induce strangers to conform to the discipline of the waiting line.[128] In much the same way, the emergence of a more general normative regime of property requires the participation of sufficient numbers of people who are willing to be complicit in a regulatory system that suppresses the private predatory instinct in favor of a new collective order. The normativity of property is the consequence of a social contract which, as one queue-watcher has said, gives effect to a "more-or-less shared disposition to impose rationality" on a situation that could easily disintegrate into unspeakable anarchy.[129] Under this *quid pro quo*, the opportunity for unrestrained self-aggrandizement is surrendered in exchange for access to mutually enjoyed advantages of freedom and security in one's economic affairs. Yet again, C. B. Macpherson's famous tension between access and exclusion as polar features of the property phenomenon finds another form of resolution.[130] But voluntary commitment to the overall normative structure—whether of the queue or of property in general (it perhaps no longer matters)—does not completely displace the primal, biosocial instinct to defend personal advantage and exclude others from it. The impulse of uncurtailed self-interest is allowed to resurface as a legitimate, socially endorsed resistance to any encroachment upon the "estate" that has been assigned within the allocative order of the collectively agreed regime. Violation of that order (whether by queue-jumping or by theft) marks a serious breach of the social contract and usually leads to significant expressions of social disapprobation.

---

127. John A. Wiseman, *Aspects of Social Organisation in a Nigerian Petrol Queue*, 17(2) Journal of Modern African Studies 317, 319 (1979).

128. Mann, *The Social Psychology of Waiting Lines*, *supra* note 43, at 397–398.

129. Brady, *Lining Up for Star-Wars Tickets*, *supra* note 1, at 161.

130. *See* C. B. Macpherson, *Capitalism and the Changing Concept of Property*, *in* Feudalism, Capitalism, and Beyond 119–120 (Eugene Kamenka and R. S. Neale eds., 1975).

Just as intriguing as the question "why?" is the question "how?" Precisely *how* do we become complicit in a normative regime that restrains self-interest for the sake of general order? By what means do we internalize the relevant normative code? How, for instance, are we persuaded to participate in the self-discipline of the waiting line? All of which touches, of course, upon the issue whether property entitlements derive from social convention or whether our conventional arrangements are dependent upon the preexistence of property. Which came first: property or contract? Which is logically prior? This remains one of the timeless, and most intractable, conundrums of legal theory. Many would argue that, without property, there would be little or nothing to contract about. Yet it might equally be said that, without a collective entry into some form of social contract, property itself would have little or no meaning.

Queue scholarship appears, at least initially, to provide some support for the surmise that "property" perceptions within the queue are a learned response rather than an expression of some instinctual or immanent sense of proprietary entitlement. Deferment of gratification is an important part of the socialization of the infant, a process of waiting that some psychologists associate explicitly with such matters as feeding protocols and elementary toilet training. The taking of turns and the instilling of respect for serial or rank order likewise play a significant role in early childhood experience.[131] Children, it is said, "learn a 'script' for queue participation," an evolving drama in which the individual child comes to understand that much of life involves a gradual progression from a position of relative insignificance (at the back of the queue) to somewhat more prominent roles (further up the queue) and then, finally, to the climax of the drama (arrival at the head of the queue and the resolution of the entire experience).[132] Again, much of the educational world of the child involves endless standing in line at school. On this basis it may be possible to argue that a number of environmental factors have helped to install a "software of the mind" that is predisposed to an acceptance of queue discipline.[133]

On the other hand, it could be said that many of the examples recited above relate, not to the assimilation of any proprietary understanding of waiting processes, but to basic requirements of institutional or systemic organization. Thus the linear formations found in the school yard might be thought to constitute

---

131. *See* SCHWARTZ, QUEUING AND WAITING, *supra* note 4, at 173–174; Frederick Gearing and Paul Epstein, *Learning to Wait: An Ethnographic Probe into the Operations of an Item of Hidden Curriculum, in* DOING THE ETHNOGRAPHY OF SCHOOLING: EDUCATIONAL ANTHROPOLOGY IN ACTION 249, 265–267 (George Spindler ed., 1982).

132. Donald Ratcliff, *Standing in the Need: Waiting in Lines in Modern Society* (http://don.ratcliff.net/conferences/q/pdf (2006)) (accessed March 30, 2006) at 20.

133. *See* GEERT HOFSTEDE, CULTURES AND ORGANIZATIONS: SOFTWARE OF THE MIND 4–5 (1997).

merely an involuntary regime of "queueing under authority"[134] and, precisely because directed toward managerial rather than distributional outcomes, not to represent true instances of normative awareness of the phenomenon of ownership. Of course, this does not in itself mean that proprietary perceptions are *not* the product of childhood acculturation.[135] But to insist that all proprietary impulses derive from processes of socialization may be to ignore the powerful pull of personhood theory in the formation of proprietary understanding. It may also underplay a significant body of evidence that proprietary motivations are presocial or instinctual[136] or, at least, are the product of a biosocial conditioning that has been in progress over millions of years. It is not without significance that some queue-watchers draw an explicit parallel between queuing and hunting. The slow, determined, appetitive quest of those who wait in line is similar to the patient process undertaken by the hunter who stalks and gradually runs down his prey. Indeed, in some languages the idea of queuing is expressed in terms equally applicable to the drama of the hunt: the ultimate objective of the queuer is to "track down" or "bag" the prize.[137] The mental software of the queuer may yet contain elements that are not so much learned as *inherited.*

Enough, perhaps, of whether we actually learn to queue. What, instead, can the queue teach us? It teaches us, first, that proprietary impulses are fundamental and that they pervade all reaches of human existence. There is no community on earth without some concept of property: property is too closely intertwined with the creation and preservation of our social and economic arrangements.[138] Embedded in the mores of the physical queue for service are plenty of coded messages about "property" and "ownership," evidenced most strongly in the various ways in which the waiting line allocates and defends the special form of spatio-temporal property held by each of its members. But, as a microcosmic replica of a property regime, the queue also demonstrates that the notion of property is much more flexible and adaptive than one might imagine. The survival of the collective order requires the presence of a high degree of solidarity and cohesion and, in Leon Mann's famous description of the queue, these qualities are assured by "establishing informal rules which are kept sufficiently general to allow individual members to adjust to the normative pattern."[139] Property, in

---

134. MacCormick, *Norms, Institutions, and Institutional Facts, supra* note 12, at 307.

135. *See* Gordon Trasler, *The Psychology of Ownership and Possessiveness, in* PROPERTY AND SOCIAL RELATIONS 35–43 (Peter Hollowell ed., 1982).

136. *See* Kevin Gray, *Equitable Property,* 47 CURRENT LEGAL PROBLEMS 157, 157–158 (1994).

137. Zbigniew Czwartosz, *On Queueing,* 29 ARCHIVES EUROPÉENNES DE SOCIOLOGIE 3, 8–9 (1988).

138. *See Koompahtoo Local Aboriginal Land Council v. Sanpine Pty Ltd* (2007) 233 CLR 115 at [74] per Kirby J.

139. Mann, *Queue Culture, supra* note 20, at 351; Mann, *The Social Psychology of Waiting Lines, supra* note 43, at 393.

short, is organic, interactive, socially defined, normatively resilient, and extremely relative.

A second lesson to be drawn from the queue is more profound. The overwhelming perception formed by its close observers reflects a clear sense of the collaborative and mutually supportive nature of the group of persons caught up in the waiting line. Neil Brady has concluded that "[p]robably the single most important feature of lines is their reliance on trust and cooperation."[140] The queue—particularly in its mass versions—is a self-help community, united both in its movement toward a common goal and in a shared commitment to making the environment of the waiting line (and, thereby, the process of waiting) more bearable. Queuers are not, in the magnificent phrase of Eugene Kamenka and Alice Erh-Soon Tay, "isolated and isolable windowless monads."[141] Instead, they relate to each other; they forge alliances; they respect, and adjust to, the needs of other queue members; and they honor debts of loyalty. The proprietary subtext of the waiting line is counterbalanced by mutuality and reciprocity. In the interdependency of the queue, rights are inseparable from responsibilities. Entitlement and obligation stand together, hand in hand, in the waiting line—a perspective on property relationships that is increasingly embraced, on a more general plane, by modern property scholars.[142] It is, indeed, this network of reciprocal duty that marks out all forms of moral community. By means of mutual accommodation and restraint, the participants in the queue are enabled to extrapolate from obsessive self-concern toward some more enlightened vision of the common good. In a context of attenuated resource, those in the waiting line understand intuitively that the maximization of welfare lies not in preemptive strikes for individual advantage, but in cooperative strategies of ordered advancement. The private property of each queuer mutates, subtly and indistinguishably, into a community property in peace, order, and good government. Furthermore, although beginning merely as a method of allocating the social value of time, the regime of the queue provides, on a larger scale, a much needed model for community survival. As Kenneth Boulding observed many years ago, the critical question for humankind today "is how to make the best of what may be quite a bad job and move toward that organisation of world society that will make the spaceship earth

---

140. Brady, *Lining Up for Star-Wars Tickets, supra* note 1, at 162.

141. Eugene Kamenka and Alice Erh-Soon Tay, *Beyond Bourgeois Individualism: the Contemporary Crisis in Law and Legal Ideology, in* FEUDALISM, CAPITALISM, AND BEYOND 133 (Eugene Kamenka and R. S. Neale eds., 1975).

142. *See* Gray, *Equitable Property, supra* note 136, at 189, 198, 207–214; JOSEPH WILLIAM SINGER, ENTITLEMENT: THE PARADOXES OF PROPERTY (2000); LAURA S. UNDERKUFFLER, THE IDEA OF PROPERTY: ITS MEANING AND POWER (2003); A. J. VAN DER WALT, CONSTITUTIONAL PROPERTY LAW (2005); Gregory S. Alexander, *The Social-Obligation Norm in American Property Law,* 94 CORNELL L. REV. 745 (2009).

tolerable."[143] The fairness implicit in taking turns may indeed be our best chance of avoiding the destructive chaos of a global free-for-all.

A third, and final, thought generated by the phenomenon of the queue relates to the elusive content of the concept that we label "property." The discipline of the queue finds its origin, at least in part, in an apprehended need to protect a particular kind of personal space from predation by strangers. In performing this task, the normative code of the queue confirms not merely an ethos of moral community, but also an especially intense perception of the individual's "personhood." The demoralization cost that the normative order seeks to avert is, in large measure, the injury inflicted upon the psyche of the queuer by disrespectful encroachments upon a special zone of autonomy (together with the erosion of priority that such invasion connotes). As we saw earlier, the waiting line has a psychological as well as a social dimension.[144] There is also a significant sense in which the entirety of the law of property is effectively a field of applied psychology. The normative structure of the queue silently underscores the point that the ultimate property relates to *human dignity*—the reinforcement of a life-enhancing self-propriety.[145] Nor should this proposition seem remarkable. Etymologically, the term "property" is linked, in a powerful network of nuances, with such words as "proper," "appropriate," and "propriety." And the ideological conflation of property, personhood, and self-regard is entirely comprehensible, given that the Latin root *proprius* (or the French and medieval English *propre*) served as the primary identifier of a relationship to the self. The semantic reality is that "property" comprises the condition of being "proper" to a particular person; and nothing could be more "proper" to oneself than one's *self*.

It was, of course, John Rawls who so strongly argued that "the most important primary good is that of self-respect."[146] It is here that we find ourselves at the confluence of a number of themes that have animated property theory, both ancient and modern. In the view of John Locke, "every Man has a *Property* in his own *Person*." Accordingly Locke was quite prepared to regard the concept of "property" as inclusive of an individual's "life, liberty and estate"—a species of inalienable and self-constituting control over one's destiny.[147] As Laura

---

143. *See* Kenneth E. Boulding, The Economy of Love and Fear: A Preface to Grants Economics 111 (1973).

144. *See* Schwartz, *Queues, Priorities, and Social Process*, *supra* note 7, at 9.

145. This is, among other factors, the source of the rapidly evolving English law of privacy.

146. John Rawls, A Theory of Justice 440 (1973).

147. John Locke, Two Treatises of Government: The Second Treatise, § 27 (at 305), § 123 at 368) (2nd critical ed. by Peter Laslett, 1967). The Lockean perspective is today replicated, with uncanny accuracy, in the German Constitutional Court's identification of "property" as comprising those entitlements which provide "a secure area of freedom where the [claimant] can take responsibility for control over his or her life" (89 BVerfGE 1, 6 (1993) (*Besitzrecht des Mieters* Case).

Underkuffler has so eloquently reminded us,[148] the Lockean formula encompasses a perception of property as "moral space"—a term that assumes a certain aptness in the normative geography of the queue. During the late twentieth century the Lockean theme was recast in C. B. Macpherson's assertion that the idea of property is gradually broadening to include a "right to a kind of society or set of power relations which will enable the individual to live a fully human life."[149] This insistence that property is intricately connected with human self-realization provides our final link with the world of the queue. The "fully human life" to which Macpherson referred has, of course, a clear temporal dimension: we are all tenants of an unknown, but finite, term of years. The jurisprudence of self-propriety—just as the jurisprudence of the queue—contains a significant and salutary recognition of the conceptual reality of property in time.

---

148. Laura S. Underkuffler, *On Property: An Essay*, 100 YALE L.J. 127, 138 (1990).

149. Macpherson, *Capitalism and the Changing Concept of Property*, *supra* note 130, at 120.

INDEX

Printed and bound by CPI Group (UK) Ltd, Croydon, CR0 4YY

The manufacturer's authorised representative in the EU for product safety is Oxford University Press España S.A. of El Parque Empresarial San Fernando de Henares, Avenida de Castilla, 2 - 28830 Madrid (www.oup.es/en or product.safety@oup.com). OUP España S.A. also acts as importer into Spain of products made by the manufacturer.
Printed and bound by CPI Group (UK) Ltd, Croydon, CR0 4YY
14/09/2026
02216307-0007